BRITISH DIPLOMATS AND DIPLOMACY

1688–1800

This book is a comprehensive discussion of British diplomats and diplomacy in the formative period in which Britain emerged as the leading world power.

Jeremy Black uses the issue of diplomatic representation in order to discuss questions about the professionalism of British government, the nature of patronage and the degree to which Britain should be seen in this period as moving towards a more modern and bureaucratic system. Supported by copious quotations from their letters, the book focuses on an interesting group of individuals in order to provide an understanding of the capabilities of British foreign policy, and examines British diplomats and diplomacy in the context of the situation in other countries. It is based on a comprehensive mastery of British and foreign archival sources by a scholar whose work has had a remarkable impact in the historical world.

British Diplomats and Diplomacy
1688–1800

JEREMY BLACK

UNIVERSITY
of
EXETER
PRESS

First published in 2001 by
University of Exeter Press
Reed Hall, Streatham Drive
Exeter EX4 4QR
UK
www.ex.ac.uk/uep/

British Library Cataloguing in Publication Data
A catalogue record for this book is available
from the British Library.

ISBN 0 85989 613 7

Typeset in 11½pt Monotype Garamond
by XL Publishing Services, Tiverton

Printed in Great Britain by Short Run Press Ltd, Exeter

For Mike Duffy

Contents

Preface

This book aims to throw light on the capabilities of British foreign policy during the period 1688–1800, when Britain became the leading world power. The nature of the British diplomatic service is seen as a valuable approach to this problem. The last book dealing with this area was published in 1961. D.B. Horn's *The British Diplomatic Service 1689–1789* was an effective study, but it has been out of print for many years and, since it was written, new issues have arisen and new archival sources made accessible. Furthermore, it is important to provide a context which examines British diplomats and diplomacy in relation to issues now of concern to scholars of the period.

This study benefits from research for my works on foreign policy, and is also intended to complement the searching assessment in my *Britain as a Military Power 1688–1815* (1999). It draws on research in a multiplicity of British and foreign archives. I am grateful for the support received from the Universities of Durham and Exeter, the British Academy, the Leverhulme Foundation and the Wolfson Foundation. Visiting fellowships at the Beinecke and Huntington Libraries enabled me to examine their holdings. I am grateful to Her Majesty the Queen, the Duke of Bedford, the Marquess of Bute, the Earl of Crawford, the Earl of Elgin, the Earl of Malmesbury, the Earl of Shelburne, the Earl Waldegrave, Olive, Countess Fitzwilliam's Wentworth Settlement Trustees, Lady Lucas, Sir Hector Monro, Mrs Daphne Bruton, Richard Head and John Weston-Underwood for granting permission to consult their collections of manuscripts, and the Deputy Keeper of Records of Northern Ireland for permission to quote from a document in his care.

Bill Gibson made many helpful comments on an earlier draft and Brendan Carnduff likewise on a particular chapter. I am also grateful for the support of an anonymous reader. I would like to thank Donald Abbott, M.Y. Ashcroft, Ian Cunningham, Roger Davey, Rosemary Dunhill, Peter Durrant, Michael Farrar, Patricia Gill, A. Goode, Victor Gray, Adam Green, Sue Groves, Steve Gunn, K. Hall, Hugh Hanley, Frances Harris, K. Haslam, Adrian Henstock, Sheila Himsworth, Steven Hobbs, Gillian Holt, D.S. Hubbard, Michael Hughes, Brian Hutton, R.P. Jenkins, Dorothy Johnston, Evelyn Lord, Sheila MacPherson, Anthony Malcolmson, Patricia Moore, Christine North, Monica Ory, Glyn Parry, Geoffrey Rice, Mary Robertson, Rosemary Rogers, Margery Rowe, Paul Rutledge, Richard Samways, D.A. Stoker, R.G. Thomas, Steven Tomlinson, Anne Trimble, Tony Wherry and Chris Woolgar for their assistance either on visits to archives or in responding to enquiries.

The archival perspective is stressed, because this study very much seeks to focus on the experience of diplomats, rather than presenting them as an anonymous bureaucratic agency. This accounts for the particular character of the work, its extensive use of examples and its repeated quotation from original sources. It is a particular pleasure to dedicate this book to a friend and fellow toiler in the archives of the period who is also a colleague.

Abbreviations

Add.	Additional Manuscripts
AE.	Paris, Archives du Ministère des Relations Extérieures
Ang.	Angleterre
AST. LM. Ing.	Turin, Archivio di Stato, Lettere Ministri, Inghilterra
BB.	Bland Burges papers
Beinecke	New Haven, Beinecke Library
BL.	London, British Library
Bod.	Oxford, Bodleian Library
C(H)	Cholmondely (Houghton) papers
Chewton	Chewton Mendip, Chewton House, Waldegrave manuscripts, papers of James, 1st Earl Waldegrave
Cobbett	W. Cobbett, *Parliamentary History of England from … 1066 to … 1803* (36 vols, 1806–20)
CP.	Correspondance Politique
CRO.	County Record Office
CUL.	Cambridge University Library
Eg.	Egerton Manuscripts
f.	folio
Farmington	Farmington, Connecticut, Lewis Walpole Library
FO.	Foreign Office
Hanover	Hanover, Niedersächsisches Hauptstaatsarchiv
HHStA.	Vienna, Haus-, Hof-, und Staatsarchiv, Staatenabteilung
HL.	San Marino, California, Huntington Library

IO.	India Office Collections
KAO	Kent Archive Office
L.	Lucas papers
Malmesbury	Hampshire Record Office, Malmesbury papers
MS.	Mount Stuart, papers of John, 3rd Earl of Bute
NeC.	Nottingham University Library, Clumber papers
Newport	Newport, South Wales, Public Library, Hanbury Williams papers
NLS.	Edinburgh, National Library of Scotland
(os)	Old Style. Until 1752 Britain conformed to the Julian calendar while most of Europe conformed to the Gregorian calendar. In this book, dates are given in New Style (the Gregorian, adopted in Britain in 1752). Old Style dates are marked (os). The New Year is taken as starting on 1 January.
Polit. Corresp.	R. Koser (ed.), *Politische Correspondenz Friedrichs des Grossen* (46 vols, Berlin, 1879–1939)
PRO.	London, Public Record Office
PRONI.	Belfast, Public Record Office of Northern Ireland
RA. CP.	Windsor Castle, Royal Archives, Cumberland Papers
RA. SP.	Windsor Castle, Royal Archives, Stuart Papers
Sbornik	*Sbornik Imperatorskago Russkago Istoricheskago Obshchestvo*
SP.	State Papers
SRO.	Edinburgh, Scottish Record Office
Trevor	Aylesbury, Buckinghamshire Record Office, Trevor papers
UL.	University Library
Weston-Underwood	Iden Green, papers of Edward Weston
Williamwood	Williamwood, Ewart papers

Place of publication is London unless otherwise stated.

1

Introduction
The Diplomacy of a Rising World Power

> In our way of life we have nothing to animate us but glory and the
> consciousness of having done our duty.
>   Thomas Robinson (Vienna) to Walter Titley (Copenhagen) 1739[1]

In our period Britain became the most powerful maritime and trans-
oceanic power in the world, but her diplomacy remained centred on
Europe. Diplomatic contacts with non-European powers became more
frequent, but they were generally *ad hoc* and much less common than with
European states. Furthermore, they were often handled by military
personnel or by the agents of British commercial companies, particularly
in Asia the East India Company, rather than by diplomats accredited by
the Crown. This reflected a lack of certainty about how best to handle
relations with non-European powers. It also ensures that a history of
British diplomats largely deals with relations with other European states.

Within Europe, the British state was formed with the parliamentary
union of England and Scotland in 1707, and this state came to play a greater
role in European power politics than it had done at the outset of the period.
Closer diplomatic relations further resulted from a series of non-British
rulers: William III of Orange (1689–1702), and the monarchs of the House
of Hanover (1714–1837), in these years George I (1714–27), George II
(1727–60), and George III (1760–1820), although by the reign of the last,
who never visited Hanover, it is more helpful to think of the dynasty as
British. Furthermore, the cartography of British diplomatic concern in
Europe broadened as concern with eastern Europe increased. This outline
describes the major developments in British diplomacy in this period,
but, like much writing on diplomacy and international relations, it is incomplete.

1

Early-Modern European Diplomacy

An unhelpful teleological emphasis similarly characterizes work on European diplomacy in general in this period. For example, the generally negative account of medieval diplomacy and consequent stress on new departures in the fifteenth century in works such as Matthew Anderson's *The Rise of Modern Diplomacy 1450–1919* (1993) can be qualified. The emphasis on the rise of strong states, centralized governments and a comprehensive states system in the early-modern period which tends to be part of this teleology does not accord with much recent research. Indeed, general works frequently fail to appreciate the nature of the dynamics of early-modern monarchies, especially the impact of dynastic considerations and the role of the monarch. This is particularly a problem with Keith Hamilton and Richard Langhorne's *The Practice of Diplomacy. Its Evolution, Theory and Administration* (1994). They criticize the tendency for monarchs to muddy the waters of foreign policy management by private interference, a serious failure to understand the nature of early-modern international relations, and they also exaggerate the potential role of training, as opposed to social skills, in *ancien régime* diplomacy. Such anachronistic assessments are examples of the 'modernization' of pre-1800 diplomacy: the tendency to search for modern elements and modernizing trends.

It is, however, also necessary to emphasize the organizational limitations of diplomacy, both European and, more specifically, British. In the eighteenth century the majority of rulers did not maintain permanent embassies in more than a few capitals, if that. This was due to the cost, the difficulty of finding suitable diplomats and the absence of matters requiring negotiation. The idea of an integrated diplomatic network ignores the minor princes (and some who were not so minor) who, in some cases, had no permanent embassies, and regarded much diplomacy as family business. Instead, they might use their courtiers for special missions, share an agent or rely on confidential newsletters. More generally, any teleology tends to entail assumptions about the calibre and skill of diplomats, but these are difficult to assess. This is especially so if the necessary social skills are considered: ability in negotiation was tested less continually than court skills, for the influence of an envoy often reflected his ability to make the right impression at court.

2

Communications

Rulers and ministers frequently complained that envoys exceeded instructions, but it was difficult to provide orders that would comprehend all eventualities. Daniel Hailes, Envoy Extraordinary in Warsaw, wrote to a fellow-diplomat in 1790, 'I know from experience how necessary it is after a warm bout in business to go home in order to explain what may not have been thoroughly understood'.[2] Furthermore, the nature of communications ensured that considerable discretion had to be left to envoys on the spot if negotiations were to advance speedily. Communications were not only slow by modern standards; they were also such that information and messages could only be confirmed by waiting for subsequent messages. There was no appreciable improvement in communications in this period. Developments at the end of the period—balloons from the 1780s and semaphore networks from the 1790s—were not exploited to aid diplomacy, and, in their then state, neither lent themselves to such an end. Instead, this was diplomacy in an age before telegraphs, railways and steamships. The global diplomacy of the late nineteenth century depended on such innovations. Prior to that, the diffusion of new attitudes, such as those manifested in Revolutionary America and France, or bold proposals for far-flung combinations, like the sixteenth-century schemes for concerted action by Portugal and Ethiopia against the Turks, were necessarily limited in their impact, in part, because of the nature of communications. This factor both hindered *ancien régime* diplomacy, and paradoxically also played a major role in ensuring it retained its character.

Structural Factors of British Diplomacy

In practice, any account of British diplomacy in this period has to take note of two aspects: first, permanent or 'structural' factors that affected its conduct and, secondly, specific political crises that qualify any suggestion of a smooth progression. Structural factors were of varying significance. At the level of the individual diplomat, the most important was the financial. The private correspondence of diplomats was dominated by issues of pay and expenses, and this had long been the case.[3] Both were commonly in arrears and each, especially the latter, was regarded as inadequate. Cost was a particular problem at the more expensive and prestigious courts where diplomats were expected to maintain a costly state, and was an additional reason to appoint wealthy men. In 1787, John, 3rd Duke of

Dorset, Ambassador in Paris, took steps to raise the matter in Parliament: 'I have written this day to Sir Robert Smyth and I have given him a hint that if he should be tempted to rise upon any question where foreign politics can be brought in part to mention the insufficiency of my salary to keep up the dignity of my place. Pitt has promised these three years to move something about it but has never as yet taken the smallest step.'[4]

Such complaints were of course not unique to the British, but they reflected several more general facets of the diplomacy of the period that are important. First, much of early-modern government was undercapitalixed. It is of course true that most government in most periods has been short of funds, but, in comparison to the nineteenth and twentieth century, governments did not benefit from an important industrial base, the infrastructure of credit was less developed, and governmental credit-worthiness was limited. These deficiencies became more acute in the late fifteenth and early sixteenth century, as the growing power of the leading European states launched a process of competitive international activity that focused on more substantial and expensive armed forces and that entailed more regular diplomacy for the major states.

The latter owed little to changes in the nature of states, their strength and government, but, rather, to the extent to which the competitive international activity of the period entailed coalition politics, both diplomacy and warfare. Indeed, on the global scale, it was the weakness, not the strength, of states that was a crucial aspect of European international relations. At the beginning of the sixteenth century, no European state wielded the power of Ming China or Ottoman Turkey. These strong states required diplomacy rather less than Tudor England, Valois France or Sforza Milan. Linked to this weakness was another defining aspect of European international relations: its multipolar character. This provided cause and opportunity for frequent diplomacy. Thus, the development of European diplomacy can be located in terms not so much of a theory of modernization through governmental development as of the contingent nature of a states system that was distinctive, rather than modern.

Parliament and British Diplomacy

The financial problems of British diplomacy, however, were exacerbated by another 'structural' feature of British foreign policy: the role of Parliament. After Henry VIII failed to use the despoliation of the monasteries in the 1530s to increase the capital base of the English monarchy, the Crown was generally dependent, especially in periods of warfare and international confrontation, on financial support from Parliament. This was rarely adequate, and fiscal exigencies therefore affected the operations of all areas of British government, including the diplomatic service, although such exigencies were scarcely unique to Britain.

This, however, was only an aspect of the role of Parliament in foreign policy, because the very existence of the institution helped to lend a sense of instability to British politics and policies, particularly from the perspective of foreign governments that had fewer problems with their representative institutions. Furthermore, parliamentary speeches could anger foreign rulers. In 1781, Hugh Elliot wrote from Berlin:

> Mr. Wraxall has thought proper to deliver a philippic against this court and its sovereign [Frederick the Great]. It is much to be regretted that a sense of dignity in the House [of Commons] does not put a stop to personal invective against foreign princes ... Wraxall's speech has been translated into all foreign newspapers and the abusive parts of it distinguished with italicks. In England where that species of writing is as usual to us as our daily bread it is scarcely remarked, here the shoe pinches and a tight shoe upon a gouty foot is apt to raise ill humours.[5]

If Parliament is also taken as the symbol and fulcrum of public politics and public political pressures in the period, then it is also important to consider the impact on British diplomacy of the reluctance of the political nation to support a substantial standing army. There were of course other reasons why the British army should be smaller than that of France. Britain had a smaller population and, as an island, had both an important alternative of military commitment, in the shape of the navy, and was faced with the problems of amphibious operations. Nevertheless, the growing gap between British and French military capability on land in the seventeenth century is instructive and the same was true, after 1660, in comparison with Austria, Prussia and Russia. Whereas Henry VIII in the 1540s and Oliver Cromwell in the 1650s had been able both to deploy substantial forces and to send them to the Continent, the British forces sent thereafter were increasingly effective only as part of coalition armies arrayed against France, were smaller than the French army, and were dependent on a favourable political environment in Britain. The reliance on allied troops added a further requirement to British diplomacy. When the favourable political environment in Britain was lost, as for example when the interventionist Whig government was replaced by the Tories in 1710, then the consistency, and thus effectiveness, of British diplomacy appeared compromised.[6]

Specific Crises

This problem was related to the specific political crises that qualify any suggestion of a smooth progression in British diplomacy. Other countries of course faced serious problems, but in Britain there was a major civil war in the 1640s (in England 1642–6, 1648), culminating in the execution of the king and a lengthy republican interregnum (1649–60). In 1688 James II was driven from the throne, an event leading to a legitimist movement, Jacobitism, that was not finally crushed until the battle of Culloden in 1746, and that thereafter remained a factor in international relations until the failure of the French invasion attempt in 1759.

In addition, Britain was not alone in facing the problems of multiple kingship, but the difficulties posed by the task of imposing British control on Scotland were to prove lengthy and considerable. In diplomatic terms, it was necessary for the government in London to ensure that it alone represented the British Isles. It was therefore essential to prevent foreign rulers from seeking to develop relations, official or unofficial, with English émigrés, Scots and Irish. This was particularly a problem in 1639–60 during the civil conflict that began with the First Bishops' War of 1639 and in the Interregnum, and then, from 1689, in the case of the exiled Stuarts, who established a rival court to which diplomats could be accredited. Thereafter, the issue was next to recur with crises of imperial power: the rebellious Thirteen American Colonies in 1775–83, and Irish radicals in the 1790s after the outbreak of war with Revolutionary France in 1793.

Diplomacy is, in part, an issue of monopolization: the monopolization of international representation from a given space that is judged sovereign. The ability of a state based in southern England to seize, assert and maintain a monopolization of diplomatic representation over the British archipelago was a crucial consequence and aspect of state-building and an important dynamic element in early-modern British diplomacy.

As already mentioned, it is misleading to think of British diplomacy and foreign policy in terms of a smooth progression. Just as mid-fourteenth century English prominence in the early stages of the Hundred Years War was followed by decline, division, usurpation, conspiracy and civil war, and the same process was repeated after the successes of the reign of Henry V (1413–22), so the highpoint of Elizabeth I's reign (1559–1603) was not maintained. In terms of the number of people involved overseas in diplomacy, her reign represented the largest commitment to diplomacy in the period 1509–1688, and, in addition, English representation increased in the Mediterranean and eastern Europe.[7] James I (1603–25) and Charles I (1625–49), especially the former, saw themselves as major international figures, but England was increasingly marginalized during their reigns, a process encouraged by unsuccessful conflicts with Spain and France in the 1620s. Nevertheless, continuity and experience helped in the definition of diplomatic practice and standards. The Jacobean diplomatic service has been described as 'a competent group of professionals, an intelligent and acerbic set of men … who for the most part did their job efficiently and well'.[8]

Diplomats and Diplomacy

The art of negotiation was not in this period a taught skill. Though the foundation of the Regius Chairs of History at Cambridge and Oxford in 1724 was designed to facilitate the training of diplomats, the scheme had little practical effect. The principal school of leading British diplomats continued to be the court in London, that of their less socially distinguished colleagues the households of other diplomats. A diplomat was the personal representative of the sovereign, as those affected by George II's parsimony were all too aware, and, in a prestige-conscious age, the ability of a man to discharge an office was believed to reflect in part his social rank. Honour was a crucial concept in diplomatic representation and, just as the rank of the official appointed, whether Ambassador, Envoy Extraordinary, Minister Resident, Secretary or a less common designation, was an expression of respect and trust, not least because representation was usually reciprocated at the same rank, so also was the social rank of the individual.

The most prestigious postings for British diplomats were Paris, Madrid, The Hague and Vienna. With the addition of Rome, where Protestant Britain had no representation after the Glorious Revolution, this list was a common European one, and, at these courts, the diplomatic world was very much aristocratic. It would be wrong to suggest that simply because most aristocratic diplomats had no previous experience, they were therefore mediocre. Several of the most impressive diplomats, such as

Philip, 4th Earl of Chesterfield (The Hague, 1728–32, 1745), were hereditary aristocrats, as opposed to ennobled commoners, such as James Harris, 1st Earl of Malmesbury. However, some diplomats, for example John, 3rd Duke of Dorset, a womanizer and a fan of cricket, who served at Paris in 1784–9, not only had no diplomatic experience, but also proved himself less than diligent in ordinary circumstances and inadequate at times of crisis.

Aside from becoming a Secretary of State, there were few promotion prospects that could not be better obtained by remaining in Britain, and many diplomats complained bitterly that absence from London hindered their careers and the pursuit of other interests. In 1783, Sir Robert Murray Keith, envoy in Vienna, complained to his cousin, 'We foreign servants of the Crown are often treated as strangers and aliens, when we return after a long absence'.[9] Although a few embassies left plenty of time for leisure, as Sir Horace Mann at Florence (1738–86) and Sir William Hamilton at Naples (1764–1800) testified, diplomats could be criticized severely if they failed to write sufficiently often or comprehensively, or if they left their posts. In his 'Observations on the Office of an Ambassador', Sir William Keith sought to set public standards: 'A state of indolence or inaction is inconsistent with the office of an Ambassador, who … ought ever to be investigating the changes which daily happen in state affairs.'[10]

Apart from a disproportionate number of Scots, benefiting from the career opportunities presented by the Union of 1707, it is difficult to see any pattern in those who followed diplomacy as a career. Some had acquired experience through posts on the staffs of envoys, although others had not. As French increasingly became the diplomatic lingua franca, language became less of a problem; many British diplomats were insufficiently familiar with other languages.

The choice of envoys was not always easy. Many individuals preferred to pursue careers in Britain. Once appointed, diplomats frequently complained about their postings. Many diplomats also complained about the absence or content of their instructions, but, even when they were frequent, fast and comprehensive, there was considerable room for initiative. The shifting nature of court factions made the diplomatic task a difficult one, and, when mistakes and misunderstandings arose, the potential damage was made worse by the difficulties of securing supplementary lines of communication that could provide a check on diplomats. Distance and protocol kept most British sovereigns from personal diplomacy, except in matters of royal marriages. This was especially so after 1760, because George III did not leave Britain, unlike his two predecessors who had made frequent visits to Hanover.

British diplomats did not enjoy the high reputation of their French counterparts and the diligence and competence of individuals were criticized. However, given the difficulties of the job and the resources available, it would be inappropriate to adopt too critical a note, not least because the French diplomatic corps was more varied than is sometimes appreciated.[11] Learning on the job could have unfortunate consequences, but it was a feature of the semi-professionalized nature of much British administration in this period.

Diplomatic Calibre and National Strength

It is difficult to point to any change in the calibre of British diplomats during the period. Instead, variations in their importance and success can be more directly ascribed to Britain's relative power. It was not therefore surprising that the most effective representatives were military leaders who also wielded political power in England: William III in the 1690s and John, Earl, and, from 1704, Duke, of Marlborough in 1701–10. Marlborough, indeed, received credentials as Ambassador Extraordinary and Plenipotentiary to the United Provinces in 1701, and then again in 1702 and retained his embassy until he was dismissed in January 1712. Each had to hold anti-French coalitions together.

Aside from this direct representation, diplomats, whatever their merit, were most heeded when Britain was seen as powerful: more important, for example, in the early 1720s than in the early 1680s. However, in a somewhat circular fashion, such power rested in part on Britain's alliances, so that British strength in the early 1720s owed much to her alliance with France, both the fact of this alliance and the absence of enmity. Conversely, victory in the Seven Years' War was less effective in transforming Britain's diplomatic position, because she ended the war with no allies other than Hesse-Cassel and Portugal. On his way to take up the post of Minister to the Imperial Diet at Ratisbon (Regensburg), William Gordon wrote from Hanau in 1764:

> the joy I felt through the whole course of my route through the Empire is not to be described. Judge what my feelings must be, when in every place through which I passed every man from the highest to the lowest was striving who should do the greatest justice to the character and

shining virtues of our most gracious master, and to the nation who has the glory and happiness to be his subjects ... they look upon us as a race of people superior to the rest of mankind.[12]

This did not bring alliances, however, and British diplomats had to become used to the position of representing what was perceived, with some reason, as the world's leading maritime power but one that had abandoned an interventionism that had been the major (although not invariable) policy since 1689.

The attention paid to envoys also reflected more general facets of the diplomacy of the period, especially the extent to which individual diplomats were seen as representing the views of the crucial figures in the government. For example, Sir Robert Walpole's brother, Horatio, successively served at Paris and The Hague when each was the capital of Britain's leading ally and when Sir Robert was first minister.[13] The ability of diplomats to represent views, indeed to act as intermediaries, was always an issue. It was particularly acute in the seventeenth century, when constitutional and political differences and clashes sometimes ensured that there was a lack of mutual confidence between the monarch and the ministers who were officially responsible for the execution of foreign policy: the Secretaries of State for the Northern and Southern Departments.

This issue remained a problem after the 'Glorious Revolution' of 1688, as first William III and later the Hanoverians sought to pursue their own agendas in foreign policy and clashed accordingly with ministers and politicians. Nevertheless, despite the serious disputes over the Partition Treaties for the Spanish empire of 1698 and 1700 in the Parliament of 1701, and over the alleged role of Hanoverian interests in 1743–4, it proved easier to reconcile royal and parliamentary differences, or, looked at differently, to finesse royal views, than had been the case under the Stuarts. In part, this was because the 'Glorious Revolution' had settled the religious issue. It was no longer the case that a royal foreign policy could be presented as Catholic or crypto-Catholic, and this greatly lessened the severity of disagreements over foreign policy, not least by weakening its ideological dimension and by ensuring that it could not be placed so centrally in domestic politics.

This diminished intensity was related to another aspect of British diplomacy. In the century from 1689 the number of British diplomatic posts in Europe increased and more posts were upgraded than downgraded.[14] Greater diplomatic representation was not, however, matched by greater or more extensive public sensitivity to Continental diplomacy. In the case of most diplomats, domestic political pressures were structural, most obviously the need to consider the roles of Parliament and trade in foreign policy, rather than specific, and, therefore, it becomes easier and more appropriate to consider their careers alongside those of the diplomats of other countries that lacked powerful representative assemblies.

The World Outside Europe

This was even more the case with British representation with non-European powers: in these cases, British diplomatic agents generally had even less need to assume that they would have to confront public criticism and pressure in Britain. The nature of the interaction with non-European powers was obscure to most contemporaries. Aside from distance, there was the difficulty of discussing and conceptualizing what was poorly, if at all, understood outside the zone of interaction. There was also the habit of conceiving of the distant world principally as an extension of the nearby, especially of its problems, configurations, and patterns of causality. Thus, for example, West Africa and India were seen principally in terms of relations with other European powers, especially France.

Relations with non-European powers were usually handled as an aspect of the military, colonial and commercial responsibilities of officials, whether those appointed directly by the Crown or those who worked for chartered companies such as the East India Company, the Hudson Bay Company and the Royal African Company. This indeed continued the role of the Levant Company in the choice and payment of the Ambassador at Constantinople, though the Company's role in the choice largely ceased from 1691, and its ability and willingness to bear extraordinary expenses was hit by commercial difficulties.[15]

Naval officers and consuls played the crucial role in relations with the Barbary states of North Africa.[16] Thus, for example, Captain George Delaval was sent on two missions to the Emperor of Morocco. In 1700, he negotiated a treaty for the redemption of English captives taken by Barbary pirates, a long-standing problem in relations, and in 1708 an agreement not to molest each other's ships. Captain Padden concluded a truce with Morocco in 1713, while Commodore Sir Roger Curtis was ordered in 1783 to renew the Anglo-Moroccan treaty of friendship of 1760–2, although instructed to discourage a return embassy as they were expensive. Thomas Thomson, Consul in Algiers, concluded a truce in 1718, while the Consul in Morocco, Matra, was made a temporary Ambassador in 1790 when co-operation against Spain was considered. A new treaty of peace with King Moulay Yazid of Morocco was concluded in 1791.

However, the use of naval officers could create problems, not least a lack of clarity as to channels of communication. In 1713, Padden was given advice by George Delaval, then Envoy Extraordinary in Lisbon, but in 1750, Commodore Augustus Keppel, who had been sent to the Barbary States the previous year, wrote from Algiers to the First Lord of the Admiralty: 'I am at a loss to know to whom I am to send my dispatches; the directions I received to obey the orders of the Lords Justices has puzzled me, whether to send to them, to your Board, or to the Secretary of State. For this time they go to the Admiralty.' Keppel reached an agreement the following year.[17]

The East India Company played a crucial role in Asia, maintaining residents at a number of courts and dispatching missions, such as that of George Bogle to Tibet in 1774–5. Diplomatic relations were crucial to England's position in Asia. For example, in the late 1780s and early 1790s, Marquis Cornwallis, Governor General and Commander-in-Chief in India, in his relations with Hyderabad, Mysore and the Marathas, especially his attempts to isolate Tipu Sultan of Mysore, faced diplomatic challenges similar to those confronting British ministers in Europe, although, even after the public furore over Warren Hastings, the constraints of public opinion and traditional assumptions were less insistent in the case of India.

The Company also faced problems from the unofficial activities of agents, self-appointed or accredited. Thus, in 1785–6, local initiative in the shape of negotiations with the Sultan of Kedah by a merchant, Francis Light, led to the occupation of the island of Penang, renamed Prince of Wales Island, as a base on the route to China. The Company was less than enthusiastic about this commitment and was reluctant to help the Sultan against his aggressive opponents.[18]

More generally, there was a question as to how far it was possible to control British commitments outside Europe. Delegating many of the functions of government including diplomacy to chartered companies only worked so far. 'Country' [private] traders were more enterprising than the East India Company and were particularly active in the East Indies and the Northern Pacific.[19] There was an obvious parallel in relations with the Native Americans in North America, while in Central America aggressive local officials and others supplied the Native Americans with arms and offered them protection.[20]

These activities created problems for government and chartered companies alike, but, more generally, as imperial issues became more important in British foreign policy, government finances and public interest from the mid-eighteenth century, so there was also greater sensitivity about the diplomatic and other policies of the companies. Relations between chartered companies and overseas agents were not only an issue for the English, but also for every European state with such companies, for example the French and the Compagnie du Sénégal in the late 1780s.[21]

In the nineteenth century, home governments were to take over diplomatic responsibility, and exceptions, such as King Leopold of Belgium and the Belgian Congo, were viewed with increasing criticism. This process was prefigured in the case of the British by the decision of the government to take a direct role in Asia and to send a mission to China. The first envoy, the Hon. Charles Cathcart MP, died en route, off Malaya, in 1788, but it was decided to send a replacement. William Grenville, then Home Secretary, wrote:

> great part of the hopes which are entertained of the success of this mission rests on the greater degree of attention which, it is supposed, the Government of China will show to a person coming there, as authorised by the King, than if he came, only in the name of a trading company.[22]

This was felt to be especially necessary, because the East India Company was opposed to any initiatives that might affect the monopoly of its 'factory' [commercial station] at Canton. It was also criticized for failing to aid the export of British manufactures to the Orient, though the advice of the Company on exports was sought by the government. George, Lord Macartney, who had earlier served at St Petersburg, replaced Cathcart, but his embassy, which left England in 1792, failed to obtain the desired commercial advantages.[23]

Macartney's varied career demonstrated the non-specialised nature of the careers of many 'diplomats'. Aside from serving in St Petersburg (1764–7), China (1792–4) and on a mission to the exiled Louis XVIII of France (1795–6), Macartney was also a colonial governor—of Grenada (1775–9), Madras (1781–5) and the Cape of Good Hope (1796–8), an MP in Ireland (1768–76) and at Westminster (1768–9, 1774–6, 1780–1), and Chief Secretary to the Lord Lieutenant of Ireland (1769–72). He was a competent diplomat, but diplomacy was not his career.[24]

The dispatch of a mission to China might not seem a world away from medieval European attempts to recruit the support of distant rulers, but it took part in a very different context. By the late eighteenth century European diplomacy was truly global. European commercial links had been forged across the Pacific as early as the sixteenth century, but the scale of European trans-oceanic trade and settlement in the late eighteenth century was greater than ever before. In 1791, the British bought 17¼ million pounds of tea at Canton. By 1793, India was contributing £500,000 per annum to the British Exchequer.

The traditional cartography of European governmental and thus diplomatic concern was also being subverted by the changing status of the New World. The newly independent United States of America sent and received diplomatic envoys and was soon to be followed by Spain's former Latin American colonies. Commenting on news that Consuls were to be appointed to South America, the *Birmingham Chronicle* of 2 October 1823 noted, 'though the Consuls intended to be appointed, it would seem, are merely commercial appointments, still it must be viewed as one important step taken towards a formal recognition of the independence of those states, which, if once made, would effectually prevent the meditated designs of France'.

Thus, even before and aside from the French Revolution, the *ancien régime* of European international relations and diplomacy was coming to a close at the end of the eighteenth century. Looked at differently, international relations and diplomacy revealed a degree of dynamism that suggests that it is misleading to regard them as static and bound to succumb, or be forced to respond and adapt to the new precepts, methods and world of revolutionary diplomacy.

The globalization of international relations certainly affected the models that could be employed to analyse or explain both diplomatic conduct and diplomatic relations. To a certain extent, the classics provided the basic frame of reference, explicit or implicit, for extra-European relations. The British appropriated Imperial Rome as a parallel state with which they wished to compare, and British officials were apt to adopt a proconsular role, seeing themselves as bringers of civilization. These values, removed from the suppositions affecting diplomacy in Europe, encouraged aggressive attitudes. Even though extra-European territorial goals in relations with non-European powers were generally limited, the mechanisms for establishing a compromise settlement were less well-developed, and policy was not in the hands of diplomats seeking a compromise. If, as in Australia and the Andaman Islands, no native state was acknowledged, then the British government and its officials could act in a bold fashion, taking advantage of established conventions, looking back to Roman law, relating to land seen as 'waste' or 'desert'.[25] The North American Native Americans were not represented in the 1782–3 peace negotiations that reapportioned their land,[26] and, in the early 1790s, Commodore George Vancouver had no hesitation in claiming the coast line of what he called 'New Albion': the Pacific Northwest coast.[27]

No such arguments were possible in India, but the officials of the East India Company became less willing in the second half of the eighteenth century to accept local notions of political conduct and sovereignty. Instead, an absolutist concept of sovereignty was increasingly advanced, and implemented by force.[28] As the Macartney mission was to demonstrate, the British found it difficult to accept the diplomatic assumptions of other peoples and polities. This reflected both great cultural and ideological divides and also a decreasing willingness to accept that difference did not mean inferiority. That the same was also true of the Chinese was scarcely surprising. Aside from a long tradition of contempt for non-Chinese people, who were seen as at the margins of a Sino-centred world, China, like Britain, was a tremendously successful power in the eighteenth century. The Chinese received tribute from most of their neighbours, although not from Russia.

The British and European Diplomacy

As Continental European commentators pointed out, the British had a self-serving, even hypocritical, notion of international relations. Successive governments sought to create and sustain what they termed a balance of power in Europe, while seeking unrestricted power in the oceanic and colonial spheres. In theory, this subverted the logic of British diplomacy, but, in practice, there were more pressing reasons why Continental states would not support British interests nor respond to British approaches. The most significant were, first, repeated British refusals to make the commitments required by putative allies, indeed to see alliances as mutual and dynamic, and to accept that allies, such as Russia, might wish to make territorial gains, and, secondly and related to the first, the nature of

15

European power politics. States such as Austria, Prussia, Russia and Savoy-Piedmont had little interest in Britain's trans-oceanic policies; and were not outraged by British gains in this sphere. This was not true, however, of other major European colonial powers—Portugal, Spain, France and the Dutch—and, to a considerable extent, they formed a different diplomatic system alongside the British.

In European diplomacy, the British followed similar practices to their Continental counterparts. Issues such as appointment, control, remuneration and training were similar and handled essentially in a common fashion. British diplomats had few problems in seeing Britain as part of a European system guided by common rules, rather than as separate from such a system. The value and beneficial nature of such a system was outlined by many commentators, especially after the abatement of persistent religious hostility at the level of international relations in the late seventeenth century led to a search for secular rationales of diplomatic policy. The maintenance of *the* [not a] balance of power became the end of diplomacy. The apparent precision and naturalness of the image and language of balance greatly contributed to their popularity in an age in thrall to Newton and mechanistic physics. Furthermore, balance served as an appropriate *leitmotif* for a culture that placed an emphasis on the values of moderation and restraint, and for an international system and diplomatic culture organized around principles of equality or at least the absence of hegemony.[29] In 1769, the influential Scottish historian William Robertson, in his successful *History of the Reign of the Emperor Charles V*, presented the balance as a product of

> political science ... the method of preventing any monarch from rising to such a degree of power, as was inconsistent with the general liberty ... that great secret in modern policy, the preservation of a proper distribution of power among all the members of the system into which the states of Europe are formed ... From this era [the Italian Wars of 1494–1516] we can trace the progress of that intercourse between nations, which had linked the powers of Europe so closely together; and can discern the operations of that provident policy, which, during peace, guards against remote and contingent dangers; which, in war, hath prevented rapid and destructive conquests.[30]

Robertson's book provided empirical underpinning for the notion of contemporary Europe as a system that had devised a workable alternative to hegemonic power, and an alternative that was better, not only because it facilitated internal development, but also because competitive, but restrained, emulation gave Europe an edge over non-European powers. Thus, Edward Gibbon argued that

> the balance of power will continue to fluctuate, and the prosperity of our own or the neighbouring kingdoms may be alternatively exalted or depressed; but these partial events cannot essentially injure our general state of happiness, the system of arts, and laws, and manners, which so advantageously distinguish, above the rest of mankind, the Europeans and their colonies … The abuses of tyranny are restrained by the mutual influence of fear and shame … In peace, the progress of knowledge and industry is accelerated by the emulation of so many active rivals; in war, the European forces are exercised by temperate and indecisive contests.[31]

This perspective—a European version of universalism—described the ideal vision of the diplomatic world of Europe between the Peace of Westphalia of 1648 and the start of the French Revolution. It was expressed in such diplomatic concepts and devices as collective security and the congress system.[32] Yet, just as Gibbon's account excluded the 'barbarians' from his 'one great republic' of Europe, so also the diplomatic world was very brittle. That this world excluded women and the bulk of the male population, and reflected the world of orders and privilege that dominated and manipulated society, is scarcely surprising, but helped to ensure that revolution, nationalism, people's warfare and people's diplomacy all posed serious challenges. Simultaneously, the combined effect of Eurocentric ideologies and a diplomacy of force and coercion was to ensure that, as European horizons widened and relative power increased in the nineteenth century, it remained natural to resort to violence. The benefits to Europe proved short-term, but many of the problems are still with us today.[33]

2

The Choice of Envoys

If this travelling education had any real advantage, we might suppose
that it would qualify our young noblemen and gentlemen of rank for
foreign employments; but if we look abroad, we shall find that there
is at this time, but one English nobleman in any public character, and
one of a noble extraction.

Craftsman, 7 July (os) 1739

Diplomatic choice was twofold: where to send envoys and whom to send.
The bulk of this chapter is devoted to the second question, but the first
set the parameters. The central issue, as far as the first was concerned, was
the nature of relations. If they were poor, then diplomatic links were
broken or downgraded. This ensured that the range and nature of representation reflected in particular whether Britain was at war. The conflicts
of 1689–97 and 1702–13 affected representation but were succeeded by
a period in which links resumed and representation was extended. In
1739–48, however, war led to an end of diplomatic relations with both
Spain and France, and had effects on links with their allies, for example
Bavaria. In contrast, as the government made a major effort to create and
sustain anti-Bourbon alliances and to ensure that they had the desired
military consequences, so British diplomacy became much more active,
certainly in contrast to the position in 1736–8.

Peace in 1748 brought a resumption of relations with France and Spain.
James Wallace, Clerk in Newcastle's office, noted 'The Peace will send
many new ministers abroad'.[1] The active foreign policy of the inter-war
period, especially the attempts to win Spanish support and to push through
the Imperial Election Scheme, gave diplomats much to do. Conversely,
during the Seven Years' War (1756–63), Britain had few allies, and much

18

of Europe was opposed to her, or unsympathetic. Diplomatic relations were cut or diminished, missions closed, and much of the business of diplomacy was limited to wartime details, such as the conduct of neutral trade, the major issue at stake in relations with the Dutch.[2] Attempts to reawaken diplomatic links or to divide opponents were generally tackled by special missions. The very scale of diplomatic correspondence diminished and was in no way comparable with the position during the War of the Austrian Succession.

Peace negotiations brought a revival in diplomatic links, and the end of the Seven Years' War in 1763 ushered in a period of revived representation that lasted until foreign participation in the War of American Independence severed relations with France (1778), Spain (1779), and the Dutch (1780).[3] Peace in 1783 led to a resumption of relations, and when Britain entered the French Revolutionary War in 1793 they were only severed with France. However, French success shattered the opposing coalition and won France allies such as Spain, which went to war with Britain in 1796. The French Revolutionary and Napoleonic Wars were to limit gravely the continuity and extent of British representation.[4]

War was the most serious instance of a breakdown in relations that hit representation. There were also other types of dispute that led to the severance of diplomatic links. Some could be long-lasting, for example the rupture of relations with Russia in 1719–30, with Sweden in 1748–63, and with Austria in 1757–63. Robert Keith was recalled from Vienna without taking leave in 1757, because the Austrian envoy had been instructed to do the same 'and without so much as leaving a Secretary to carry on the business'. Reciprocity was an important factor, and was central to the issue of honour, for honour was implied by reciprocity. It allegedly prevented the dispatch of the Earl of Portmore as envoy to Parma in 1732 to congratulate Don Carlos on becoming Duke. In 1750, Newcastle observed:

> the King does not well see how he can send a minister to Stockholm, till a proper person is named to come from thence to His Majesty's court. You know, there is a person in Sweden who keeps a constant correspondence with me. I cannot say, any great advantage arises from it; however, we hear something, by that means, of what passes; and I wish, he were more regular in letters.[5]

Aside from the issue of mutuality in deciding where to send envoys, there was also that of effectiveness. Thus, there was an extension of the diplomatic network. New posts were created in Germany (Cologne, Dresden, Munich), Italy (Florence, Naples, Venice), and eastern Europe (St Petersburg, Warsaw). In some cases, such as Venice, there had earlier been British envoys, and the creation of a post reflected a resumption of links. In the case of Naples, a new state was created from the Austrian dynastic amalgamation when Don Carlos was made king after the Spanish conquest in 1734. In 1753, Sir James Gray became the first British Envoy Extraordinary in Naples. Greater representation in Italy reflected the importance of the peninsula in the power politics surrounding and following the War of the Spanish Succession. It was also pressed by Davenant on commercial grounds, although it is unclear how important these were.

At the same time, there was clearly a sense that the key decisions were still taken outside the peninsula and that states such as Genoa, Parma and Tuscany were of limited importance. This encouraged the expedient of the envoy with a commission to all the princes and states of Italy or responsibility for all or most of them: Charles, 3rd Earl of Peterborough (1713–14) and John Molesworth, who, although Envoy Extraordinary and Plenipotentiary in Turin (1720–5), was also regarded as Plenipotentiary to the courts of Italy and resided in Tuscany 1722–3. Molesworth left Turin on leave in May 1725 and did not return. George Tilson, an Under-Secretary, complained that August: 'Is there no one at Turin; or does Lord Molesworth leave the world to shift for itself there. That king is worth minding and if we had no better for that purpose he might be lost.'

In addition, there were diplomats accredited to Tuscany and Genoa at the same time: Sir Lambert Blackwell (1697–8, 1702–5), Dr Henry Newton (1704–11) and Henry Davenant (1714–22). However, this method posed problems. A critical Davenant wrote in 1721:

> I believe the King of Sardinia, who stands very much upon ceremony and is very jealous of his dignity, will not care for a Minister with characters to other courts; … a great trade to protect in these parts, and that a minister though not always necessary, might very often be wanted, more especially at Florence since the late disposition you have made of the state of Tuscany, and the dying condition of the Great Duke.

Francis Colman was appointed Resident in Tuscany in 1724, and in 1729 was sent back from leave because of the need for representation there.

When Colman was ill in 1732, Essex complained 'the want of a Minister at Parma leaves me in a perfect state of ignorance as to what passes there'.

The decision to create a new embassy or to upgrade an existing post was taken by the monarch. At the same time, suggestions were made by diplomats, generally keen to define an opportunity both for themselves and for Britain. Thus in December 1740, Sir Cyril Wych, the long-standing Envoy Extraordinary at Hamburg sought a post at Cassel and Frankfurt; the election of a new Holy Roman Emperor was due to take place at the latter. Wych admitted that a Hanoverian envoy might be the best representation at an imperial election, but argued that it would be good for the British government to have an envoy to provide direct accounts.[6] He was unsuccessful.

Wych's correspondence also throws light on another dynamic driving the allocation of posts: the incessant process of solicitation and intercession. In this way, diplomatic posts were no different to the rest of government patronage. For example, in 1725 he sought a post at St Petersburg, in 1728 a Copenhagen post to add to his in Hamburg, and in 1741 a post in Stockholm.[7]

Sometimes approaches for a new appointment made reference to the views of the state in question. Thus, in 1792, John Trevor informed Grenville that 'the Swiss Cantons wanted an envoy and proposed his secretary Thomas Jackson'.[8]

Diplomacy was not taught, but was an adjunct of gentility, a consequence of breeding. Diplomats were the personal representatives of the sovereign, and their readiness for office was seen as a product of their social rank. This was often closely related to the diplomatic rank of the official appointed. Thus selection was an expression of regard, respect and reciprocity. To show his friendship and regard for Charles Emmanuel III, George II sent the Earl of Essex to Turin in 1732. Essex was the first British envoy to that court with the rank of Ambassador, and had been a contemporary of Charles Emmanuel at Turin Academy.[9] In 1749, the French were upset that they had been sent an Earl (Albemarle) and not a Duke (Richmond);[10] the latter was concerned about inadequate allowances,[11] although the failure of France to offer an envoy of equivalent rank was also cited as a reason.[12]

The same year, Arthur Villettes, the long-serving and effective Resident in Turin, was replaced by an Envoy Extraordinary and Plenipotentiary: 'the King judging it proper, in the present circumstances of affairs, to send a person of rank and quality to the court of Turin (as a mark of his great regard for his Sardinian Majesty) has made choice of the Earl of Rochford.' In 1740, ministers were divided about sending Harrington to Berlin: 'the Chancellor said if no person of distinction went from England any future miscarriage would be attributed to that, then they both came into it.' When Earl Harcourt was appointed Ambassador to Paris in 1768, the Secretary of State reflected, 'there cannot be the smallest doubt but that his most Christian Majesty [Louis XV] will look upon the nomination of a person of his Lordship's high rank, distinguished abilities, and amiable disposition, as a fresh proof of the King's constant desire to preserve a good understanding between the two courts'.[13]

In turn, poor relations with his nephew Frederick the Great of Prussia (1740–86) were reflected by the representation of George II at Berlin by a mere Secretary in 1745 and 1747, and by nobody from May 1747 until the following April, again from November 1748 until 1750, and from 1751 until May 1756. Burnaby was sent to Stockholm in 1739 as a Secretary, Harrington noting 'In the situation we at present stand with your court, the King did not think fit to appoint a minister of a higher rank'. Similarly, poor relations with France led to representation at Paris from October 1740 until the French declaration of war in March 1744 being assigned to Antony Thompson, the former ambassador Waldegrave's chaplain. Reciprocity was cited as a factor in Anglo-Russian representation in 1721.[14] Reciprocity had another dimension. If the British were happy with a foreign envoy in London then it was necessary if they replaced their own to do so at the same rank, as otherwise the foreign envoy could expect to be recalled.[15]

Diplomats were rarely career civil servants. Indeed, the career officials in foreign service, the bureaucrats in the offices of the two Secretaries of State, spent their careers in those offices and were not rotated abroad. An apparent exception was Richard Neville Aldworth, who served as Under-Secretary in 1748–51, and was subsequently Secretary of Embassy (1762–3) and Minister Plenipotentiary (1764) in Paris. However, this should not be seen as an example of career progression, but rather of the role of patronage. Aldworth was a protégé of the 4th Duke of Bedford, served as Under-Secretary when the Duke was Secretary of State, and accompanied him to Paris when the Duke negotiated the Peace of Paris. Far from this role acting as a preparation for further promotion in the diplomatic system, Aldworth then became Paymaster of Pensions. Earlier, he had been recommended a long list of texts by Joseph Spence in order 'to make an ambassador of you'.[16] However, for Aldworth, as for many others, diplomatic service was simply one option among the governmental posts available to reward and promote factional service.

Diplomats were seen as in a different bracket to the career bureaucrats. They were privileged servants of the Crown, whose period of diplomatic service could alternate with other posts that today would be seen as in different career patterns. Many were parliamentarians, including no fewer than 34 MPs in 1715–54,[17] and some were in the military.

Diplomatic service could enhance the chance of holding a great office of state that was also a major political appointment: one of the Secretary-ships of State. A number of diplomats were thus promoted, including Methuen, Craggs, Carteret, Townshend, William Stanhope, Robinson, Chesterfield, Holdernesse, Rochford and Grantham.[18] Others, such as Whitworth in 1717, were discussed for such promotion. In 1713, Thomas, 3rd Earl of Strafford, an experienced diplomat then a Plenipotentiary at the Congress of Utrecht, was told that he would be recalled thereafter by Queen Anne 'since your services would be wanted here, and since she should not have the occasion of so high a character in Holland'. Benjamin Keene enunciated the theory of diplomacy as a preparation for office in 1754, 'Employments of this sort are generally given as trials of people's integrity and capacity, and then serve as steps to something solid at home'.[19]

Promotion, however, was often to posts where diplomatic experience was of no value. Waldegrave was well pleased with the promise of the Governorship of Barbados, 'a very advantageous post', on his return from Vienna, although in fact he went to Paris.[20] Abraham Stanyan returned from Constantinople in 1730 to become a Commissioner of the Privy Seal, and Edward Finch MP from Russia in 1742 to become Groom of the Bedchamber. When Finch had begun his diplomatic career, Sir Roger Mostyn had welcomed it as 'a most likely step to still greater favour at home'.[21] Philip, 5th Earl of Chesterfield never took up his post as Ambassador to Spain, because the Spaniards did not reciprocate with an appointment at that level.[22] Having returned from France he was successively Master of the Mint, Joint Postmaster-General and Master of the Horse. Thomas, 2nd Lord Walsingham, who also did not go to Spain because of 'the etiquette of an interchange',[23] also became, instead, Joint Paymaster-General.

Household posts were filled with former diplomats. Poyntz became Governor to the Duke of Cumberland, and Fawkener the Duke's secretary. Thomas Robinson returned from Vienna in 1748, 'a great favourite with the King',[24] to be a Lord of Trade (1748–9) and then Master of the Great

Wardrobe (1749–54), rather than the embassy to Spain that was mentioned,[25] until he became a Secretary of State in 1754. Dorset found the household more congenial on his return from Paris in 1789; he became Lord Steward and held that post until shortly before his death in 1799. Thus, just as the royal court was the best training place for diplomatic life, service abroad in foreign courts as the king's personal representative suited one for court office at home. In January 1755, George II was reported as wanting Rochford to move from being envoy in Turin either to Paris or to being First Gentleman of the Bedchamber.[26]

Such appointments are a reminder of the extent to which diplomats were royal servants, rather than officials of an impersonal state. If they fell foul of the monarch, as Henry Legge, for example, did in 1748, when he was sent to Berlin, then they were in a dire position. The inexperienced Legge, a good parliamentarian, was criticized by George II for being 'dazzled' by Frederick II and thus supporting an Anglo-Prussian alignment. George III was unimpressed with William Eden's conduct in France: 'I cannot say I am pleased with the tone of Mr. Eden's letters and think it highly advisable that one who had admitted a French minister to hold every sort of sore language should be got from thence, when I am confident it will of itself cease'.[27]

Conversely, royal favour could be important as, for example, with the appointment of Waldegrave and Essex. In 1724, George I turned down the proposal from his Secretaries of State that William Finch, then in Sweden, go to Florence:

> His Majesty being entirely satisfied with the services you have done him at Stockholm, and convinced by your dispatches of your being so thoroughly acquainted with the affairs of the North that it would be difficult to supply your place there with one equally versed in that part of his business, we found him very averse to the removing you from thence, but as an encouragement to your continuing there His Majesty chose rather to add to your present allowance that of Plenipotentiary.[28]

The role of the king and the need to manage him was captured in a letter of 1750 to Hanbury Williams from his ministerial ally Henry Fox:

> The Duke of Newcastle, Mr. Pelham, the Duke of Bedford, have all agreed that you should go to Turin, Sir James Gray to Poland, and

Mr. Villettes to Venice; The Duke of Newcastle proposed it to the King who approved of it, but added that the Czarina having desired it, it was necessary a minister from him should go to Warsaw *now*, and unfortunately you are the only one who can ... when you are at Hanover you must, if you would act discreetly, behave as one who is trying to be well with, and agreable to His Majesty rather than as one who may presume he is already so, which last I fear is not your case.

In order to help, Fox had 'begged', George's mistress, the Countess of Yarmouth to assist the envoy. Newcastle saw her as responsible for royal views on embassies.[29] Dorset was very much George III's choice for Paris in 1784.

Royal favour was important not only for who was chosen, but also for the rank at which they were chosen. Appointed Envoy Extraordinary to The Hague in September 1739, Trevor wanted the additional appointment as Plenipotentiary, which would have given more money and status, but found George II resistant. Horatio Walpole was able to write in December 1740 that the king 'began to relent on your account, but complained of the great sums employed, in support of his foreign ministers'. It was not until the following July that Trevor gained the promotion he coveted.[30]

Equally, royal favour was affected by, and usually mediated through, the ministerial politics of the period. This was not simply a case of the relevant Secretary of State, although he was usually important, even if by not taking a role. In addition, diplomats could owe their promotion to ministers other than the Secretary with whom they corresponded. For example, in the 1720s and 1730s, Keene, Mann, Robinson and Leheup were Walpole connections, although in 1736 Robinson could refer to 'belonging to the Duke of Newcastle'.[31] Thomas Robinson, later 2nd Earl of Grantham, Ambassador in Spain (1771–9) and Foreign Secretary (1782–3), owed his first post, at the age of 22, as Secretary of the British Embassy to the peace congress of Augsburg (which never met), to a meeting at the ball given by the Knights of the Bath between his father, a former Secretary of State, and Charles, 2nd Earl of Egremont. The latter, who was soon to be made a Secretary of State, had been ordered to find a Secretary 'who by making a proper use of such an employment might become fit for His Majesty's further notice and service'. Robinson senior agreed as long as Newcastle and the Yorkes agreed. Egremont told Bute, the newly appointed Secretary of State for the Northern Department. He agreed. The Yorkes unsuccessfully pressed another candidate, and

Robinson junior under Egremeont's patronage got the post. The other Secretary of State, Pitt, played no role.[32]

The appointment of foreigners to represent British interests was an aspect of royal power. It was particularly important under George I (1714–27), although not without problems, and there was criticism of such appointments.[33] In 1716, the Swiss-born Luke Schaub was informed:

> that foreigners by the laws of England are precluded from receiving any salaries from the Crown and though you yourself are an instance of the contrary yet the necessity of affairs requiring somebody to serve the King during the absence of his minister at Vienna he thinks a great difference may be made between establishing a fixed pension for a length of time and paying you for the intermediate time you serve.[34]

Townshend, however, assured St Saphorin, also Swiss-born, that nationality was not important to him as George I would be in control in any event.[35] However, he also noted that the issue of a replacement for Francis Colman, Secretary in Vienna 1721–4, was difficult, as there would be problems over St Saphorin's status there if Colman, with whom his relations had been good, was replaced by someone of distinction.[36] Schaub and St Saphorin were both well-integrated into the diplomatic world of Europe. Another British diplomat wrote of the latter in 1727 'I am persuaded you are satisfied that nobody knows the affairs of Germany better than him'.[37]

In any case, this very largely ceased to be an issue in the late 1720s. The two powerful Swiss diplomats whose careers had developed in the 1710s— Schaub (Paris, 1718, 1721–4) and St Saphorin (Vienna, 1718–27)—lost their postings and thereafter enjoyed less influence. Plans in 1727 to give several Hanoverians responsibility for British and Hanoverian interests only materialized for the Stockholm posting, where Baron Diescau, the Hanoverian envoy, represented Britain from late 1727 until October 1728. Subsequently, however, Diescau fell foul of Edward Finch and was recalled in 1730, partly due to Finch's complaints.[38]

George II also decided to appoint the Hanoverian diplomat Friedrich von Fabrice as Hanoverian envoy in Dresden and considered giving him responsibility for British interests there. This was particularly insensitive, as Saxony was a very significant posting, because Augustus II was willing to act as a go-between in the restoration of Anglo-Austrian and Anglo-Prussian relations. In addition, Fabrice was an old enemy to Townshend with very different views on European matters. Townshend had failed to get Fabrice sacked as one of George's chamberlains in 1726, and, thanks to postal interception and deciphering, the ministry had discovered that Fabrice was in touch with hostile foreign envoys. Fabrice had used their information to try to dissuade George I from anti-Austrian steps. In the event, excessive personal demands ensured that Fabrice was not sent to Dresden, but it had been a source of tension.[39]

Concern had been voiced by Cardinal Fleury, the leading French minister, leading the government to define its position:

> ... the Cardinal's apprehension of the consequence that the King's sending German ministers to some courts of the Empire might have both here and abroad ... tell him ... as to the success of the negotiations abroad, His Majesty never thought of having them carried on separately as Elector and King, but the employing of German ministers in some places is indeed unavoidable, there being some things to be transacted in the King's behalf as Elector, which cannot be properly negotiated by a British minister; and his Majesty has been so good in the choice of those who act on the part of the Electorate, as to take particular care that they shall be such as will in everything perfectly agree with his British ministers abroad, so that they will rather add weight than the contrary, to any negotiations that may be carrying on.[40]

This theory had not survived circumstances and, thereafter, there was relatively little interest in employing Hanoverian envoys to represent Britain. When, in 1728, the Hanoverian diplomat Reck was sent to the Congress of Soissons, Townshend ordered the British Plenipotentiaries to tell him nothing about the negotiations for a Wittelsbach alliance, adding 'He had no powers nor anything to do at the Congress, and was sent by the King with no other view but to inform and assist your Excellencies in the affairs of the Empire'.[41] The Hanoverian network did not expand, and some Hanoverian envoys, such as Tronchin du Breil, the Resident in Paris 1724–31, were not very conspicuous. Instead, British envoys could find themselves expected to serve Hanoverian ends. The resumption of Anglo-Russian diplomatic relations in 1730 was not matched in the case of Hanover, and from the 1730s Hanoverian interests, such as the import of Russian grain in the 1740s, were handled by British diplomats.

However, although no longer regularly represented in France and Russia, Hanoverian diplomats were present in Paris during the winter of

1741–2, while the regular representation in Vienna and Regensburg under-lined the continued importance of German disputes and matters of imperial jurisdiction. Hanoverian diplomats provided George II with sources of information and channels of communication that were outside the control of the Secretaries of State.

British diplomats encountered difficulties as a result of the actions of their Hanoverian colleagues, although it was also convenient to blame them for problems that were not their fault. In 1741, Frederick II drew attention to serious discrepancies between what he was told by the royal and Electoral envoys, telling Hyndford 'when you Mylord call a thing white Sweicheldt calls it black, and when you call it black he calls it white'.[42] Such problems made some envoys very uneasy, as did instructions to act on behalf of Hanover. Whitworth found that British and Hanoverian views on relations with Prussia clashed.[43] In 1734, Horatio Walpole wrote to his brother about orders received from George II to correspond directly with Johann Philipp von Hattorf, the head of the Hanoverian Chancery in London:

> this cannot go on for long without being perceived in the office, and consequently by Lord Harrington … as it will I suppose relate to His Majesty's demands concerning a negotiation about Bergh and Juliers; and as I am afraid these demands will be unreasonable and break off the negotiation; it may not be proper that the correspondence should appear in the office, and indeed by my writing directly to Hattorf it will be kept out of it.[44]

The following year, Wych wrote to Tilson:

> If the German ministers hear that there is a design of giving me creden-tials to the circle of Lower Saxony and employing me at some other courts they will oppose it with all their strength because they would never have an English minister employed in Germany but when they have brought themselves into some scrape to help them out again, but this reason is strong enough … to induce an English ministry to make use of their own people.[45]

Relations between British and Hanoverian envoys were not always poor—Waldegrave and Saladin were on good terms in Paris in the early 1730s, and Saladin wrote a report for Horatio Walpole,[46] but there could be tension and differences, particularly at Vienna.[47]

Aside from Hanoverians, there was little use of foreigners other than in a minor capacity, principally in Switzerland, where Armand Louis de St George, Comte de Marsay, remained envoy to Geneva or the Helvetic Republic from 1717 until 1762. Formally he was a Hanoverian, not a British envoy, but he dealt mostly with British issues. Jerome de Salis was envoy to the Grison Leagues 1743–50. The Frenchman Lewis Dutens, who was James Mackenzie's secretary at Turin in 1758–61, was in charge in the absence of envoys in 1761–2, 1764–5 and 1781.

In 1735, Horatio Walpole was approached by Baron Mark de Fonseca, formerly an Austrian representative in Paris but now seeking employment:

> he hinted he could be of great service at Brussels: that he knew, on account of his religion, he could not be an avowed minister to the King: that he had no design of removing Mr. Daniel, who was an honest and industrious man; but yet he insinuated, that he could be much more useful to the king there than it was in Mr. Daniel's power to be.

The approach was not followed up.

Foreigners did not tend to be used later in the century, but in 1788 Hugh Elliot complained about Charles Keene who had been Sir Thomas Wroughton's secretary and who was left in charge at Stockholm between Wroughton's death in August 1787 and Liston's arrival in August 1789:

> It is exceedingly to be regretted that the English chargé des affaires at Stockholm is peculiarly disagreeable to the King and his ministers. Mr. Keene is not an Englishman, his father, I am told, is or was the Russian Postmaster at Warsaw, and I am sorry to add that the most impartial people complain of the total devotion of that gentleman to the King's enemies ... I have subjected myself to great expense in placing Englishmen and men of merit, either with myself or others at foreign missions, and I presume that upon no account English foreign ministers ought to be allowed to take up with the first idle foreigner as a secretary whom they find able to write a letter in English.

Four years later, after Colonel Louis Braun, the long-serving envoy in Switzerland, died, it was requested that he be replaced by a British subject, and one of 'parts and suitable education', not like Robert Colebrooke, Minister in 1762–5, 'whose house was a mere gaming house'.[48] He was indeed replaced by a British subject.

Foreigners were sometimes used when diplomatic relations were ruptured. Disrupted Anglo-Spanish and Anglo-Austrian relations in the late 1720s led to reliance on friendly diplomats. Francis Vandermeer, the Dutch envoy in Spain, provided regular reports on developments,[49] while Berkentin and Tarouca, the Danish and Portuguese envoys in Vienna, sent in a number of reports. Tarouca, who was close to Prince Eugène, also acted as an agent of influence on behalf of Britain.[50] St Saphorin praised Berkentin, Tarouca and the Sardinian Breglio as sources of accurate information on Austrian policy. He characterized Berkentin as clever and close to the Austrian Chancellor, Count Sinzendorf, and Tarouca as possessing a rank that enabled him to be on familiar terms with members of the Austrian government. This praise for Tarouca was repeated by the next two British envoys in Vienna.[51] In the late 1720s, Cramm, the Wolfenbüttel envoy in St Petersburg, was suspected of being a British agent, and the government of Wolfenbüttel sought money from Britain, on the grounds that it helped British interests in Russia.[52] Cramm's Paris counterpart, Johann Christoph, Baron Schleinitz, provided information to the British and their French allies in the late 1720s.

The collapse of Anglo-French relations in 1731 made it more important for the British to develop links in Paris. Diplomats who helped in the 1730s included the Swedish envoy, Baron Gedda, a correspondent of Horatio Walpole, and possibly his Portuguese and Russian counterparts. In 1741, Newcastle received information from the Russian envoy in London which he had presumably received from his Parisian colleague:

> The Duke of Newcastle laid before their Excellencies an extract of a letter communicated to him … by Prince Scherbatow; giving an account, that it was reported at Paris, that the French intended to fall upon the English in Scotland and Ireland; and that they were, for that reason, sorry to hear of the return of Sir John Norris with his squadron to the English coast.[53]

In a similar fashion, British ministries received reports from the diplomats of allied powers during mid-century disputes with Prussia and Sweden. Such diplomats acted as both intermediaries and sources of information. In 1753, the government turned to the Dutch envoy in Prussia, while two years earlier they had sought information from the Russian envoy in Stockholm.[54] In thus expanding its diplomatic network, Britain benefited both from allies that had a large diplomatic corps, especially the United

Provinces and (between 1716 and 1731) France, and from good relations with a number of second-rank powers that were not always engaged in the conflicts of the period. The Dutch retained diplomatic links with France in the War of the Austrian Succession after they had been severed between Britain and France in 1744, until France invaded the United Provinces in 1747. Charles Emmanuel III of Sardinia remained neutral in the Seven Years' War, and his envoy in London, Count Viry, both provided the British ministry with information on French plans, and, in combination with his colleague in Paris, acted as a valuable intermediary in Anglo-French negotiations.

The intervention of foreign diplomats was not always welcome. The attempt by the Modenese Resident in London, Giuseppe Riva, to improve Anglo-Austrian relations in early 1729 met a cool response,[55] and that by Genoa to help settle disputes with Spain was not encouraged.[56] However, the value of friendly diplomats as sources of intelligence was clear, and this helps to explain British anger when diplomats of friendly powers, such as Abraham van Hoey, the Dutch envoy in Paris in the 1730s and 1740s, failed to act as expected.

Disrupted relations also threw an added responsibility on British envoys in other posts. Nearby embassies could be expected to provide information. Thus, in September 1792, after Gower had been recalled from Paris, Elgin was instructed to send from Brussels accounts of developments in France.[57] Envoys at posts where there were also diplomats from the power with whom direct relations had been severed could be expected to carry out negotiations.

The extent to which a diplomatic service with professional ethos may be discerned depends in part on which diplomats are being scrutinized. It is certainly possible to detect elements of career progression and specialization in the case of some diplomats. Robinson served in a junior capacity in Paris (1723–30), before taking on responsibility at Vienna (1730–48), being a Plenipotentiary in the peace congress at Aix-la-Chapelle (1748), and serving as a Secretary of State (1754–5). Andrew Mitchell, one of the talented and energetic Scots in British diplomacy,[58] proceeded from Brussels (1752–5) to Berlin (1756–71). Rochford served at Turin (1749–55), Madrid (1763–6) and Paris (1766–8) and became a Secretary of State (1768–75). Joseph Yorke was Secretary of Embassy at Paris 1749–51 before serving at The Hague from 1751 until 1780. He was briefly appointed to Berlin in 1758 and was considered for a Secretaryship of State in 1778.

Longevity in service was important, because, as in most spheres of public life, training was on the job. Experience was crucial. Some diplomats gained training and patronage through posts on the staffs of envoys, such as Robinson and Trevor with Horatio Walpole and Keith with Sandwich. In 1789, John Mitford referred to a nephew who 'had a desire to add to his military profession the diplomatic, and for this purpose has been studying under Mr. [Thomas] Walpole at Munich and Mannheim … it occurred to him that Lord Auckland, to whom he is in some degree known, might want a private secretary who had some knowledge of French, and a little of the habit of the corps diplomatique'.[59] Townshend wrote to St Saphorin in 1724 about Charles Harrison, the newly appointed Minister in Vienna: 'de mes parens … it apprendra avec plaisir son metier de vous, il etudiera vos leçons, et tachera de se former sur vôtre modèle'.[60] However, there were also examples of the appointment of aristocratic and non-aristocratic envoys to responsible posts without any such experience.

Envoys were also briefed in London. In 1728, Poyntz read Horatio Walpole's dispatches from recent years. En route for Vienna in 1752, the Earl of Hyndford wrote to Onslow Burrish, then at Munich: 'Before I left London I went through all your correspondence for above eighteen months past, with the Duke of Newcastle, and I admire your distinctness and punctuality.'[61] Three years earlier, the government were keen that Villettes on his way back from Turin should meet Rochford en route there as his replacement, so that Villettes could inform him of the situation at the court.[62] The papers of envoys sometimes include the dispatches of predecessors that were clearly obtained as a form of information. Thus, copies of diplomatic correspondence from Warsaw in 1733 were apparently prepared for the later guidance of Hanbury Williams.[63] In preparation for his embassy at The Hague, Auckland in 1789 read all the correspondence from Malmesbury's embassy and also sought information from him on the Dutch government, on diplomats at The Hague and on issues of etiquette and dress.[64]

The *ad hoc* manner in which diplomats were 'trained' or at least instructed contrasted with suggestions for more systematic instruction. These were very few, most prominently the creation of the Regius Chairs of Modern History at Cambridge and Oxford in 1724. This had very little impact,[65] and, despite the scheme, few Oxbridge graduates went into diplomacy. One who did, John Burnaby, made it clear that patronage was still important. After graduating, he 'was then put into the Secretary of State's office by Mr. Walpole's recommendation'.[66] For those who lacked connections, experience continued to be seen as of greater importance than formal qualifications. In 1741, Frederick Frankland MP wrote to Robinson to recommend a Swiss chaplain as a secretary, adding 'I think he promises much better than any raw young fellow from the University'. Daniel, Lord Finch, who unsuccessfully sought an embassy, clearly felt that an appropriate education would have helped, but what he described was not a course followed by those who did gain posts:

> I know the German language is despised and thought of no use. I cannot say much for it. But however I wish I had spent the four last years of the Queen [Anne] in this country [Germany] and some part of the time in any of their academies where one might have learned their language and by dipping a little into the Civil Law and what they call the Jus Publicum of the Empire might have been in a capacity even in your Lordship's opinion of having been employed at the beginning of this reign.[67]

Other than the regius chairs, singularly little governmental, political or press attention was devoted to the issue. There was, however, one exception, an article, anonymous in the fashion of the period, published in the *Centinel*, a London newspaper, on 27 September 1757. Arguing that the British were frequently duped in negotiation, the article called for the establishment of a political academy for the formation of statesmen, although the tone was that of a Swiftian condemnation of the foibles of the world. The academy was to include:

> a Dancing-School ... address and a graceful appearance have some influence in all courts, and often contribute to the carrying of great points. It is at least very improper that a person invested with a public character, which represents his sovereign, should be so far destitute of all breeding, as not to know how to come into a room with tolerable grace, or to behave himself when he is there. In this school might likewise be taught the ceremonies and punctilios of honour, which ought to be observed in conversation with ladies, or other persons of high rank
>
> ... a Geographical School; in which our young students in politics should be instructed in the knowledge of the globe and maps.
>
> ... the Ambassador's School; where I would have Monsieur Wiquefort's book upon the functions of that high office, carefully

explained to the students; and no person should ever be sent abroad with a public character, who is not a tolerable proficient in the interests, manners and characters, of the chief persons of that court, at which he is to reside. The Professor of that school should take great pains to instruct his disciples not to be imposed upon and led by the nose (as some ambassadors have been) by the tricks, subtleties and finesse of artful ministers ...

In another school I would have the whole modern art of treaty-making explained by a professor, well acquainted with this part of political knowledge.

He must be a man of subtle, prevaricating genius, a perfect master of ambiguities, double meaning, and equivocal expressions; which are of great use, when it is not proper to let the sense of the contracting parties appear in public. He must likewise be well versed in secret and separate articles, saving clauses, and counter-stipulations; which make the greatest part of modern treaties, and give either party an opportunity of breaking through them when occasion requires, without any apparent violation of public faith, by distinguishing between the letter and the spirit of a treaty.

In 1752, Onslow Burrish had to select a secretary. The recommendations he received throw light on what was expected at junior levels and how, even at this more 'professional' level, personal connections played a crucial role. The eventual choice, William Money, was 'very sober, honest ... writing a very tolerable hand, which is capable of improvement ... having some knowledge both of the French and German languages, but, particularly, of the latter'. The son of a clerk in the office of the Southern Secretary, Money was only 15, but was recommended by the Duke of Newcastle, one of the two Secretaries of State.[68] Similarly, ministerial promises were crucial in the choice of Robert Sutton as a secretary to one of the plenipotentiaries at Cambrai.[69]

Yet, appointments made in response to connections did not please all envoys. Whitworth asked Tilson in 1721 'why are not you more cautious at first in the choice of those you encourage and employ. Many a man of wit may be dangerous, and many an honest man may be impracticable'.[70] In 1764, the young, immature and impecunious Thomas Bunbury MP was not acceptable as Secretary of Embassy in Paris to the envoy, the Earl of Hertford, who had already offered the post to David Hume, nor to others. Lord Beauchamp exploded: 'I have just heard that Mr. Bunbury is appointed … what a potent counsellor! What a wise and experienced nego-tiator! In one word he is Mr. Fox's brother in law, and that is at present sufficient to gild a character with all the lustre it can wish.' In Munich in 1782, John Trevor considered appointing a Catholic as his secretary, explaining:

> The system of young gentlemen secretaries except in the idea of obliging some parent or friend seldom answers—a steady chancellis-tical sort of a German qui connoit sa place—who is sensible and well informed, *writes* English well, and is master of German and French is certainly a much more useful and convenient personage—I have met with such, but they have not been Protestants.[71]

However, the notion of diplomacy as a form of outdoor relief continued. Auckland referred in 1806 to 'a respectable attempt on the part of the young man to escape so creditably from London dissipation. But I conceive that the convulsed and broken predicament of foreign courts will induce Mr. Fox to send, if they can be found, ministers of experience and resource, or at least of a certain age and weight as well as of rank'.[72]

Diplomacy was not well paid. In 1704, George Stepney pressed for his recall from Vienna on the grounds of cost, estimating that he had person-ally lost £2,260. In 1697, the credit of John Robinson (Stockholm) came near to collapsing. The cost of behaving appropriately was a particular problem. This was especially so at the more expensive and prestigious courts where diplomats were expected to maintain a costly state. The Duke of Shrewsbury aroused complaints in Paris in 1713 by going to bed too soon and not having a party on Queen Anne's birthday.[73] The cost of diplomacy was an additional reason to appoint wealthy, or, at least, credit-worthy men.

Aside from the issue of choice on the part of Crown and ministry, there was also choice by envoys and potential envoys. The former could seek different posts, while the latter could refuse to accept a post or could only accept it on terms. In 1747, Hyndford wrote from St Petersburg, 'I have now the spleen for the first time; I long more than ever to change my situation to some warmer climate, and less expensive court, excepting only the court of Berlin, from which, I hope, the King will dispense me for reasons very well known to His Majesty'. Russia was clearly a difficult post to fill. 'Who would marry a man that is going to Petersburg?' complained Wych in 1741, a point repeated by Harris in 1777.[74] Hyndford did not think the post suitable for a wife. 'I cannot wish you Russia though you were ambassador', was Henry Fox's verdict to Hanbury Williams. In 1754, Joseph Yorke resisted pressure to go to St Petersburg, at the same time providing evidence of the criteria adopted by an experienced diplomat:

> I have neither strength of mind nor *body* for it … nothing but an absolute order from the King, under good conditions, should force me into a post which would throw me out of the way of everything, where I should get neither honour nor credit, and from whence I might by some sudden revolution mistake the road, and take a trip to Siberia instead of Middlesex.[75]

Arriving in Russia in 1758, Robert Keith attempted to leave without success the following year. Holdernesse broke the news:

> You know of what importance it is for us to keep forms with the Court of Petersburg even at this time, and the necessity of having a person of trust and ability upon the spot to be ready to treat the moment a favourable opportunity offers, and at this time you could not be removed without disgusting the Empress [Tsarina Elizabeth] … so that my inclination to serve you must for the present yield to necessity and public utility.[76]

Such an argument did not encourage service, although Keith was an experienced diplomat and continued at St Petersburg until October 1762. Fitzherbert was against the post because of the cost.[77] Climate was not only a factor in Russia. In 1721, Whitworth confessed that he was fed up with the rough climate and tempers of northern Europe, no longer wished to serve at Berlin, and, instead, hoped to be a Plenipotentiary at the peace congress that was to meet at Cambrai.[78] His complaint throws interesting light on the need for patronage and the desire for progression held by long-standing and thus 'professional' envoys:

> I was quite weary of being continually exposed to new changes and acquaintance, and of losing my superiors by that time I had any tolerable share in their esteem: you may remember I was just in the same case when Mylord Townshend went out formerly [1716]; the same was then entirely new to me, but having since had the opportunity of gaining some place in my poor Lord Stanhope's friendship and

confidence, I just lost him when it begun to be most agreeable, and would probably have been of most use to me … nothing would have encouraged me to continue longer in this uncertain dependence, but my Lord Townshend's return, and his continuing to remember me in so obliging a manner.[79]

This patronage was designed by Whitworth to help him escape northern climes:

You know I have waited several years, only for an occasion to go out of the foreign employments with a good grace, which was my chief view in the congress at Brunswick; for otherwise it would not have been very agreable to be coupled there with Poles and Moscovites: But that congress is like to come to nothing, and the other being thus filled up, there is no more left for me to hope abroad; and as it is too great a discouragement to have the drudgery of business continually left on my hands, whilst the posts of pleasure and reputation are disposed in favour of others, all my thoughts are now turned seriously towards coming home: If I do not live there with much distinction, I shall at least without chagrin, and enjoy much more of life in every article than I can possibly here, though with the appointments of ambassador.

Whitworth's concern with his ranking within the profession was apparent. He suspected that:

Lord Carteret's friendship for my Lord Polwarth or some insinuations from Lord Cadogan or Count Bothmer to my disadvantage have done me this ill turn. I have spoke truth on several occasions and that may have displeased. The King of Prussia could not have taken amiss my being removed to so advantagious a station. On the contrary I ran a risk of losing my credit here since they find I have so little at home … Had you sent Lord Stair, Lord Cadogan, or any person of their rank out of England, I should not have complained; but when you sought for a minister in the North, I had hopes I should not have been passed over, after so long a course of service, especially since I had treated these very matters at The Hague, and was intimately acquainted with almost all the foreign ministers who are to assist at that congress. I own I look upon it as a very great slur on my reputation, and the world must think it so, to see me left in an obscure and disagreable situation, instead of being employed in a place where the most important affairs of Europe are to be settled; and where I might have acted with satisfaction and distinction, and had hopes of gaining to myself some new merit by my services to His Majesty and my country.[80]

Vienna was preferred to Berlin, Morton Eden seeking transfer in 1792: 'for, although in despite of its good pay it is subject to great expenses, it is a paradise in comparison of Berlin in every point of view, locality, society, country, business etc.'[81]

More seriously, there was a reluctance on the part of many to serve. Observers, British and foreign,[82] frequently commented on the difficulty of finding envoys. L'Hermitage, the Dutch agent, thought it would be difficult to replace Stair at Paris in 1720, because diplomatic posts were unpopular;[83] indeed Sir Robert Sutton had to be threatened with dismissal in order to get him to go.[84] Waldegrave commented in 1728 on 'the want of proper subjects to fill up foreign embassies'. Four years earlier, Horatio Walpole thought Robinson would 'prove extremely useful in the knowledge of foreign affairs, which is a talent not very common amongst our young gentleman in England'.[85]

Ministers sometimes voiced the same point, although the difficulty was at times due to the sensitivity of the post and the need to balance different claimants. Stanhope told the French envoy in 1719 that Whitworth was the only diplomat who could be sent to Berlin. The following year, Craggs was unimpressed by Cadogan, noted that Schaub 'labours under the difficulty of being a foreigner' and added 'I see all our foreign affairs subsiding in a manner for want of people to set them a going'. In 1755, Newcastle remarked on the difficulty of replacing Albemarle at Paris.[86] It was a very sensitive moment in Anglo-French relations, and the French wanted the post filled.[87] There were a number of possibilities—Rochford, Halifax, Egremont and Hertford—in part because Paris was not a distant exile comparable to St Petersburg. Newcastle wanted Hertford, as he felt sure of his support. The French envoy felt that on grounds of birth, dignity and personal qualities he was a good choice.[88]

Seven years earlier, when Newcastle had unsuccessfully offered Sandwich the Paris post and had also complained about a shortage of diplomats,[89] the experienced Sardinian envoy Ossorio, who was close to the government, put his finger on the political factor:

... le manque de sujets du second ordre bien capable d'une telle commission [restoring good relations with France and Spain] et dans lesquels les ministres puissent en même tems mettre une confiance parfaite comme il faudroit pour ce qui regarde leurs vues et leurs interêts particuliers dans la nation et dans le Parlement.[90]

In 1758, Pitt and Newcastle both complained that it had been very difficult to find someone for Madrid, and that several who had been approached had refused, while, conversely, several who had sought the post had been rejected.[91] In the end, George, Earl of Bristol, the envoy in Turin, was appointed as Ambassador. He was replaced by James Stewart Mackenzie. The Sardinian envoy thought him 'peu versé dans les affaires' but noted his personal qualities including wealth, sociability, honesty and distinguished parentage.[92] Later in the century, the situation improved. In 1783, when peace brought new opportunities, there were numerous candidates for diplomatic posts, 'as the reduction of civil offices has made them more valuable'.[93]

Courtly skills were important. As a pamphleteer pointed out 'that some of our ministers can neither dance nor sing, would not be a reproach to them, if they had but somebody with them that could; for, as long as courts exist, the social virtues will influence the most serious transactions'.[94] In 1727, Waldegrave was instructed to inform the French envoy at Vienna, the Duke of Richelieu, 'that you choose rather to imitate his example of politeness and good breeding, than to follow the steps of Mor. De St. Saphorin, who has been censured as having acted too rough and forbidding a part'.[95] While waiting in Paris to proceed to Vienna, Waldegrave's diary reveals that he spent much of his time at formal diplomatic dinners. In addition, there was wild boar hunting (17 October), stag hunting (18, 24 October), shooting (19 October), and roe deer hunting (25 October). In 1735, Horatio Walpole was to think Waldegrave better suited by his 'suppless and address' than Horatio to seek to win over Chauvelin, the French foreign minister, though, the same year, he complained of Waldegrave's 'pitiful and weak conduct' towards the French.[96]

Aristocrats could expect to be appointed young: Holdernesse to Venice in 1744 when not yet 26. In 1752, Hanbury Williams wrote of the Habsburgs, 'there is no treating with that House unless much more able ministers are employed, there must be a Duke with a blue ribbon [garter] at Vienna', a theme he returned to in 1753.[97] Grantham was sorry to see James Harris depart from Spain as Minister Plenipotentiary:

He is spoken of with the greatest regard by the principal persons here, for the behaviour which he observed in the late critical conjuncture and they love him for having most judiciously fallen into their manners and customs. It is not a very easy matter for an Englishman to become a Spaniard in a day; but I can assure you I shall not be wanting in my endeavours to execute that part of my duty which consists in culti-vating and living on an easy footing with the ministerial society here however different their sentiments, prejudices, habits, and manners may be from others.[98]

However, well-connected individuals posed problems, not least because they had interests in Britain that required cultivation, and envoys were aware that 'les absents ont toujours tort'.[99] In 1784, Torrington complained to Harris, 'so few people think of their friends, when once they have passed the river Lethe [i.e. the Channel] that I am astonished when anyone ever mentions my name'.[100] In January 1747, Sandwich requested leave to return in order to tend his electoral interests, as did Dorset in 1784.[101]

Aristocrats were particularly worth the government cultivating as English peers all had seats in the House of Lords, while their Scottish counterparts formed an electoral college out of which sixteen Scottish peers were elected. Thus, in January 1784, Dorset sent Carmarthen his proxy vote in the Lords to give 'to anybody the King approves'; as a diplomat-peer this was his first obligation.[102] However, despite the social skills that gained him important entrées at court, Dorset was less than diligent in sending reports, possibly because his habitual laziness was exac-erbated by a minor stroke in 1785.[103] This forced a role upon the other diplomats in Paris, Hailes[104] and Eden.

The importance of selecting aristocrats as envoys was not restricted to royal courts. Aristocratic envoys were also sent to The Hague and to Venice. The latter was no longer an important post, but status was very important there and it had a reputation for pleasure that could be expected to attract many aristocrats. Chesterfield was posted to The Hague, 'as the King ... has obliged me to undertake it',[105] while the long-serving Joseph Yorke was the son of an earl. Indeed, The Hague contained a princely court, that of Orange, which was closely related to the British royal house. In 1734, the Princess Royal married William IV of Orange. In 1748, the influential Dutch politician William, Count of Bentinck wrote to Newcastle from The Hague that he hoped that, if Sandwich did not continue to serve, an envoy would be sent 'dont nous puissions être sûrs par rapport à ses principes et à ses liaisons avec vous'. These political criteria were accompanied by social considerations:

> il seroit très à propos que ce fût quelqu'un d'un rang et d'une naissance distinguée. Je suis persuadé que cela seroit plus agréable et que cela auroit un beaucoup meilleur effet, que si les affaires étoient mises entre les mains de quelqu'un, qui, étant d'un moindre rang, n'auroit pas les mêmes agréments pour sa personne que pourroit avoir son supérieur. Je crois, que ceci est un point très important.[106]

On receipt of this letter, Newcastle wrote to the Duke of Cumberland: 'We must find some person of quality to send to The Hague, I wish your Royal Highness would let me know, who you think would do there'.[107]

Rank, however, involved cost, which was always of concern to monarch and ministers. The cost was generally financial, although high-ranking envoys could also press for marks of royal favour, such as honours.[108] Cadogan was sent to The Hague in 1716 on the understanding 'that after his Lordship has paid the compliment to the States, he may return to England, and that the business at The Hague may be carried on without the extraordinary charge of an ambassador'.[109]

Pressure for higher rank came not only from diplomats but also from a sense that only envoys of high rank had an impact abroad. Stanyan suggested in 1713 that it 'would be more for the dignity of the Crown generally to employ ambassadors rather than envoys, and they should be in greater number than they are at present ... but the Lord Treasurer has still views of retrenching'.[110]

Eleven years later, Whitworth wrote about a potential Resident at Vienna:

> It will exclude him in a great measure from the best company, or at least make him very indifferently looked upon there; for the title of Resident in that Court, is generally given to men of no family, or figure; and he will have occasion of very distinguishing parts, and a long acquaintance before he can wear out this prejudice; for though he may have audiences of the Emperor, yet he won't be on the same footing as Envoys Extraordinary.
>
> The title of Minister in general will leave Mr. Harrison to act with much more liberty, and to make his way at Court, according as he behaves himself.[111]

Lists of the establishments of posts make it clear that there were major discrepancies in expenditure between diplomatic ranks. At The Hague in 1734 and again in 1739, the annual charge including extraordinaries for an Ambassador was £6,800, for an Envoy Extraordinary and Plenipotentiary £2,990, for a Resident £1,695 and for a Secretary on the royal payroll (as opposed to the private secretary of an envoy) £730. An Envoy Extraordinary who was not a Plenipotentiary received an ordinary allowance of £3 daily less.[112] In 1748, Newcastle assured his brother, Henry Pelham, the First Lord of the Treasury, that 'in the disposition of our foreign ministers, I have had the greatest regard, I could, to the doing it, in the cheapest manner'. The same letter revealed the extent to which the notion of rank was intertwined with that of connectability. Well-connected envoys were seen as more likely to be successful, because their connections were both testimony to the importance attached to the mission and the means of furthering its success. Newcastle revealed that he had suggested Joseph Yorke for Paris: 'I think him the properest person on all accounts. The relation he has, to His Royal Highness [he was Cumberland's aide-de-camp]; and his being My Lord Chancellor's son; will add weight to his commission, and make him very agreable to the French ministers.'[113]

Such considerations do not accord with the presentation of Britain as a dynamic commercial economy with the accompanying values. In part, indeed, a contrast can be discerned within the diplomatic service between those who focused much of their attention on trade and others who did not. The former group did not only include Consuls but also envoys and agents who were primarily entrusted with commercial negotiations.

What is less clear is whether these individuals and commercial negotiations in general received insufficient support and attention and whether trade itself featured too little in the activities of diplomats. This can be seen as reflecting the minor role of commercial interest and interests in their selection. A pamphleteer of the 1800s complained:

> I should suppose, that after negotiating with the respective courts where ministers are accredited, the next point of duty would be to study the commerce, genius, and locality of the country they often reside in during so great a part of their lives; but many of our English, as well as French ministers, leave the country with little more local knowledge than they brought into it. The French government, aware of this, have now their *Commercial Agents*, who, being paid for the office they hold are not (like our consuls) necessitated to follow trade, but apply their

time and talents in investigating the political and commercial nature of the country they live in, whilst the ambassador has only to look to the formal part of the business, and do the honours of his office.[114]

Envoys who lacked any prior knowledge of commerce, almost by definition most of the landed order, were not necessarily anti-trade, but commercial considerations certainly played scant role in the appointment of most. Few diplomats would have subscribed to the view expressed about 'the most solid department of an ambassador; it is chiefly to him his nation looks for an extent of its present commerce, and for plans of future enterprizes; since no one has so favourable an opportunity of discovering and pointing them out'.[115] Indeed, in 1730, Claudius Rondeau, who was soon to be appointed Consul-General in Russia, where he was already working, criticized his predecessor Thomas Ward, who became Minister Resident that year:

> I was very much surprised to hear from England, that some people thought Mr. Ward would soon have a character sent him, though he is a very honest man and a good merchant, being actually engaged in a considerable trade. I believe nobody who knows him, thinks he will make a good minister, and that if such a step was made by our court it would be his ruin, and that of our interest here, for it would be but a bad beginning to name a person who is now contracting to buy and sell goods.

The last was a very clear expression of the social politics of diplomacy.[116]

This social politics was a product not only of British values, but also of an assessment of how far an envoy was likely to be acceptable. Representations could play a role in the latter. Edward Finch was intended for Turin in 1727 but was sent instead to Stockholm in 1728, after the Sardinian envoy had indicated that the Protestant zeal he had displayed as Minister Plenipotentiary to Augustus II of Saxony-Poland would make him an unacceptable choice. William, Count of Bentinck pressed against Sir John Goodricke going to Brussels as Resident in 1750. He did not go.[117] Acceptability related both to general manners and ease of access and to relations with specific individuals. In 1774, Langlois (Vienna) wrote to St Paul (Paris):

> Frequenting all men and receiving all men is a necessary and indis-

43

pensable duty in your situation. Though a man may go about a great deal and learn very little, yet it gives him the reputation of activity at home; and the contrary conduct will infallibly and with great justice be imputed to him as a neglect of and indifference to the duties of his employment.

Wych suggested that Frederick II's knowledge of his musical talent would make him an appropriate choice for Berlin.[118] He was not, however, chosen. Schaub went to Saxony-Poland in 1730–1 in response to a request from the Saxon minister Count Hoym, although the ministry was dubious about this and took pains to retain Woodward in the post so that Schaub could be rapidly withdrawn if the mission did not work out as intended.[119] Newcastle asked foreign diplomats in whom he had confidence, such as the Sardinian envoys, what they thought of prospective appointments.[120]

The frequent appointment of military men reflected not simply the absence of notions of specialization and technical training in diplomacy, and their already-demonstrated willingness to serve the Crown and availability in peacetime, but also the sense that such envoys were especially appropriate for particular courts. This was especially true of Berlin. Thomas Wentworth, Lord Raby, later 3rd Earl of Strafford, who was in Berlin in 1701 and again in 1703–11, had served in the army throughout the Nine Years' War. He only accepted his diplomatic post on condition that he should continue to receive his army promotion as if serving, and in 1707 became a Lieutenant-General. The previous year, he had accompanied Frederick I of Prussia to the Low Countries and taken part in the War of the Spanish Succession. Strafford served at The Hague in 1711–14, and was one of the joint Plenipotentiaries at the Congress of Utrecht. Also at Berlin, Colonel, from 1727 Brigadier, Charles Du Bourgay (1724–30), was followed by Lieutenant-Colonel Sir Charles Hotham (1730), and then by Captain Melchior Guy Dickens (1730–41). John, 3rd Earl of Hyndford (1741–4) was a Captain in the foot-guards. Hugh Elliot (1777–82) failed to obtain the military career he sought but he had been to the military school at Metz and had served as a volunteer with the Russian army against the Turks in 1772. John Dalrymple (1785–8) had served as a Captain in the War of American Independence.

A far more distinguished veteran from that war was sent to Prussia in 1785. His mission is worth stressing, for Earl Cornwallis does not appear in Horn's *British Diplomatic Representatives*; nor indeed in his monograph.

The former exclusion is important, because the list is commonly seen as definitive; and thus as offering the basis for statistical investigation. Alas, as Horn made clear, he concentrated on diplomatic agents, thus excluding consuls, commissaries and secret agents, but also on those with credentials or creditive letters. Cornwallis went to Prussia to attend the military manoeuvres, but was instructed to act in a confidential manner, without any ostensible mission, in order to probe the possibility of improved relations. He received written instructions from the Foreign Secretary and made a written report. George III appreciated Cornwallis' efforts, and in 1786 he was appointed Governor-General and Commander-in-Chief in India and awarded the Garter. Brigadier Richard Sutton had been intended for Berlin in 1726,[121] but, instead, went to Cassel (1727–9) and (now Major-General) to Wolfenbüttel in 1730–1.

Other military envoys included Colonel, later Major-General, Joseph Yorke, who indeed went to Berlin in 1758. Tyrawly (Lisbon 1728–41, 1752, Russia 1744–5) was a Colonel with experience of service in the War of the Spanish Succession when appointed, with 'an education more military than ministerial'.[122] Tyrawly sought military promotion[123] and was successively promoted to Lieutenant-General and in 1762 combined diplomatic and military roles when he was appointed commander of the British forces sent to Portugal as well as a Plenipotentiary. Lieutenant-General, William, 2nd Earl of Albemarle (Paris, 1749–54), and Lieutenant-Colonel Ruvigny de Cosne (Paris 1751–5, Madrid 1757–60) and Yorke were all protégés of the Captain-General, the Duke of Cumberland.

The use of military men was common throughout Europe, and less so in Britain than, for example, France or Prussia.[124] Many were polished aristocrats, and, irrespective of this, military envoys could fit easily into certain court circles. They were especially appropriate when wartime co-operation was at issue or when drawing on memories of such alliances. For example, Lieutenant-General William, 1st Earl Cadogan, was envoy in The Hague 1707–11 and 1715–21, and was sent to embassies to Vienna in 1715 and 1720. A protégé of Marlborough, he was a prominent commander in the War of the Spanish Succession and in the suppression of the Jacobite rising of 1715–16. However, Cadogan's conduct as an envoy was criticized by Horatio Walpole. This reflected their very different personalities, but also Walpole's experience of Dutch politics:

> General Cadogan was indeed a great military officer and acted in negotiating more like an officer than a minister. He thought the pen and

the sword were to be managed with the same fierceness, impetuous and impatient of opposition, and, at the same time, to remove the present difficulties, as lavish of promising things that could not be performed.

More specifically, Cadogan's personal sympathy for the Orangist cause led him to anger their opponents, a common problem of defining a middle way for British envoys in the United Provinces.[125]

Stair (Paris 1715–20) was another blunt ex-General who caused offence, leading to French pressure for his recall.[126] Yet two other distinguished veterans, James Stanhope, who was envoy in Spain 1706–10 and 1718, in Paris in 1718 and in Berlin in 1720,[127] and William Stanhope, who was in Spain in 1717–18 and 1729 and in France in 1719 and 1728–30, were both successful, popular and socially adroit.

More generally, British ministers had to be aware of the social politics of *ancien régime* Europe, the emphasis on social rank and the frequent hostility to those seen as *arrivistes*. There was a sense that affecting the fate of nations was a role that required envoys of distinguished status. This was captured in 1791 by the hostile Barthélemy when he referred to Ewart as 'ce petit parvenu, qui s'est acquis la triste gloire d'avoir agité de vastes empires'.[128] Horatio Walpole had been extensively criticized by the opposition for a lack of dignity and decorum.

> He damn'd a Plenipo' in France,
> Because he had not learned to dance; …
> That slovens are the most unfitting,
> To be the ministers of Britain'.

David Gray, Morton Eden's secretary, who was left in charge of affairs for a year at Dresden in 1788–9 while Morton took leave, was described by a British visitor as 'as dirty a dog as ever I saw in my life. I could swear he never washes himself but on Sunday morning when he goes to church.'[129]

In contrast, a natural courtier of cosmopolitan upbringing such as Waldegrave easily fitted into the world of a Catholic court and made many influential friends.[130] Thomas Villiers, the second son of the second Earl of Jersey was another envoy who fitted well into court society, and was, indeed, praised as a 'citizen of all countries' by Frederick II.[131] After a diplomatic career from 1737 to 1748, Villiers followed a career in domestic politics, and in 1776 was created Earl of Clarendon; he was also given a Prussian title.

Well-connected and successful envoys could expect promotion in the peerage. In 1729, William Stanhope obtained that peerage he had been seeking for many years.[132] Waldegrave, a favourite of both George I and George II, was made a Lord of the Bedchamber by the first (1723) and an Earl (1729) by the second. Harris was created Lord Malmesbury (1788) and Earl (1800). Social skills did not always make for a successful envoy. James Hare, a talented man about town and former MP, but also 'a broken macaroni', was appointed Minister Plenipotentiary to Warsaw in 1779 in order to get him away from his gambling losses, but the latter were so extreme that in 1780 he resigned without having gone.[133]

The balance of required characteristics was captured by Auckland in 1790:

> there is a gentleness in Fitzherbert's temper together with a proper mixture of firmness, which would give him great advantages over so peevish a minister as Count Floridablanca [Spanish first minister], who is very open to the convictions of good sense, if presented to him with due management and perseverance.

Two years later, he thought his brother, Morton Eden, appropriate for Vienna not only because he spoke German 'perfectly' but also because he had a good income and 'pleasant' manners.[134]

In addition, the ministry had to consider individual appointments as part of a system, at once a system of patronage that included domestic politics and government, and also a foreign service in which there should be some notion of training, career development and promotion. Thus, in 1792, Grenville rejected Gower's suggestion for the Secretaryship of the Embassy at Paris as his recommendation was not in the diplomatic line, 'especially when he must have come over the heads of two or three young men of merit whom I wish to bring forward into situations where their talents and activity may be of use'.[135]

Equally, diplomats saw themselves as being chosen within a diplomatic system. Those who sought to pursue a career were well aware of having to respond to and manoeuvre in this context. Thus, concern about rank was not simply a matter of remuneration. Indeed, issues of rank were linked to social politics and status, as diplomatic ranks were not treated equally throughout Europe. Edward Finch was given a rank at the Imperial Diet in 1724 designed to free him from difficulties that had been encountered in the past:

> … and then he might live as he pleased, and not be entangled in the formalities of the place.
>
> Mr. Harrison is to be sent Resident to Vienna; a new character in our books for that Court. Pray my Lord what figure do Residents make at Vienna? Have they access to the Emperor, audiences etc. as Envoys? He is to be our English Minister with some character to give in memorials though St. Saphorin will have the business in the main.[136]

John Mitford was anxious for his nephew on the same head in 1789. He wanted to know whether if Auckland had a private secretary at The Hague he would be received at court, as in Germany such officials were not.[137]

Aside from rank, there was concern to gain posts and tasks that could yield repute. Thus, in 1721, Whitworth was keen to be a Plenipotentiary at the forthcoming international congress:

> As such entangled and important interests are to be treated at the Congress of Cambrai; and such difficult tempers, as those of the Imperialists and French, to be managed there at the same time. I thought it a very proper scene for a man of spirit and business to exert himself. The reputations assemblies of this nature will always have in the eye of the world, and the honour of succeeding to the late Lord Stanhope and mylord Carteret were very strong reasons to make it still more desirable … The business of Berlin did not then seem to me very essential; the chiefest transactions were likely to pass between Stockholm and St. Petersburg; and whenever the peace of the North comes to be made and that the defensive alliance is settled here, the ordinary occurrences of the place will not be sufficient to keep up the opinion of merit and service, and then the ministers must of course grow out of fashion by degrees.[138]

Such a consideration was not at all uncommon, especially for that group of envoys who can be regarded as professionals eager either to make their career through diplomatic service or to foster their career through a period as a diplomat. Such a search for high-profile negotiations was less important to 'envoys of title' than to 'the men of business'. Instead, they were more likely to see representation as their key task and to regard their presence and manner as the crucial requirements of this representation. Such 'envoys of title' commonly had little notion of a career in diplomacy, and were more likely to focus on service to the sovereign and thus on issues, and rewards, of rank and prestige. Much of the problem in judging British diplomacy derives from the habit of putting both groups together in order to produce an overall judgement. Although in many cases the differences were readily apparent and sometimes commented upon, there was no rigid divide between the groups. Nevertheless, the presence of these two contrasting groups makes questionable any overall judgement that does not make reference to this issue.

In July 1695, George Stepney, a 'man of business', wrote to Trumbull:

> it is now nine years ago that I offered you my service when you was going to France but you was already provided: so I launched into this German-Empire, and have been tumbled about here ever since. I spent 3 years at Hamburgh with Sir Peter Wyche, 2 with Mr. Johnston at Berlin and one more there as my own master; one at Vienna, and two in Saxony. Having thus rambled near one third of my life, and finding the proverb of the rolling stone, that gathers no moss, but too true (for you sir, who are acquainted with foreign employments know very well no profit is to be made by them for men who mean honourably) and seeing but few examples of ministers provided for at home when their commission abroad is at an end, (except they can recommend themselves by an extraordinary capacity, and services like those you have done your country) and lastly considering the slowness or loss of our payments by tallyes, (notwithstanding I have one in the Treasury who was once my friend and is now my patron) I, even resolved when I was last in England, to settle there, if I could find any footing either for love or money (as we call it) for I would have employed a small sum my mother left me last winter towards procuring me some sort of establishment; I had my eye upon, Clerk of the Council, but I find the number of super-numeraries increase daily, and I have not patience to wait the death of men younger than myself; and I am so little acquainted with England, by reason of my long absence, that I know not the nature of other employments, nor any other that I am fit for. Upon this consideration I came abroad once again, and must be contented to play the mercury, till a more favourable conjuncture offered some moderate settlement for me at home, which I would infinitely prefer to this shadow of greatness in

a strange country: But as I see no prospect of that, I have turned my thoughts another way, and am willing to renew my lease of travelling till we can have a peace.

The question then is where I would wish to be? Or rather where I can pretend to find my admittance? His Majesty perhaps does not yet think it seasonable to send envoys to the Northern Crowns, and has reason to be contented with Mr. Robinson and Mr. Grey who serve well in their stations. Mr. Cressett and Sir Paul Rycaut seem to have taken possession for life and Mr. Woolsely loves £5 a day too well, to be in earnest, when he threatens to throw up: and the same may be said of Mr. D'Hervart. The season is not yet come of sending a Minister to the princes of Italy, or if it be, some nobleman will snap at that employment so that unless His Majesty were willing to entertain an Envoy with the Electors and Princes on the Rhine, I see no sphere for me but Brandenburgh, Saxony, Ratisbon or Vienna. These two first may easily be joyned together, (Mr. Ham the Dutch Envoy has 'em so) and I should have my two houses as Mr. Cressett has his three; but Mr. Ham, whom I have mentioned, has perfectly monopolized the Court of Berlin and by his extraordinary credit with my Lord Portland (which I may venture to say is his chief merit) will do the King's business, as well as the States, which made Mr. Johnston very uneasy, and so would any other Englishman be who was to go thither; otherwise that should have been my request long ago, for (I know) the Court was desirous I should come thither.

Vienna is a court where all business centers, I am known to the Emperor and his ministers, and without vanity may be useful: But would not obtrude myself so as to make my Lord Lexington uneasy, nor be there so as to depend on him, after having been my own master. I therefore hope to have a credential as Resident if I go; or have offered to Mr. Blathwayt, as an expedient, to be there under the title I had at Dresden Ministre du Roy auprès des A.E. de Saxe, as if I only attended him to the Imperial Court, where I may remain on the foot of a stranger till my Elector returns from the campaign ... .[139]

The light Stepney threw on the problems both of pursuing a diplomatic career and of finding a suitable post clarify the difficulties successive ministries encountered in filling posts.

3

Effectiveness

I conceive that not only a Plot, but a Peace may be made by Receipt, … I have by Accident seen one of these Receipts, and I find that the first Rule recommended to the Minister, concerns the choice of the Person whom he is to appoint to negotiate with the neighbouring States, in which it is incumbent upon him to be very delicate, and he ought, if possible, to find out a Person of a very *thick Head*, the *thicker* the better, for such men are apt to follow their Instructions with a more implicit Obedience, and seldom are observ'd to raise Objections against anything, either absurd in itself, or contrary to the true Interest of their Country; a Fault which Men of Sense are but too liable to fall into; and they are the best Tools to work with upon these Occasions;— if he be intirely a Stranger to all publick Affairs, and even ignorant of the Address of a Gentleman, it will be never the worse.

He should be a little vers'd in *Ambiguities*, and, above all Things, make himself Master of that profound Science, call'd double *Entendre*, that in everything he transacts, there may be Matter left for Dispute and Contention; as, for Example, if anything should be negotiated concerning a Fortress, a City or a Province, in Dispute betwixt two Powers, the Articles should be so contriv'd and framed, that it may remain doubtful whether they are to be given up or preserved, for every Treaty and Negotiation ought to be so managed, that there should be a Necessity for another Treaty of Negotiation to explain or mend it; thus the Publick Business may be always doing, but never be done, and, if I may be allow'd the Familiarity of the Expression, a Plenipotentiary must do his Work like a Tinker, who, in stopping one Leak, contrives to make two or three.

Fog's Weekly Journal, 29 Aug. (os) 1730

The success of a minister, in his foreign negotiations, depends almost
as much on the credit he is supposed to have, and the figure he makes
in his own country, as on his address and superior personal abilities.

Anon., *The Present Influence and Conduct of Great Britain
Impartially Considered* (1741), p. 16

The British diplomatic service was frequently criticized during this period.
In October 1733, British ministers were able to read an intercepted report
from the Danish envoy, John, claiming that Britain was very badly
informed of European events, and blaming this on her foreign service.
John stated that, when diplomats were appointed, no attention was paid
to their merit or ability, but simply to the influence they, their friends and
relations possessed in Parliament. Furthermore, good service was not
rewarded, a discouraging factor, and the ministry was unwilling to spend
the necessary sums to create 'correspondances secrètes'. A far more distinguished observer passed comment in 1781. Frederick II (the Great) of
Prussia, who had experienced over forty years of British diplomacy, and
been much angered by Hanbury Williams' hostility, criticised an inaccurate report by Robert Liston, and continued,

> depuis quelque temps cette couronne n'est nullement délicate dans le
> choix de ses ministres et secrétaires d'ambassade, et qu'elle les envoie
> partout, sans se mettre en peine s'ils connaissent ou ignorent parfaite-
> ment le local des états de la cour où ils vont résider.[1]

Such themes were not only voiced by foreign commentators, although
domestic criticism, such as that cited from *Fog's Weekly Journal* above, has
to be placed in the context of partisan political debate. In Parliament in
1734, Sir William Wyndham, the Tory leader in the Commons, bitterly
attacked the leading minister, Sir Robert Walpole, for 'in foreign affairs
trusting none but such whose education makes it impossible for them to
have such knowledge or such qualifications as can be of service to their
country, or give any weight or credit to their negotiations'.[2] Five years later,
the *Craftsman*, a leading London opposition newspaper, attacked Benjamin
Keene, noting:

> in former times it was always usual, upon such important occasions,
> to employ men of the highest rank and eminence; who, by their dignity,
> might add a weight to their negotiations abroad; and, by their fortunes,
> give pledge to their own country for the integrity of their conduct—

this was certainly a wise precaution, which ought always to be observ'd; for a man of mean birth, and low fortune, may be tempted to sacrifice the publick interest to his own; or, at least become the subservient tool of a minister by whose indulgent hand he was raised.[3]

In 1750, another opposition newspaper, *Old England*, criticized negotiations with the French over the Canadian border:

> Though it is notorious that the *French* circumvent us in negotiations, yet we are stupidly fond of falling in with every opportunity to try our skill with them; like losing gamesters, who are led on by false hopes of recovering what they have lost; and rather than not be doing at all, we are forward to employ ourselves in undoing what may have been better done than we can amend.[4]

Lady Mary Wortley Montagu had complained about the low calibre of British diplomats nine years earlier. Criticism of British diplomacy continued in the second half of the century. On 17 October 1761, the *Monitor* complained:

> Britons were never celebrated for the arts of negotiation. We have never attempted to practice it but to our loss. While we have been bewildered by intricate debates about trifles or matters that serve only to disguise the truth, and to hide the real object, many opportunities have been lost, and we have given up that by treaty, which war could never have taken from us.

Philip Thicknesse claimed that 'Britain is alone distinguished for suffering ignorant, inexperienced, and ruined people, to be among the numbers of its foreign, residential Ministers'. Sandwich, as Secretary of State, 'never saw a worse memorial than' one drawn up in 1764 by Francis, Earl of Hertford (Paris 1763–5). There was criticism of the Consuls in Spain for failing to communicate relevant political and military information. The Hanoverian Ernst Brandes observed in 1787 'We take your Resident at Berlin, Ewart, to be exceedingly well informed of continental politics, which is not generally the case of the English Ministers abroad'.[5]

Aside from general attacks on the diplomatic service, there were also attacks on individual diplomats. To take the period 1720–40, Horatio Walpole was condemned for being duped by the French both in the late 1720s and during the War of the Polish Succession:

Clumsy is a near relation of Sublimate's and by him employed as his agent to Doctor Balance. The poor fellow has the misfortune to be born a blockhead, and to be bred a clodhopper … we hear that a certain ancient crown-jewel called the balance of Europe hath been missing some time; and that it is supposed to have formerly stolen out of the hands of a certain person in France, who was entrusted to carry it abroad with him.[6]

Waldegrave was castigated for being duped by the French, while Keene was criticized for allegedly surrendering national interests in the late 1720s, the early 1730s and, more particularly, during the Anglo-Spanish negotiations in 1738–9.[7] When this is combined with those diplomats found wanting by the government in this period, the list becomes an impressive one. To take the latter, St Saphorin's 'ill-timed heat and haughtiness' (Vienna, 1718–27) played a major role in the deterioration of Anglo-Austrian relations,[8] although St Saphorin himself blamed Austrian hostility, not least over religion, and an absence of 'any true cordiality'.[9]

Isaac Leheup (Stockholm, 1727) was recalled in disgrace for being rude to Frederick, Prince of Wales, at Hanover en route to take up his post. He had allegedly told him that the Whigs had kept the Hanoverians on the throne and that, if they did not act satisfactorily, Leheup would turn Jacobite.[10] Du Bourgay (Berlin, 1724–30) was reprimanded on several occasions for exceeding orders.[11] The intemperance of Lord Tyrawly (Lisbon, 1728–41) had to be restrained frequently. George, 7th Earl of Kinnoull (1729–35) was recalled after reiterated complaints that he was pro-French; he refused to leave when his successor Fawkener arrived, leading the latter to suspect that he wanted to play a continued diplomatic role.[12] William Finch (The Hague, 1733–4) was a poor representative who failed to note the Dutch move into neutrality in 1733. Ten years earlier, he had been criticized for failing to send prompt notice of Russian moves from Stockholm.[13] The Earl of Essex (Turin, 1732–6) found his posting boring, constantly sought leave for travel, and complained about a lack of attention from London.[14]

Furthermore, in these years, as throughout the period, envoys quarrelled, especially with consular officials or others in the same post. John Molesworth, envoy in Turin, criticized Henshaw at Genoa for being timorous and insufficiently determined to defend British trade.[15] Walter Titley (Copenhagen, 1729–68) quarrelled with Tigh, Consul at Elsinore,[16] and Robert Daniel (Brussels 1722–45) with John Deane, the Consul at

Ostend, while Brigadier James Dormer (Lisbon, 1725–7) was recalled after a dispute with the Consul, Thomas Burnett, led to violence. Earlier, each had complained of offensive behaviour by the other, and Burnett had already been told he would be replaced. The immediate spur in 1727 was Burnett's decision to hold a party on George II's Coronation Day. Dormer saw this as a disparagement and had him publicly and severely beaten by seven of his servants. John V of Portugal was greatly offended, not least because the attack took place on his birthday.[17]

William Stanhope feared that Keene would report on him. Essex had a feud with Edmund Allen, Secretary in Turin, and successfully recommended his own secretary, Arthur Villettes, for promotion to this post,[18] while Tyrawly had a bitter dispute with Admiral Norris during the latter's stay in Portuguese waters in 1735–7. Envoys also criticized the failure of their colleagues to keep them informed: 'I should, I think have done more service, if I had been once informed by Lord Hyndford. Egotisms are not enough in business', complained Thomas Robinson in 1741.[19]

Disputes between envoys and consuls were but one example of the problem posed by having more than one representative in a state. This problem was accentuated when two envoys were accredited to the same court. This was especially so if the senior diplomat saw the other as a counter-balance. Thus, Waldegrave was resentful of Thomas Pelham, who was Secretary of Embassy in Paris in 1730–6,[20] Hertford refused to accept Thomas Bunbury as Secretary of Embassy in Paris,[21] and Dorset had clashes with Hailes, who was Secretary of Embassy (and Minister Plenipotentiary during the Duke's absences) in Paris in 1784–8, and was also made livid by William Eden,[22] who used his authority to negotiate a trade treaty in order to seek to influence Anglo-French relations in general and British foreign policy. Thomas Wroughton blamed Keith for the Russian refusal to receive him as Minister Resident in 1762. Relations between the two were poisonous. Sir William Norris' mission to Mughal India (1699–1702) was handicapped not only by his own lack of emollience but also as a result of the rivalry of the two English trading companies in India. He also quarrelled with Thomas Pitt, President of Fort St George.

Complaints about individual diplomats were not restricted to the 1720s and 1730s. In October 1746, the French Plenipotentiary at the peace congress at Breda argued that the choice of Sandwich as his counterpart proved that the British government did not wish to settle the war at Breda: 'c'est un blanc bec, qui à rendre l'esprit des belles lettres, a peu d'experience et beaucoup de pedanterie'.[23] Such complaints did not only come from foreign pens. Sandwich's lack of experience had been criticized in the British press. Cumberland responded to the collapse of the Dutch war effort by writing to Newcastle in 1748, 'I think our friend Lord Sandwich greatly to blame in sending us the sanguine accounts he has done both by his private and public letters'.[24] On 14 January 1777, the *Westminster Gazette* complained that Stormont had been 'bambozzled' by the French.

In 1756, Keith totally failed to anticipate the 'Diplomatic Revolution', the rapprochement between Austria and France. Indeed he wrote, 'it is the general opinion that this court will hardly enter into engagements with France'.[25] Keith's failure was shared by Hanbury Williams. This was very serious as Britain was already in a state of war with France; but it is worth noting that most European observers were wrong-footed by the rapidly changing international relations of that year.

One must add the problems inherent in diplomatic arrangements. Poor communications meant not only that the arrival of letters was unpredictable and subject to interference by allies and enemies, as well as frequently late, but also that envoys could only rarely return to Britain for discussions. The absence of distinct and unpolitical agencies for the conduct of foreign policy and the close relationship in most countries of foreign policy and domestic politics ensured that diplomats in many countries, including Britain, had to face difficult choices. Should they seek to lend support to domestic opponents of governments following antagonistic policies? Edward Finch ended his Swedish mission (1728–39) disastrously through so doing. Should they seek to gain the support of the reversionary interest (the heir to the throne)? Instructions on these, and other, points were often ambiguous and outdated. Newcastle sought to clarify the matter when writing to Horatio Walpole in 1723:

> it is certainly right for foreign ministers to apprize themselves of, and enter into the affairs of the court to which they are sent, whenever there is any stroke of consequence which must really affect the interest of the power they are employed by, so it is impertinent and trifling to be entering into every little quarrel and pique which no ways concern their master's interest.

The last was directed at Schaub,[26] but the distinction was difficult to draw.

Language skills were another aspect of communications. Certain British envoys were gifted. Keene was good at Spanish, John Robinson at Swedish, and Paul Methuen at Portuguese. Tyrawly was able to speak Portuguese with John V of Portugal, upstaging Admiral Norris who did not under-stand the language. Seeking appointment to Berlin in 1740, Hyndford wrote, 'I have the advantage of possessing the German tongue', while, that year, Sir John Lambert mentioned his knowledge of Italian as well as 'having been brought up to business' when seeking the Venice consulship. Dickens had German 'in perfection', and Wych's German similarly qualified him for Northern courts. Gray mentioned his knowledge of Italian and Spanish when seeking the Naples post in 1750.[27]

Secretaries were frequently expected to make up for linguistic defi-ciencies, for example in German, the necessary language of business at St Petersburg in the first half of the century. Edward Finch felt his lack of the language 'extremely'. Jezreel Jones, who was secretary to Paul Methuen for part of his embassy, was very fluent in Arabic, Portuguese and Spanish. He did not succeed in being sent as secretary to Sir William Norris on the latter's embassy to Mughal India, but he was sent to Morocco in 1704. William Poyntz, appointed Consul-General in Portugal in 1715, knew the language very well. At Paris, Horatio Walpole sought a secretary 'that can talk and write French well, not a forward fine gentleman, but [one] that will be contented to be in a lower class'. In 1747, Sandwich pressed successfully for the appointment of Edward Wortley Montagu as Secretary at the Congress of Aix-la-Chapelle and for his recall to the Congress after the opening of Parliament, because of 'his knowledge of the Dutch language, which he writes and translates extremely well'. William Kirkpatrick, Resident to the Maratha Prince Sindia in 1786–7 and to the Nizam of Hyderabad in 1794–7, wrote a *Grammar of the Hindoo Dialect and an Arabic and Persian Vocabulary* (1782), which was published with the support of the East India Company.[28]

Although Charles Boyd was unsuccessful, it is interesting to note the qualifications he mentioned to Bute: 'as I write and speak French with the greatest ease, and as I have a general notion of the political interests of the different European courts, I might perhaps (if I had the honour of being known to your Lordship) appear not improper to be made Secretary to some Embassy.' A recommendation of Solomon Dayrolle, nephew of James Dayrolle, Resident of The Hague, included 'understands most languages'. Dudley Cosby, Minister Resident at Copenhagen in 1764, defined the best qualifications for his successor, 'The German language, a good temper and easy address are the most material qualifications'. In some cases, embassy staff played a role based on their linguistic skills. Mr Wadsworth, Chaplain to the embassy in Spain, taught the Infanta English, and later converted to Catholicism.[29]

Many envoys, however, suffered from linguistic deficiencies. Sent to Cassel in 1727, Richard Sutton complained of 'the little French I am master of' and of his inability to read a word of the letters sent to him in German by the Regency in Hanover. The same year, Woodward noted, 'neither is my tongue very glib yet in the French language; for all I can pretend to is to make myself understood with some *hums* and *haws*'. Robinson was worried about the appointment of a Spanish envoy in Vienna who spoke no French. As Richard Oswald, who was sent to Paris in 1782 to negotiate with the American commissioners, did not know French, the government appointed an interpreter.[30] Others made an effort. In Copenhagen, Glenorchy learned German 'which is of the most use in all these Northern countries'. Poyntz took 'a pull' at learning German 'though to the great danger of spoiling my voice'.[31]

Languages were also a problem for the officials of the Secretaries of State and Foreign Office. In 1723, Tilson referred to 'high Dutch, which you know our office don't understand'. George Aust responded to the death of James Manby in 1786 by writing to the envoy in Madrid: 'As we have now nobody who can translate Spanish, I have some thoughts of attempting that language, and shall be much obliged to you to recommend me to any books'.[32]

Criticisms should be noted, but they also must be qualified. Patronage played a major role in appointments, but this was scarcely unusual in British government of the period, or, indeed, in Continental states. Most diplomats filed regular and comprehensive reports. If they tended to concentrate on court and ministerial factions, this was both something they shared with other diplomatic services, and an understandable response to the sources of power and policy. Most British and Continental diplomats devoted little attention to broader social and political developments. They lacked the resources to do so, the information was not readily available, and it was generally believed to be of slight significance.

Most British diplomats in the period were conscientious reporters and worthy, rather than brilliant, negotiators. Judging between these two functions is difficult. Scholarly attention tends to concentrate on diplomats as negotiators, because it was then that their activity, perception and ability were most significant, and also apparent to contemporaries, both within and outside the government structure. However, most of the time, diplomats were reporters, and this role has left the biggest trace in the archives, although it tends to be underrated by scholars. To the governments of the time, this role was more important than is generally allowed in scholarship, and thus more significant in the assessment of individual diplomats. The French envoy Destouches praised Whitworth in 1722 for being able to provide a perfect account of German affairs.[33] In September 1738, Harrington informed Robinson that

> though nothing could give the King a more sensible concern than the present great distress of the Emperor's situation, as it appears in your last dispatches, yet His Majesty expressed a particular satisfaction in the fullness and exactness of your accounts concerning the affairs of the campaign, together with the just observations you have made yourself thereupon.[34]

The last point was important. Diplomats were expected to provide a gloss on the news in order to make it explicable. Craggs complained to the French envoy about Stair: 'que ses depesches etoient succintes, ne marquoient que les principaux evenemens qui se passoient en France, et n'entroient plus dans aucun passoient detail ni dans aucun raisonnement'. Tilson was exasperated by contradictory faults: 'William Finch at The Hague does well: but he is too laconic a writer. Edward Finch at Warsaw is refined and almost incomprehensible. If he keeps quiet it is the best thing he can do.'[35]

Part of the job of diplomats was contextualisation. In 1735, Everard Fawkener reported from Constantinople his difficulty about providing an accurate account of Tatar activity:

> I am very sorry, Mylord, I can only send your Grace reports which so flatly contradict each other; I dare not attempt to reason upon them, but I will hazard my opinion to your Grace's indulgence, which is, that the Tatar Han has not been able to pass forward; my reasons are that the Russian accounts are uniform, though possibly the particulars may be aggravated, and the Tatars vary in theirs and are inconsistent: Had the Tatar Han passed in the manner they relate, there has been time sufficient for them to have had a particular account of it from him, which they would not have been wanting to have published in all its circumstances.

Experience clearly helped in contextualization and, far from favouring a regular rotation of diplomats, there was a stress on its value. In 1792, Burges was sorry to hear of Robert Murray Keith's departure from Vienna as he had 'become so complete a master of every political matter'.[36] Long service was seen as beneficial in developing a relationship of trust with superiors.[37]

In turn, diplomats urged their experience when pressing for appointment, reappointment, or promotion. Francis Manning, Secretary to Abraham Stanyan as envoy to the Swiss Cantons, was in charge of affairs during Stanyan's absence from Berne in 1708–9, Secretary to the Grisons at Coire in 1709–13, and Stanyan's secretary thereafter until he returned to England. In 1715, he wrote to Sunderland, asking to be sent back to Switzerland: 'for which post I don't find there is now any competitor with me ... I may be supposed to be more useful there to his Majesty, than others who are unacquainted with the genius of that nation.'[38]

Diplomats welcomed approbation, Joseph Yorke writing to Weston in 1761:

> I am very glad you found anything in my scrawls which were worth communicating, it is really discretion when I don't trouble Lord Bute with such articles in my dispatches, because I am apprehensive of appearing to go out of my line, and presuming to intrude my vague accounts, in opposition to what you must receive much better authenticated from other quarters.

Drake sought Burges' advice on his official correspondence.[39]

The qualities expected in dispatches were clearly noted by Tilson in 1711—'method, clearness, and expressive brevity'—and most diplomats obliged successfully. Dunant, Robinson's secretary, who was left in charge during the envoy's absence in 1737–8, reported, 'Mr. Robinson advised me to write nothing but facts, and to avoid entering into reasonings and speculations'. Robinson himself commented on his methods to a fellow envoy:

> When I write upon hearsay, I say so: when I write upon probability, I mark what I think to be only probable: But when I have a voucher for affirmation, I promise, vow and affirm; for if you are deceived, it is not I, but my voucher, who deceives you.[40]

Further insight was offered by comments from and about foreigners concerning the standards expected in other diplomatic services. Waldegrave's secretary, John Burnaby, reported in 1735 that Fleury, the leading French minister, praised Vaulgrenant, because he states his facts clearly and makes faithful reports of whatever comes to his knowledge, that he thinks can be of any service, distinguishing always in his intelligence what is doubtful from what is certain, and leaving it to the king, and his ministers to infer from thence the consequences, they think proper.[41]

Lapses occurred, but, on the whole, London was well informed of the politics and policies of other governments.[42] Warnings of advance information were given about many of the surprising international moves of the period, for example the Sardinian alliance with France of 1733 and the Austro-French peace of 1735. The difficulty of evaluating information, on which decisions would be based,[43] vied with the need to make frequent reports. Hyndford noted the problem in 1741—'unless my intelligence is very certain, I am unwilling to write every report, what I may be obliged to contradict immediately afterwards'[44]—but such certainty was fragile. Six years later, Hanbury Williams noted, 'I find by my letters that I am often forced to contradict by one post what I wrote by the last, but in this Court it is impossible to do otherwise, and I think it my duty to send all I hear from hands that most deserve credit, though they often do not'.[45]

Most diplomats appear to have discharged their tasks to the satisfaction of the Secretaries of State. As many of the latter had been diplomats, they were well aware of the problems of diplomacy. Diplomatic skill and influence were of course difficult to assess. Hindsight does not make the situation any better, although it can provide additional insights. The most valuable is that offered by the opening of foreign archives. These provide information on the views held by foreign rulers, ministers and diplomats, and also offer accounts of events and intentions against which the accuracy and perception of British envoys can be assessed. Unsurprisingly foreign views were mixed.

One major insight is that on the integrity of British envoys. No major British diplomat appears to have provided information for foreign powers, as the French diplomat and Foreign Office official François de Bussy did for the British to whom, from the 1730s, he was agent 101. Robert Sutton, Secretary of Embassy at Paris 1720–4, was believed by a Jacobite agent to be 'entirely devoted' to the Pretender, but it is unclear with what result, and similar hopes of his uncle, Brigadier Richard Sutton, seem far fetched.[46] The French informed the British that Robert Sutton's father, Sir Robert Sutton, formerly Resident at Vienna and Ambassador at Constantinople and Paris, was in touch with the Jacobites.[47] Kinnoull had been imprisoned in 1715–16 on suspicion of supporting the Pretender and in 1722 was accused of being aware of the Atterbury Plot, but was still appointed to Constantinople in 1729. He did indeed appear to have broken with the Jacobites.

Suspicions about Waldegrave, the son of James II's illegitimate daughter Lady Henrietta Fitzjames, were unjustified but persistent. In 1732, he had to deny rumours that he was bringing up his sons as Catholics: '... the stupidity of the principles in which I was educated ... It is hard upon any man to have the misfortune of his education reaped upon him as a ground of suspicion ... is it not then very hard that because I send over for my sons, it should be thrown out that I design to breed them up papists'.[48]

Nevertheless, suspicions continued,[49] as did a sense that Waldegrave was insufficiently firm with the French.[50] In 1740, the cantankerous Earl of Bristol observed:

> ... no information from our alert and vigilant ambassador at Paris of what has been sometime doing at Dunkirk, in manifest breach of the only express and valuable article of that exploded treaty of Utrecht; but all people rightly ask, How could Sir Robert expect more faithful service from a grandson of King James's.[51]

Yet, the very 'supplesse and address' that could pass as a lack of firmness could also be seen as a crucial way to win confidence, and, while Waldegrave was praised for having them, Stair was found lacking in 'insinuation'.[52] Similarly, the choice of Charles, 3rd Duke of Richmond, as Ambassador to France in 1765–6 was criticized on the grounds that as a French peer he might display insufficient firmness,[53] but this also gave him more entrées into the French elite.

Aside from effectiveness in the sense of accurate reports and skilful negotiations, there was also the question of the nature of the British diplomatic network, both the extent and character of representation. There were criticisms that both were inadequate. Essex complained from Turin in 1733: 'We have not in all Italy a person in whose advices we can confide; our consuls, Skinner alone excepted, being much more taken up with their private concerns, than thoughts of the nation's.'[54] Indeed, representation in Italy was an issue on a number of occasions, and there was, for example, criticism of the delay in sending a high-ranking diplomat to Naples.[55] In addition, there was concern that a failure to maintain appropriate representation in Berlin in the 1730s hindered good relations.[56]

A caveat must be entered before any conclusion is offered. A notion of effectiveness depends in large part on a clear sense of national interest or a clear sense of a professional role and objective; but when, instead, there were a range of attitudes and policies being pursued from within government, then much judgement was necessarily subjective and has to be located within an, often polemical, context of contention. Lord George Germain pointed out to his nephew in 1784 that

> the most disagreeable part of your employment is that when you are writing to the minister of your own court, you can not be certain but that your whole correspondence may be laid before Parliament for the inspection of the Public.[57]

Envoys were not abstracted from political disputes, especially in key postings, and rivalry between ministers could extend to attempts to win over the diplomatic protégés of rivals, as in 1723 when Newcastle advocated detaching Schaub from Carteret.[58] Political considerations were central to appointments. As Cadogan pointed out to Stair (Paris), 'your station requires a person of the greatest ability and dexterity, and personal attachment to His Majesty'.[59] The situation was no different at the close of the century, although loyalty was focused as much on the ministry, and that was assumed to reflect royal wishes. The role of political considerations make any assessment of effectiveness in terms of administrative criteria somewhat limited. This point will be addressed again, but an understanding of its politicality is central to any assessment of foreign policy in this period.[60]

In considering effectiveness, it is crucial to note that the diplomatic system was little better elsewhere. Throughout Europe, most diplomats owed their appointment to patronage; rank was at a premium and pay frequently in arrears; while aristocratic amateurs were not always a success. Other states might possess a single foreign ministry (which Britain did not gain until 1782), but it was frequently difficult to get diplomats to obey orders, while many ministers corresponded in secret with envoys and conducted what was in effect a personal foreign policy. Whatever the impact of Parliament and public opinion upon the formulation of foreign policy, the conduct of diplomacy was not noticeably different to that of other European powers.

4

The 'English Plan' of Diplomacy

I never knew a foreigner who had an adequate idea of England.

Thomas Robinson, 1744[1]

The 'English Plan' was the term employed to describe the system of conducting negotiations through British envoys rather than foreign diplomats in London. This was seen as characteristic of British diplomacy.[2] It had clear attractions. It was usually easier for British ministers to control such negotiations and to limit the impact of British domestic politics on them. Furthermore, foreign envoys in London were seen as likely to enter into intrigues with British opposition politicians. At times, indeed, their conduct could lead to serious tension, as with the collapse of Anglo-Prussian relations at the close of the Seven Years' War. Michell, the Prussian envoy in London, actively intrigued against the government. He was far from alone in this. Other examples included the Spaniard Monte-léon in 1718, the Austrians Palm in 1726–7, Kinsky in 1730 and Strickland in 1734–5, the Prussian Reichenbach in the late 1720s, the Frenchman Chavigny in the 1730s, and the Russian Voronzov in 1791. As examples of the 'English Plan', the abortive discussions for an Anglo-Austrian alliance in early 1729 were conducted by Waldegrave in Vienna. His successor, Robinson, handled the negotiations in 1730–1 that led to the Second Treaty of Vienna.

However, such a 'plan' did lead to more reliance being placed on British envoys, and not all were equal to the task. In particular, there was a danger that British diplomats would 'go native' and become overly sympathetic to the views of the court to which they were accredited. It was certainly the case that some diplomats became very popular at their posts: Titley at Copenhagen was possibly the best example. Newcastle praised Horatio

Walpole in 1735: 'You know all the Dutch people; You can sooth and frighten and do both'.[3] In 1758, when Andrew Mitchell was recalled in response to the wishes of William Pitt the Elder, a Secretary of State, although for the Southern Department, Frederick II made it clear that he wanted him to stay, as he indeed ended up doing.[4]

The danger for envoys was more complex. Whatever the length of their mission, and despite instructions 'to have as little as possible to do in the broils which are now at that court',[5] there was the possibility that diplomats would become overly involved with a group or faction at their post, and that this group would be unsuccessful. The fault was most excusable if the group was pro-British, but diplomats risked alienating other ministers or courtiers if they overly committed themselves to such a party. At times, they were indeed instructed to support such ministers,[6] although many diplomats appreciated the need for caution in order to avoid alienating support. In 1726, the Portuguese Infante, Dom Francisco, approached James Dormer, the British envoy, told him that John V was pro-Spanish, and suggested that Britain intimidate Portugal with a powerful fleet. Dormer responded cautiously, and Newcastle congratulated him on avoiding giving encouragement or offence.[7] In accordance with his instructions, Joseph Yorke set out his goal in 1752, which was:

> My predecessor's fault was to have been too particular in his acquaintance. I am sure no foreign minister will ever succeed, or be able to send good accounts if he is so, his business is to see and converse with all sorts of people, and to make himself if he can agreable to them.[8]

Involvement in internal politics, and indeed diplomatic links in general, proved a particular problem in heavily factionalized courts, such as Russia in 1734, and far less so where government was less divided and factions under greater control. Edward Finch felt that ministerial changes in Sweden put him in an impossible position in 1739:

> when foreign ministers have no share of the confidence and good will of the Prime Minister they are to treat with, their most innocent steps are always seen by him in a false light and wrongly interpreted ... after losing all my friends in the Senate and Chancery ... my ministry must become as useless to the King's service as it will be hereafter miserable to myself.

He left that November. The previous month, John Burnaby, the newly arrived Secretary, was told by General Diemar, a Hessian minister of Frederick I of Sweden with long links with the British ministry, to report to London separately from Finch, and a minister told him that 'they would have no dealings with me till Mr. Finch was gone'.[9] Moving on to St Petersburg, Finch declared

> that I never thought it the business of a foreign minister to meddle with the domestic affairs of the Court where he had the honour to be employed, but that for the service of his master he ought to apply in an open, honest way to the government he found actually subsisting at the time.[10]

This was not easy in practice.

The fate of Edward Finch's Swedish mission was far from unique. In 1721, Whitworth presciently observed to Tilson: 'I am of your opinion that St Saphorin's passion against the Vice Chancellor carries him too far; and that it is no easy task to overthrow a minister in credit.'[11] In 1756–7, Hanbury Williams's links at St Petersburg to the court of the heir, the future Peter III, and his wife Catherine, harmed Anglo-Russian relations. Frederick II pressed for his recall, although he subsequently changed his mind as he decided that links with the young court would be useful. Hanbury Williams was seen 'more as a Prussian spy than as an English Ambassador'. The reversionary interest in Russia had to wait until Elizabeth died in 1762.[12]

Yet, at the same time, what can be presented as an over-commitment to local interests can also be seen both as a response to opportunities, and as policy informed by the potential of the situation. To take the Mitchell case, it is all too easy to cite Pitt the Elder's denunciation and his claim that British policy was being distorted:

> I find to my extreme concern, Mr. Mitchell's letters so constantly in the same strain, with regard to sending British troops, to reinforce the army in the Electorate [Hanover]; and his chief and favourite object seems to be so particularly to nourish the King of Prussia's mind, with the fitness and practicability of that impossible measure, that I can't forbear, on reading his last letter from Breslau, to express to your Grace my strong alarm at so extraordinary a proceeding. I love to speak plainly. Andrew Mitchell is not a fool, and therefore he must be something not fit to be the instrument of the present system of

administration … it is evident to whom he belongs, and whose work he is doing … Thus it is, My Lord, in every part of government, the tools of another system are perpetually marring every hopeful measure of the present administration. In a word, if your Grace is not able to eradicate this lurking, diffusive poison a little more out of the mass of government, especially from the vitals, I think it's better for us, to have done. I do not intend for one, that Andrew Mitchell shall carry me, where I have resolved not to go.[13]

Pitt was concerned that Mitchell was representing the views of Carteret, now Earl Granville, a former Secretary of State who was committed to Continental interventionism, and his determination to replace Mitchell was part of an attempt to gain control of British foreign policy. Allegedly, this also led him to seek the recall of Ruvigny de Cosne, the Secretary of Embassy in Madrid, who was seen as a protégé of the Duke of Cumberland.[14] In practice, however, Mitchell was representing the need for a military commitment if the Anglo-Prussian alliance was to be sustained, and this indeed became British policy before the year was out, and one that Pitt strongly supported.

Furthermore, if envoys were possibly over-associated with particular factions or politicians, allowance must be given for the difficulties posed by exclusion from particular circles. These were particularly pronounced when relations were very poor. Keene complained from Spain in 1727:

If it was possible for me to think of any place disagreable, where I had the least prospect of doing His Majesty service certainly I should be of that opinion at present, where both friends and enemies equally avoid me … even some of the Jacobites that I have acquaintance with dare not come nigh me for fear of losing their interest at court. I am lodged in a tent, just big enough to hold my bed, but when I go out, I have the king's walls and gardens to myself, for no one joins with me.[15]

In the mid-1730s, Robinson angered the Austrians by what they saw as his bullying manner, but, in addition, the ministers to whom he was closest, Eugène and Starhemberg, lost influence, and Eugène died in 1736. Robinson's relations with Bartenstein, the Secretary of the Imperial Conference and the leading minister of the late 1730s, were poor, and Robinson complained that he did not keep him informed.

Involvement could entail financial support for particular ministers and courtiers, and such a policy, often, but not always, no more than bribery, was especially common in Constantinople, St Petersburg and Stockholm, such that any comprehensive footnote would cover British relations with all those courts. Keith was authorized to spend up to £20,000 in St Petersburg in 1759 and up to £100,000 in 1762; Burnaby (Stockholm) was sent a more modest £4,000 in 1740.[16] Such intervention reached a high point with attempts to overthrow unwelcome ministers or factions. In 1787 Harris played a major role in committing Britain against the Dutch 'Patriots' and in support of the House of Orange. His role was more direct than that of the British in 1747.[17]

Aside from the problem of the reliability of British envoys, there was the difficulty that the 'English Plan' could not avoid the issue of distance, in this case the need for envoys to report back for approval and/or fresh instructions. In April 1721, Whitworth noted:

> … for these three weeks past, that I have been acting on contrary principles, and almost against His Majesty's intentions, for want of a little light in time: I continued on the scheme which I thought to be the foundation of all our proceedings for some years.

Two months later, he was able to add:

> I am extremely glad that His Majesty and Mylord Townshend have approved my conduct and notions about the affairs of the north …
> I should not have engaged so far in the discussion of them had I not thought it absolutely necessary for their service. The same object to persons in different stations shows itself in very different views; Had I been in England and known the secret springs of what passes there, I don't question but I might have been of Mylord Townshend's opinion at first; and had his Lordship resided here, and seen what has been for some time, and is now acting, I am persuaded he would have fallen naturally into my way of thinking.[18]

Sent to Berlin in late 1793, Malmesbury pressed Grenville on the need to avoid this problem by leaving him considerable powers: 'Whatever decision may be taken at home, your Lordship will be good enough to give me if possible such instructions as may not make it necessary for me to refer for explanations as the effect of the whole depends on its being done quickly.' In 1694, John Methuen lacked orders on whether a Portuguese offer of mediation would be welcome.[19] The issue had been addressed for Hyndford in 1741, when Harrington noted the difficulties of keeping up with the opportunistic Frederick II:

> ... almost impossible to send you any particular directions from hence for your future conduct ... especially considering that the impetuous tempter of the Prince you are to treat with, the quick turns he is liable to take, and the peremptoriness with which he expects an immediate compliance with his ideas and determination must necessarily oblige you in most instances to resolve with yourself what you shall think best.

There was no time to seek orders. As an experienced former diplomat, Harrington had extensive experience of the issue.[20] Charles Delafaye, an experienced Under-Secretary, pressed the need to take initiatives:

> Poor Keene is quite scared. I write what I can to keep him in heart ... and tell him ... that a minister should upon occasion exceed his orders, and hazard the mortification of being disavowed, rather than throw things into confusion, or miss an opportunity of doing signal service.[21]

Paget complained in 1690 of insufficient instructions, of the need for new ones due to changes in circumstances, and of not being kept informed about English policy. Eden reflected in 1786, 'I continue without one word from England ... I suffer deservedly for having left London without securing either more specific instructions, or more discretionary powers',[22] although his complaints have to be considered in the context of the Foreign Secretary's distrust of France. Thus, policy, as much as personal or instructional delays, was at issue.

Aside from envoys facing the problem of delay in the transmission of instructions, there was also the difficulty posed by changes in the views of the British government. This was accentuated when there was political instability in Britain. According to Whitworth in 1714, 'the unhappy constitution of our nation is such that, instead of being a merit, it is a disadvantage to have served when the Government is in hands that are not liked'.[23]

Sir Robert Walpole wrote to Waldegrave in 1737, 'Your Lordship will not very much wonder that we have been behindhand of late in our foreign correspondencies, considering how fully we have been employed in our domestic broils and contests'. John Burnaby, an Under-Secretary, added to Robinson during the final crisis of the Walpole ministry, 'the Ministers are so employed in domestic affairs that they have no leisure to think on what passes abroad'. William Fraser defended the government in 1782 from complaints about not receiving instructions: 'You must make some allowance for sudden changes.'[24] In late 1755, Joseph Yorke complained about the consequences of parliamentary disputes over policy:

> It is hard to be fighting your cause as I am in a manner without instruc-tions, but they say that your house calls for so many papers, they have no time to do anything but copy old things and consequently the new must be neglected ... brick without straw is difficult to make ... get me instructions'[25]

Then it was the case not only of actual changes in orders, but also the continued possibility of such changes. Dorset suggested in 1784 'we want nothing but stability in our government to talk a proper language to this court'. Aside from this, the 'multiplicity of business' that the session brought had an effect on diplomatic correspondence.[26]

There was the risk that the states to which British diplomats were accred-ited would be overly prone to suspect change in British policy.[27] This could make it far harder to negotiate with them, either more difficult to maintain and operate alliances or, conversely, to exert pressure. As a consequence, British envoys talked up the stability of country and ministry as well as defending particular policies. Thus, in 1722, Thomas Lumley had to explain the imposition of a tax on the Catholics in Britain to the Portuguese, and in 1727 Dormer was told to stress Parliament's support of British foreign policy. He translated the relevant parliamentary resolutions into Portuguese.[28]

The problems posed by actual or potential instability within Britain were not restricted to the formal diplomacy of the Crown. They also affected the agents of other bodies, particularly the East India Company. Thus, in 1770, Warren Hastings wrote from Fort St George:

> The Company's affairs have suffered very much, and their authority weakened for some years past by the continual contests at home. Their servants doubtful which party would continue in power, and dreading a change of rulers have been prevented from acting with that confi-

70

dence and vigor which all public measures require, in the execution of the orders before them, by the apprehension of counter orders, and of reproach from the new Directors who may think differently from the old.[29]

Governmental changes affected the Secretaries of State, and the Under-Secretaries lacked the authority to provide continuity in policy. In most cases, envoys were not directly affected by these changes, but some were. This was especially true of those who were MPs or peers and in periods when there were major political changes. By the 1760s it was increasingly common to refer to the Paris embassy when considering Cabinet reshuffles.[30] Some envoys went in changes of government and others thought they might. Thus John Trevor wondered whether the fall of the North ministry would lead to him leaving Munich;[31] it didn't. However, Joseph Yorke found himself out of favour: 'if at the end of three and thirty years foreign service, I am to be thrown aside like waste paper, I can only say I would never advise a relation or friend of mine to go into the same line.'[32] Carmarthen added, the following February, when Shelburne's peace preliminaries were defeated in the Commons, that 'this convulsion' would prevent him going to Paris.[33]

When Pitt replaced Fox–North, it was necessary to appoint new envoys to Paris and Madrid, because their followers were either dismissed or sought to undermine the new minister by a collective resignation. This led to the departure of the envoys, George, 4th Duke of Manchester and John, Viscount Mountstuart, as well as Anthony Storer, Secretary to the Embassy at Paris and an MP. The previous May, Elizabeth, Duchess of Manchester had warned her husband, 'I think it may be *prudent* not to engage any house till the stability of this ministry is a little more certain'.[34] By backing Fox in the Regency Crisis, Malmesbury condemned himself to the political wilderness from early 1789.[35] Had Fox prevailed, Dorset and William Eden would probably have lost their posts. Dorset was certainly very uncertain on this head.[36] However, political links did not always prevent appointments or lead to dismissal. Yorke did not go out with the Hardwicke–Newcastle connection, in 1762, because, as his brother pointed out, 'he has all along kept out of the way of our disentions at home'. Harris was chosen for The Hague in 1784 despite his affiliations.[37]

Instability, in the shape of the possibility that a new ministry would seek to discredit its predecessor, was partly responsible for another aspect of the conduct of foreign policy, namely the attempt to prevent diplomats from committing the government on paper. Thus, in 1756, Holdernesse, a diplomat turned Secretary of State, reprimanded Keith for communicating an extract of a letter from him to the Austrian Chancellor, Count Kaunitz:

> … has been the source of great part of this ill-humour, and was a step, which His Majesty greatly disapproved … I am to acquaint you with His Majesty's express command, that you should never give any thing whatsoever in writing to the Court where you reside, unless you have leave so to do.[38]

This approach, however, hindered the so-called 'English Plan'. Three years earlier, Guy Dickens had responded from St Petersburg to similar criticism:

> With regard to the displeasure I had incurred for taking upon me, without orders, to give a memorial in writing, the Great Chancellor desired me to tell your grace that it is impossible you should be unacquainted that, at this court, there are only two methods of transacting affairs with foreign ministers, which are equally the same: the one, by way of promemoria; the other, in a conference with him and the Vice-Chancellor, where everything is taken down at *protocollum*; that, were this not the established rule, his, the Grand Chancellor's surprise would not be the less great at its being expected in England, that, upon a loose verbal report, he should have taken upon himself, without the privity and communication of the other ministers of his department, to induce the Empress to enter into measures of such great importance, as those proposed … if we were not content, in England, to conform to the established method of treating affairs here, the best way would be to give over all thoughts to having any serious or important transactions between the two courts.[39]

The 'English Plan' therefore left British foreign policy dependent on the negotiating procedures followed in other courts. However, this should not be exaggerated, not least because much was in fact handled in London. During the Falkland Islands disputes in 1770–1 between Britain and Spain,

> early despatches demonstrated the problems involved and what emerged as an effective deployment of existing resources. Robert

Walpole and James Harris's services were deliberately confined to court duties, intelligence gathering and maintaining communications. Serious discussion was thus the more readily confined to London and the services of those politicians closest to the King.[40]

Concern about envoys could encourage the handling of issues in London.[41] In 1761, Bute wanted Austria approached via the Dutch not via Joseph Yorke, the envoy in The Hague, because of the latter's links with Newcastle. Monarchs did not wish to lose control of particularly sensitive issues such as marital diplomacy. Thus, in 1728, Du Bourgay was ordered to 'confine yourself to the orders you receive from hence, and not enter further in the affair of the marriages, but only hear what may be told you'.[42]

A major problem posed by the 'English Plan' was that of reconciling the varied views of foreign powers. When Britain was trying to reconcile the interests of other powers, for example Austria and Sardinia in 1732–3 and 1742–3,[43] Austria and Spain in 1731–3,[44] and Austria and Saxony and Sweden and Russia in 1741, it was all too easy for her envoys to side with the courts to which they were accredited, or to be seen to be acting in this light. This could lead to contradictory commitments, thus creating problems for the government. In 1746, Harrington felt it necessary to caution Hyndford about pushing Russia to guarantee Prussia's acquisition of Silesia: 'be careful to act in it with such caution and prudence, as neither to give handles of complaint to one party by an over officious zeal, nor to the other by any visible coldness and neglect.'[45] A variant on this general problem was that of having to warn envoys not to intervene in subjects that were being discussed at congresses of the powers.[46]

The difficulty of this situation was accentuated by the habit of British diplomats claiming that their counterparts at other courts had 'gone native' and that their views should be discarded. In 1751, Hanbury Williams, ever ready to make criticisms of others, explained why he would welcome a posting to The Hague: 'The difference between that place and Vienna is that at The Hague you may do yourself honour and yet be a good Englishman. But at Vienna you must often give up England in order to be thought a good Austrian—Keith never contradicts them and so is very well there.' Robinson, however, claimed that service in Paris did not have this effect, and that indeed it was 'the most contagious for the old English way of thinking'.[47]

Harrington responded to clashes between Hyndford and Robinson in 1741 by admonishing the former that 'different impressions of things and persons, may be easily taken at different courts, and the variety of senti-ments arising from that source is as easily capable of being improved into a personal disagreement'.[48]

Accusations of exceeding orders were not restricted to an alleged undue favour to the government the embassy was accredited to. Paget was criticized in 1690 over his tactics in opposing the grant of an important Elbe toll to Denmark. Du Bourgay was reprimanded in 1729 for suggesting that the British, French and Dutch envoys warn Prussia about its policy in the Jülich–Berg crisis, while, in 1743, Villettes was accused of exceeding orders for suggesting that Naples and Sicily be ceded to Austria.[49] He had been warned the previous year not to say what was not 'warranted' by his instructions.[50]

Envoys had to respond to criticism from London knowing that much of it was likely to be inspired by complaints from other powers, whether conveyed to British diplomats at these courts or by foreign envoys in London. In 1747, Lieutenant-General Thomas Wentworth, who was sent to Turin to try to improve Austro-Sardinian relations, reported to Newcastle on Austrian anger:

> It may possibly be insinuated, that I may be sometimes mistaken in the relations I send to your Grace, which I certainly may, but I can safely affirm, that I neither have, nor ever will on any consideration, write what do not then appear to me to be matter of fact to the best of my knowledge and judgment.[51]

The experienced Trevor had glanced at another cause of irritation the previous year: 'I am too sensible how delicate it is for a minister barely to recapitulate the objections, replies, and arguments that a state where he resides opposes to him … without more or less appearing to give into and adopt the same himself.'[52]

Another serious problem with negotiating abroad was that diplomats lost touch with domestic politics, governmental views, parliamentary pressures, public opinion, and, more generally, the compromises that underlay decision-making. This was a particular problem with long-serving envoys, such as St Saphorin, and with those who became attached to alliances, for example Horatio Walpole and France in 1730, Mitchell and Prussia in 1762,[53] and Ewart with Prussia in 1791. Horatio Walpole complained in 1726 'St. Saphorin is a good judge of the Court of Vienna, but not of the House of Commons'.[54] Robert Murray Keith wanted a 'general coalition' in 1784, not a policy that recommended itself to Pitt the Younger.[55] More generally, a careful reading of diplomatic correspondence, both public and, more clearly, private, suggests that many envoys lacked sympathy with the nature and consequences of public debate in Britain.

In part, this was an aspect of what was more generally true of diplomats, a sense that they were misunderstood at home and that the policy-makers were insufficiently sensitive to events abroad. However, in addition, there was a specific disquiet about the public debate that reflected a social disdain for the character of popular politics. In 1718, Robert Walpole, then in opposition, attacked Robert Jackson, representative in Stockholm, about an answer to Parliament deemed offensive: 'that gentleman having lived so long in a despotic government, where petitions and representations of that nature are accounted capital crimes, that he had forgot the rights and privileges of his countrymen.'[56] Robinson complained in 1739: 'The warmth of your parliamentary debates do no good abroad ... Foreigners have not an adequate notion of our constitution.' He proved an unsuccessful Secretary of State, not least because he was a poor orator.[57]

In 1761, Mitchell could not 'persuade' himself 'that the people of England *en corps* are competent judges of matters of state'.[58] An out-of-touch Joseph Yorke wrote to Newcastle in 1762 from The Hague about withdrawing British troops from Germany: 'I can never be brought to believe that it will be a popular measure when carried into execution, however it may please in theory, the multitude, uninformed and giddy as they are, love national honour, and if peace does not accompany the recall of the troops,' Yorke warned that it would be unpopular.[59] He completely failed to judge the national mood in Britain.

Such problems could be lessened if higher-ranking envoys were sent out on special missions, when relations were at a delicate stage. Thus, William Stanhope was sent to Spain in 1729:

> If the treaty is to be made there, it is inconsistent with common sense that we should have there only a minister of the second rank and our allies each one of the first when our affairs are the foremost in debate; not that anything can be said against Keene who behaves like an angel, but they do not seem to regard him so much as I hope they would a person of greater dignity.[60]

Six years later, while the British were seeking to negotiate a solution to the

War of the Polish Succession, personal representation by Horatio Walpole was thought essential:

> His Majesty thought it absolutely necessary that, instead of answering the Cardinal's last letter which would serve only to lose time that is very precious, I should go through France in my return to Holland, and confer with the French ministers upon what has already past, in order to know what we must expect for the future.[61]

However, the problem of diplomats losing touch with the political situation at home could not be solved by such episodic missions. It directs attention to the means of control available to British government.

5

Means of Control

Let me hope for your protection, Sir, under the disagreable and dangerous task I am involved in of representing unpalatable truths to my master.

Robert Trevor to Henry Pelham, 1744[1]

It does not appear to me that there can be any necessity to maintain so very regular a correspondence as you advise. Were such a measure to be adopted, I am well convinced that there would be no time for anything else; and, while we were establishing a reputation on the single ground of ceremonious punctuality, we should effectually lose it on every other. When foreign ministers go from us to the different European courts, they carry with them general instructions, by which their conduct is to be regulated. It is their duty to act upon them on all occasions to which they can apply; and it is also their duty to transmit to their own court regular accounts of what is passing by every mail. Should anything in these dispatches require an answer—should a change of circumstances render a change of instructions necessary— or should the foreign minister himself desire the advice or appui of his own Court—in such cases, the Secretary of State for the Foreign Department, in his wisdom and knowledge of the interests of the several parties concerned, will act properly by transmitting to the minister abroad his sentiments and instructions.

James Bland Burges, 1789[2]

In 1785, a long-standing British diplomat, Sir James Harris, delivered a pungent and oft-cited verdict on the need for diplomats to follow their own head:

our Principals at home are too much occupied with the House of Commons to attend to what passes on the Continent; and, if any good is ever done there, it must be effected through the King's ministers abroad, and not by those about his person. Long experience has taught me this; and I never yet received an instruction that was worth reading.[3]

Harris' comment can be supported by reference to the complaints of other diplomats, not so much about the content of their instructions, but about their infrequency. This was not a new problem, and it can be seen throughout the century, more particularly in peacetime. In 1734, Tyrawly (Lisbon) complained that in nearly seven years he had acted 'without any support from home, or even a correspondence kept up with me'. In December 1738, Villettes (Turin) noted that he had had no instructions for a year.[4] Such a neglect had a consequence for diplomats' conduct. Essex (Turin) complained in 1734 when Charles Emmanuel III was one of the participants in the War of the Polish Succession, 'I am kept in the greatest ignorance of what is doing anywhere; so don't know how to behave', and Dunant added from Vienna three years later:

> I have not received a syllable either from England or from any of His Majesty's ministers abroad for several posts, I had not a word to say either to the Imperial, or to the foreign, minister here, and I began to find a good deal of coldness when I visited any of them … everyone expects some sort of reciprocity on my part.[5]

There were serious complaints about Francis, Marquess of Carmarthen and later 5th Duke of Leeds, the Foreign Secretary in 1783–91, especially from Sir Robert Murray Keith in Vienna,[6] but also from William Eden during commercial negotiations in 1786.[7] In part, political and diplomatic circumstances played a role. This was obviously the case with the failure to send Eden the instructions he sought while the government was in turmoil during the Regency Crisis of 1788–9; and also with the failure to keep Keith informed in 1787–8 when relations with Prussia, not Austria, were crucial.

In part, however, there were also particular problems arising from the transition in 1782 from the system of two Secretaries of State to the Foreign and Home Secretaries.[8] Under the former system, the absence of one Secretary from London or his ill-health did not prevent his colleague from filling his role.[9] Although the colleague would not necessarily be conversant with the details of a particular negotiation, he would be well aware of the general developments in British foreign policy and would sometimes be an experienced diplomat. However, differences between two Secretaries could also cause division and/or disorganization. In 1736, Horatio Walpole noted the problems of trilateral negotiations when writing to Trevor:

> I do not wonder at your embarrass in our negotiations; consultations and orders are carried on in England with such confusion, and in so indigested a manner; the affairs of Turkey are in the province of one Secretary, the directions to be sent to The Hague belong to the department of another. These two I believe see one another but little, and I perceive that one [Harrington] writes nothing at all and the other [Newcastle] will not suffer nobody but himself to think or write anything that may concern his province.[10]

Joseph Yorke thought 'two Secretaries for Foreign affairs a wrong arrangement for business'.[11] To Abraham Stanyan, the solution was a 'Council for Foreign Affairs'. This seemed the best way to deal with variations in the dedication of Secretaries of State. Stanyan explained to Bolingbroke that the latter's predecessors had been remiss in corresponding even though important matters had been in negotiation:

> ... to be feared, when you quit it, that your successor will let the business relapse into the former track, I hope it will be part of the glory of your Lordship's ministry, to settle the management of foreign affairs upon a lasting good foundation.[12]

This idea got nowhere. The relevant advisory body to the Crown continued, formally, to be the Privy Council and, less formally, to be the Cabinet, with the Secretaries of State answering to the king for the execution of policy. Such a system lacked the conciliar structure of the Boards of Treasury, Admiralty and Trade, but there is little sign that such a structure would have increased effectiveness, especially as political differences played a major role in the formulation of foreign policy.

Whatever the disadvantages of two Secretaries, there were problems if there was only one. During Carmarthen's tenure of the Foreign Office, when he was busy on other duties, for example attendance at Parliament,[13] ill,[14] or otherwise absent, diplomatic business suffered. No other minister had served as a diplomat or taken a regular role in foreign policy, let alone having any experience in fulfilling the functions of the Foreign Secretaryship. Carmarthen responded to Eden's complaints that negotiations 'cannot always be regulated according to the ordinary course of common post days'.[15]

Harris' claim should be treated not as a verdict on the entire period, but rather on the situation in the early 1780s, when Britain faced a serious internal crisis. At other times, the position was less bleak. For example, in 1715–40, only James Stanhope on his missions in the late 1710s and Horatio Walpole in the mid-1730s enjoyed the independence that was claimed by Harris. Partly this was due to ministerial stability and experience, both of which were in shorter supply in 1782–5; partly, possibly, to firmer royal control by the experienced George I. Under George, obstreperous diplomats were disciplined. The Earl of Stair (Paris, 1715–20) was removed because his criticisms of French policy were held to be endangering the alliance. Stair's embassy was also unpopular in France because of the success of his chaplain, William Beauvoir, in attracting over 100 converts to Protestantism and the popularity of his services. Henry Davenant (Envoy Extraordinary to several Italian states, 1714–22) was recalled for being overly pro-Austrian. He became an Austrian pensionary, who was used in order to encourage pro-Austrian sentiment.[16]

Clearly, then, and at other times, domestic commitments and the awareness of the problem of distance led the Secretaries to allow much independence to the diplomats. In 1730, George Tilson, an Under-Secretary, wrote to Robinson: 'I don't see by your relations [reports] that you wanted any instructions. You on the spot with those just notions of the true state of affairs will always act better than we can bid you from hence, unless something new should arise.'[17]

This was certainly true for unimportant postings, and for periods when the ministry had no particular policy to advance. In 1748, Everard Fawkener sent his successor at Constantinople, James Porter, a copy of the recent Treaty of Aix-la-Chapelle:

> I know how much a remote minister, and who is not in the circle of those affairs which is the object of immediate attention, is ordinarily neglected, and that it is therefore very probable you may not have any notice of this transaction, in some time, or at all any papers relative to it.

When the situation was very different, supervision was close. A courier could easily get from London to Paris or The Hague, and return in a week. Benjamin Langlois pointed out in 1774 that 'Paris and London are too near for any step not to be known and aggravated'.[18]

Such correspondence could be too slow at crucial moments, such as in the developing crisis with Revolutionary France in late 1792. Nevertheless, it was still relatively quick compared to the situation with respect to British embassies further east in Europe. There, distance exacerbated the difficulties that arose for all British diplomats from their country's island character. Adverse winds could prevent messengers sailing, or lead to their being blown off course. At a crucial moment in November 1757, a courier from Andrew Mitchell in Berlin landed in Whitby, not Harwich. The following month, Mitchell found himself under 'the greatest perplexity', because contrary winds had detained Holdernesse's instructions. And the 'state of affairs' had recently changed considerably.[19] Earlier, on 16 September, Mitchell could only respond to Frederick II's news that George II had signed a neutrality agreement with France by saying that his last letter from England was of 16 August and from the Duke of Cumberland, the commander of the Hanoverian army, of 2 September. In March 1731, at a crucial moment in Anglo-Austrian relations, Delafaye referred to the 'unpardonable … slowness of our couriers', and, later, to a courier from Vienna being 'delayed by bad roads and contrary winds'. They clearly were not the only problems for he also wrote, 'French and Spanish couriers may have some advantage of them in getting post horses; but with all the allowance that can be made in their behalf, their slowness [to Spain] is inexcusable', and, later, 'our messengers are beat so shamefully by the French and Spanish'.[20]

It was not only couriers who were affected by difficulties in travel. Envoys had to be prepared for difficult journeys. En route for Constantinople, William Harbord spent thirteen days at Gravesend in December 1691. He was to die at Belgrade in August 1692; his predecessor, Sir William Hussey, had died there the previous September. Even short voyages could be very difficult. Having left Harwich at 10 am on 19 January (os) 1745, Chesterfield, who was not on his first crossing, arrived at Helvoetsluys at 2pm on the 20th 'a good deal disordered after a very sick and rough voyage'.[21] In June 1784, Dorset 'had a most unpleasant rough passage of eight hours and a half owing to the *cowardly behaviour* of the French seamen who would not venture out of Calais harbour in a boat to take us in'. For William Grenville, it took 'twenty four hours seasickness, and eight hours jolting in Dutch wagons' to reach The Hague in 1787.[22] In November 1793, Malmesbury explained his belated arrival at The Hague: 'An uncommonly long passage from Dover to Ostend and the badness of the roads since'. 'A good deal of night travelling on the dykes in Holland … exhausted' Malmesbury's 'bodily strength', and once into Germany his journey was delayed by poor roads. Malmesbury was no more fortunate the following May: 'After a passage of three days and as many nights we are just arrived—you will readily suppose that the wind was contrary the whole way and that my female companions were very sick … this long passage has lost me a great deal of valuable time'.

Longer voyages could be far worse. Stephen Poyntz encountered terrible storms on a passage to Gothenburg in 1724. In 1799, Thomas Grenville suffered shipwreck and the loss of most of his possessions en route to Berlin. Conversely, in late 1794, Morton Eden congratulated himself on his speedy journey to Vienna. Sailing from the Nore on 29 November, and 'having had a favourable passage to the mouth of the Elbe, I was enabled to reach this place, on the night of the 13th [December]'.[23]

A century earlier, the absence of a method for prompt communications from Lisbon under the control of the envoy led John Methuen to urge that the Admiralty provide an advice-yacht. James Dormer was detained by contrary winds at Plymouth while on the way to Lisbon in 1725. On his return in disgrace in December 1727, Dormer was detained by contrary winds at Lisbon for several days; the eventual voyage to Plymouth took twelve days. The following March, Tyrawly was delayed for fifteen days by contrary winds. The Spanish-Portuguese war panic of 1735 led John Burnaby Parker, Consul at Corunna, to press for the addition of another packet on the Portugal run.[24]

When Britain's main alliance axis moved from being with The Hague or Paris, where it had been in the period 1689–1730, to being with one of Vienna and Berlin, for most of the period 1731–62, there were serious problems with communications; these were to be resumed in 1788–91 (with Berlin) and from 1793 (with Vienna). Messages took longer and were more prone to disruption. The Harwich–Helvoetsluys crossing was longer than the Dover–Calais route and more subject to interruption, especially to the westerlies that stopped the Harwich passage. Delays came to play a greater role in correspondence. For example, on 6 August 1756, Holdernesse noted that Mitchell's of 23 July from Berlin had been delayed by contrary winds.[25]

Problems with communications were not restricted to crossing the sea.

There were also many difficulties facing travellers within Europe. Roads were frequently poor.[26] Facilities could be very limited. Leaving Paris on 21 September, William Stanhope was delayed by bad roads made worse by heavy rains, and by the difficulty in securing sufficient mules for his baggage in north Spain, but he still reached Seville on 25 October. En route overland for St Petersburg, Edward Finch wrote from Königsberg (Kaliningrad):

> Courland, at all times a desert country ... everything necessary for the subsistence of myself and servants must be carried with me, since I am assured that it will be impossible even to find bread and salt in any place nor in many so much as water ... there is no such thing as posting, so that I am reduced to make use of the same horses ... to Riga.[27]

Overturned carriages were a problem. George Woodward was delayed on the way to Paris in December 1726 while en route to take up his post as Secretary at Vienna:

> ... having had the misfortune of the axle tree of my chaise breaking in the night at above a league's distance from Montreuil. The getting it to the town and the time in mending of it detained me more than a whole day. Just before the accident, I was overturned into a hollow way, and was so lucky as to escape with a little bruise only, though Mr. Smith fell upon me; he was so much hurt that he is still lame. Such is often the fate of travellers.[28]

Poor health exacerbated and was accentuated by the strains of travelling. Harbord's bad gout delayed his journey from The Hague to Frankfurt in the winter of 1691–2. He was subsequently affected en route for Vienna not only by gout and bad weather but also by the closures of passes caused by the outbreak of plague in the Habsburg dominions. William Fawkener who, unlike Harbord, reached Constantinople, travelled there via Hanover, where he saw George II. Reaching Vienna, he reported, 'I was detained upon the road by little accidents befalling my coach, and by bad weather and worse roads during the latter part of my journey, longer than I expected'. It then took a month to reach Belgrade, 'a very pleasant but slow journey, occasioned by the lowness of the water. It was necessary I should change my boats, the providing others has occasioned my stay'. Leaving Belgrade on 12 November, Fawkener reached Constantinople on

19 December, but reported that it was still a quicker journey than if he had gone by sea, as his equipage did.[29]

Difficulties were also exacerbated by bad weather and by the impact of the winter. Post from England was very slow to reach the Imperial Court at Augsburg in late 1689. This left the Envoy Extraordinary, William, Lord Paget, unaware of what was expected of him and unable to act through lack of instructions. In March 1742, Wych was delayed at Gdansk en route for St Petersburg by the difficulty of crossing ice-filled rivers.[30] Road and river traffic were affected by winter ice. In January 1715, Horatio Walpole was delayed by ice en route for The Hague after he had reached the United Provinces. In January 1791, Auckland reported from The Hague: 'The roads are so bad in consequence of this long continued course of wet and open weather, that the posts from the north arrive with great difficulty.' In January 1795, Wickham wrote from Berne, 'It is dreadfully cold here, and I fear the Rhine will be frozen over. If so, the messenger will be obliged to go round the Lord knows where.'[31] Nevertheless, summer travel could also be difficult. Travelling from Prague to Vienna in June 1743, Robinson faced a tiring journey and had to put up with a bad inn.[32] Furthermore, winter cold could be better than spring thaw and autumn rain. Glenorchy wrote from Copenhagen in November 1724, 'Till the frost comes the roads are intolerable, and that seldom is lasting till after Christmas'.[33]

Distance also put more pressure on the King's Messengers, the couriers employed. Their work was hard. In October 1733, the traveller John Ward met a King's Messenger on the Calais–Dover packet. In order to take only seven days from Turin to the boat 'he had not been in a bed since he left Turin'.[34] This system had its limitations. Although the Russians murdered a Swedish courier returning from Stockholm to Constantinople in 1739 and seized his dispatches, no British courier, or foreign courier travelling to or from London, was thus treated, although communications during the attempt to mediate a settlement to the war between Austria and Turkey in 1693 were affected by the murder of a foreign courier between Hermannstadt in Transylvania and Constantinople, while it was alleged that William Stanhope was 'privy' to the robbing of a Portuguese courier from Madrid in 1725. More generally, couriers could be affected by injury and illness. Messages entrusted to the post could be intercepted and deciphered, and this led to delays. Newcastle replied to Essex's complaints of neglect in 1735 by referring to 'the impossibility of trusting anything of a secret nature by the post'.[35] Nevertheless, the British were far more effective at interception and decipherment than their rivals: there are a few

British intercepts in foreign archives, for example Vienna, but very few. The need for quarantine on arriving from the Ottoman Empire was a particular problem in communications with Constantinople.

Communications became more of a problem in wartime. War with France led to the suspension of the cross-Channel packet services. Couriers and diplomats could still travel via Ostend or Helvoetsluys, but the journey time to embassies such as those in Italy increased. These routes could also be affected by French advances. Ostend was occupied in 1745–8 and again from 1793, while the United Provinces was overrun in 1794–5. This forced the British to turn to North German links. In 1727, as relations with Spain deteriorated, the packet boat *Boscawen* was seized at Corunna. Routes were also affected even if Britain was not a combatant. In 1757, France's ally Austria cut all communications between the Austrian Netherlands and Britain although they were not at war. This severed the Ostend route.[36] It was rare for diplomats to be harassed in wartime, but in 1744 Holdernesse was arrested in Franconia while en route to Venice by hussars of Britain's ally Austria. War hit communications even when Britain was neutral. In July 1735, Harrington wrote from Hanover about the envoys in the Southern Department, 'the great distance of some of the places where they reside, and the irregularity of the posts in this time of war, may have occasioned many of their letters arriving here very late'.[37]

No British envoy in Europe experienced the treatment recorded in the *Original Mercury, York Journal: or, Weekly Courant* of 24 September 1728. A week earlier, in London,

> the Secretary of the Ambassador of Tripoli going over into Southwark, with Jezreel Jones Esq., who speaks the Arabic language, to see the diversions of the fair, was met by a disorderly drunken fellow, who perhaps from a dislike to the Secretary's habit, or to his being a foreigner, was so civil as without any ceremony to strike him a violent blow in the face; which almost swelled up one of his eyes, for which he was heartily caned by Mr. Jones, and committed by Justice Mitchel to prison for assaulting a person under national protection.

Due to distance, in Central and, still more, Eastern Europe, envoys, such as Kinnoull, Harris and Ewart were better able, or perforce felt themselves obliged, to follow initiatives of their own, not obviously that they saw these as diverging from British interests and policy. Envoys in distant postings were certainly given more leeway in deciding how best to implement their orders,[38] although that created problems.

Control and responsibility during periods of intense activity were clearly an issue, but they cannot be seen in isolation from periods when there was a different level of activity and supervision. In March 1792, Auckland wrote to his brother, Morton Eden:

> You seem to think it odd that you have so few official letters since your arrival at Berlin: but this is always the case with respect to all the missions during a session of Parliament and at a period too when there is no matter of foreign discussion that materially engages the anxieties of administration. Under such circumstances it sometimes happens with respect to missions even of the first rank not to receive a syllable in six months. The case would be very different under a Secretary of State so efficient as your present principal [Lord Grenville] if there were anything that necessarily required frequent despatches from him.[39]

The impact of government direction was lessened both by experience of its episodic character and by the extent to which many diplomats were long-serving and had careers that spanned several ministries. Prominent examples included Keene, Titley, Keith and Ainslie. Walter Titley served at Copenhagen from 1729 until his death in 1768, being promoted from Chargé d'affaires to Minister Resident in 1731 and, after failing to get the post in 1736, Envoy Extraordinary in 1739. Such a long posting would not have been possible had an ambassador had to be sent, and, indeed, in the last forty years of the century major embassies were increasingly treated as similar to major political posts, ensuring that there were changes when ministries fell, as in 1783. Long postings encouraged a degree of familiarity with their problems and language.

Some long-serving envoys were at relatively minor embassies, such as Florence, Naples and Venice. Sir Horace Mann served at Florence from 1738 to 1786, and Sir William Hamilton at Naples from 1764 to 1800. Venice was referred to as 'the hospital for Foreign Ministers'.[40] Sir William Pulteney unsuccessfully pressed for his brother to succeed Mann as the climate would help his poor health and 'I considered the office as not at all important with regard to the public business'.[41]

However, this situation was not true of all long-serving envoys; and it is clear that diplomats such as Ainslie and Keith were greatly influenced by their earlier experience of their posts, and that this created the context within which they responded to new developments and to their instructions. For example, the attempt to improve relations with France in 1786 and early 1787 cut across the views and experience of most diplomats. In this respect, there was some basis for Harris' maxim, not least because, in the relative economy of experience, at least initially, both Carmarthen and Grenville as Foreign Secretaries were at a disadvantage compared to many of their envoys. Many other Secretaries of State served far more briefly.

Irrespective of their experience, Secretaries of State faced some difficult individuals. Aristocratic envoys were used to getting their own way, both because they were aristocrats and because many had limited diplomatic experience and had not been habituated to the system. In 1762, Hardwicke wrote about John, 4th Duke of Bedford, an ex-Secretary of State, who negotiated peace with France:

> a person of His Grace's temper and turn, liable to such sudden starts and changes, as he is … as zealous for power as he is, he may take a sudden offence; start at some particular point, especially when he is to be the hand to act … he had some such particular sallies in the negotiation of last year. If that should happen, he is as likely to break a negotiation as any man I know. In another light, no man is more likely to take a disgust at instructions that may be sent to him; or at the ministers here differing in opinion from him; or not agreeing to everything His Grace shall propose. I am sure I should not wish to be the Secretary of State to have the correspondence with him.[42]

There were indeed problems. Bedford complained about his instructions: 'For God's sake what occasion was there, for sending a minister to this court, if the whole was to be transacted from ministry to ministry, and why was I selected for this contemptible employment of transmitting *projets* only to my court.' Complaint did not suffice: 'I had been obliged, in order not to lose the whole, to exceed, in things of no real moment the limits, to which I was bound by my instructions.'[43] The French, however, were more impressed with Bedford.[44] Three years later, Macartney disobeyed explicit instructions in negotiations for a treaty with Russia.[45]

In 1794, Lord St Helens wrote to Burges about two recent incidents. In Florence, Wyndham had publicly horsewhipped Count Carlotti for advocating neutrality, while in Copenhagen, Hailes was inflicting 'political horsewhippings'. Burges was unimpressed:

Nothing certainly can be more distressing than the conduct of some of our Foreign Ministers. With respect to Mr. Hailes, his conduct both in taking up the idle business of the libel, and his subsequent proceedings have been much disapproved of. He has received a long letter from Lord Grenville on the subject, to which he has sent a very civil answer, which however shows he is not much convinced by what has been said to him. This is the second hint of this sort which he has received since I have been here. The first was a very strong check from the Duke of Leeds, in consequence of his behaviour to the King of Poland. I am afraid his present ill humour will not be very serviceable in the preservation of good harmony between us and Denmark.[46]

The representation in Florence had also created problems earlier in the year. John Udney, the consul in Leghorn, reported that John, Lord Hervey, the Envoy Extraordinary, had employed 'too much violence' in manner and language in trying to gain Tuscan assistance, and had accordingly failed. In addition, 'Lord Hervey refused to deliver me up the public papers and correspondence'.[47] The previous year, a visitor suggested, 'They deserve the bold truths he has told them but it is a bad diplomatic practice to call the sovereign a fool and the Prime Minister a knave'.[48]

Yet, the complaints of 1794 reflected, in many respects, an extreme position, as also, for example, did Robert Murray Keith's complaints of neglect by Carmarthen in 1788. More often it was the case not of defiance or neglect, but of the difficulty of providing prompt and pertinent instructions and reports. Understaffed Secretaries of States offices contributed in the case of instructions. Weston referred in 1750 to 'the machine of our foreign affairs', but the springs seemed rusty to many diplomats.[49] This was a particular problem for less prominent embassies. Envoys in such posts, for example Brigadier Richard Sutton in Cassel in 1728, were especially apt to complain about a lack of instructions.[50] Kinnoull reflected, 'our Court almost forgot that there is such a country as Turkey in the world'.[51]

The formulaic character of instructions was a problem, as was the implicit notion that if anything was unclear the envoy should write in for fresh instructions, a method that neglected the constraints of time. In 1739, at a crucial moment in Anglo-Spanish relations, Keene informed Sir Robert Walpole that his letters 'always explain the loose general expressions office letters are usually composed of'.[52] Conversely, in 1755, Keene informed Robinson that his private letters underlined what was in the official correspondence.[53] The root problem was the difficulty of providing what was required on time.

Envoys not only felt that they were not provided with ample and prompt instructions, but also that they lacked adequate information from home and from other British envoys. The former was important in order to present the best gloss on developments within Britain and, in particular, create an impression of strength and stability there. Furthermore, it could help ingratiate diplomats. Whitworth wrote to Stanhope in 1717:

> The Queen advises me to take all opportunities of writing to the King of Prussia, by sending him any little news I can though I should be sure he had the same directly from Bonet [Prussian envoy in London]; Her Majesty thinks this would by degrees introduce me into a sort of confidence, and give me occasion of mentioning other matters, and preventing the impressions some here are very industrious to give: If you think this for the service some little advices from the office ... might be of use. [54]

Knowing that there was nothing new to say was also regarded as an advantage.[55]

Information from other British envoys was seen as necessary, and indeed often featured in diplomatic instructions, because it was felt that it made envoys more authoritative. In November 1755, Hanbury Williams complained from St Petersburg to Keith that the latter had never sent 'one paragraph of news ... I have known no more from you of what has been doing at Vienna for this last summer than of what has been doing in China'. Titley complained in 1734 about not being kept informed by Edward Finch.[56] A year earlier, however, Robinson had replied robustly to complaints from Essex:

> as to the holding a regular correspondence, and reasoning with them [other envoys] upon affairs it is what I pretty much avoid for the few following reasons:
> 1. That is mighty well for ministers to do it, where they are left to guesswork and speculation, but for me who seldom write anything but what I learn from the source and by way of confidential communication, I should be afraid to diminish that confidence, were my letters opened.
> 2. That it may not be imputed to me as if by my own reflections I was

willing or presumptuous enough to prevent the orders that should naturally go from England.

3. You cannot but easily believe I would rather not write at all but in the greatest necessity than to sit down in the uncertainty of knowing what is proper or not to be written. But the misfortune is everybody thinks his own business is the only business of everybody else.[57]

Being kept informed was far less of a problem for embassies through which communications were routed. The Hague and Paris were the central points in the British system. As a consequence, envoys there were kept alert to developments. Townshend wrote of The Hague in 1724: 'This post being reckoned the best and most agreable of any abroad', and presented it to William Finch as 'the just reward of the good services you have done in him [George I] in Sweden'. Newcastle wrote to Sandwich in 1748, 'I can never think of your quitting The Hague: that is, and must be, the center of all business, both of peace and war'.[58] In 1751, Hanbury Williams thought The Hague a 'desirable' posting 'in our trade. The Minister at that court has the secret lodg'd in him and may make a figure.' In contrast, difficulties were caused when the secret was withheld. William Eliot wrote from The Hague in 1793:

> Lord Henry Spencer before he left the Hague stated to me several times the disagreable situation in which he was more than once placed by the messengers who passed through here carrying all their dispatches sealed; for as frequently the ministry here got intelligence from Mr. de Nagel [Dutch envoy in London] concerning the object of their journey and sometimes even copies of their papers it made him, Lord Henry Spencer, appear extremely reserved towards this government which it certainly is not the wish of our minister either to be, or seem to be. I understand it is not usual at the office to send the dispatches in the absence of the ambassador under flying seal through the Hague,

and therefore Eliot proposed to ask Grenville to change the rule.[59]

Aside from the information available, envoys in key posts, such as Horatio Walpole in Paris, could also, if trusted, be given authority to modify orders to other envoys sent under flying seal and thus co-ordinate foreign policy in particular spheres. Horatio was also sent important dispatches that he would not otherwise have seen.[60]

Irrespective of the information available, there were problems with control. Ensuring that envoys fulfilled instructions was made more difficult by the absence of a notion of bureaucratic service. Furthermore, the habit of choosing well-connected envoys potentially lessened their obedience. The personal representative of the sovereign, envoys felt able to ascribe orders they disliked to particular political combinations, and thus to justify following their own views. In this respect, the aristocratic or House of Commons background of many envoys was potentially a disadvantage.

At the same time, the means of control were complicated by the number of individuals who might give envoys instructions, by potential differences between them, and by the lack of any automatic procedure for resolving such differences. In 1747, Robinson wrote, 'What I wish is steadiness and union in and amongst those who are at the helm'.[61] In 1787, British envoys in Paris were in touch not only with the Foreign Secretary, but also Pitt the Younger, First Lord of the Treasury, and Lord Thurlow, the Lord Chancellor. The previous year, Eden had explained why he had had to write 'so many long letters' to Pitt 'but my business will never advance without the aid of your energy and decision'.[62]

This problem was exacerbated both by the importance and sensitivity of foreign policy issues and by the nature of some of the individuals involved. The cantankerous George II (1727–60) was a case in point. Aside from his concern with the dignity and prerogatives of his post, George also sought to use British diplomacy to further the security of his beloved Electorate of Hanover. Envoys were instructed to co-operate with their Hanoverian counterparts,[63] and Hyndford was ordered to provide information to George via the Hanoverian Chancery.[64] Diplomats were also aware that prominent ministers might help them circumvent royal instructions. The private papers of diplomats showed this process in operation. In 1722, Carteret sent Schaub a private letter in his own hand:

> I return you your private letter of the 14th, which I received this day; and desire that you will send it me, as a particular letter, write over again, in the same form; with the private articles concerning the particular matters, left out. It contains many necessary and important things to be shown to His Majesty, but I can not show it on account of those two articles, which I have scratched out, concerning Countess P—[Platen]. For the future pray never mingle private letters with politics.

In 1736, Tilson informed Titley that he had shown a letter from the latter to Horatio Walpole 'but did not let it go to the King who might take it as a design to elude his orders'.[65] At the same time, the king held the ultimate whip hand, as Horatio Walpole noted when discussing Trevor's salary in 1739:

> I am sure he knows our master too well, as to be convinced that he is not to be moved in a point of this nature, where he has once declared his resolution; although I have pressed my brother to renew his instances, I am afraid if he does it will only end, as it did in Mr. Robinson's case, in the king desiring him to nominate another minister instead of Trevor to succeed him.

There were fewer problems over the royal role as Elector of Hanover during the reign of George III, although it remained a sensitive matter. Grenville wrote to Morton Eden in 1798:

> On consideration of your letter separate of the 11th August it did not appear to me that there was anything in its contents that might not with the greatest propriety be laid before the King, who is indeed I believe well aware that the instructions sent from the Hanoverian Chancery do not always exactly correspond with the sentiments or interests of the English government.[66]

The theme of royal control over the diplomatic service and direction over policy were frequently reiterated in the correspondence of diplomats and ministers. In 1740, Trevor wrote to Harrington about 'a general rule which His Majesty has laid down to himself of establishing a certain gradation in his foreign service'.[67] Sixteen years later Holdernesse wrote to Keith that George II had seen his recent private letter to the minister and 'was very much pleased with the accounts you send of the interior of the court where you reside'.[68] The sole royal spouse who played an important role was George II's wife, Caroline, who died in 1737. Aside from her general influence, she was particularly important when George II went to Hanover and she was (invariably) left in London as Regent. Horatio Walpole wrote 'long letters' to her about foreign affairs.[69]

The suspicious, frequently paranoid, Newcastle, Secretary of State in 1724–54, and the equally paranoid Pitt the Elder, Secretary of State in 1756–62, were both very difficult. Waldegrave thought Newcastle 'childish' about his coming to Paris: 'takes it to be an encroachment [in his Department] threats used to make me decline it ineffectual ... no sorts of lights given me from Duke of Newcastle's office.'[70] In 1748, Keith en route for Vienna, was reprimanded at Hanover for having earlier visited Sandwich. He wrote to Sandwich that Newcastle had told him:

> that His Majesty was particularly dissatisfied with that part of my journey, as it had very much the air of going to receive private instructions whereas *the King pretended that his servants were to receive orders from nobody but himself, or those immediately entrusted by him.* This part of the Duke's conversation I own astonished me beyond anything I had ever met with. However I answered him directly that I had no design in going to Aix but to have the pleasure of passing two or three days with you, and to have the opportunity of thanking you in person for the civilities I had received from you ... that I was neither fool enough to think myself of consequence enough to have any particular views of my own, nor knave enough to mean any harm to my benefactors ... Your Lordship may easily conclude from all this, that my situation is not very agreeable, as I shall go to Vienna without a character and probably with very small appointments; besides the certainty of being out of favour with the Duke of Newcastle, who was the person from whom I expected my greatest, I may say my only support in this mission.[71]

Sandwich, in turn, was keen to clear himself of Newcastle's suspicions: the Duke saw him as overly critical of Austria. Sandwich emphasized the difference between private doubts and public views, a distinction Newcastle generally ignored:

> I give you my word no advantage shall ever be taken from any part of my behaviour to authorize a diffidence of our proceedings in the Court of Vienna; nor shall my private apprehensions ever appear in any public transactions more than I imagine would be agreable to your Grace.[72]

Yet, the previous year, Newcastle had had to warn Sandwich: 'Great jealousy ... is taken at your correspondence with the Duke of Bedford and me; and therefore I wish it might be as seldom as possible; and only upon great and extraordinary occasions.'[73] Differences between ministers and envoys interacted with those among the latter. This was exacerbated when plans foundered in difficult circumstances. Thus, a lack of success in the War of the Austrian Succession divided ministers and diplomats over whether to grasp at chances for peace and over how best to handle allies. Trevor's career was one victim, as his advice was rejected by Newcastle.

Such differences became more serious when Britain was an active part of an alliance, as during that war, because allies could be given a misleading impression of government policy. Negotiations between an alliance and other powers were particularly difficult as the British discovered on numerous occasions. Canning welcomed the Peace of Lunéville between Austria and Napoleon in 1801 with the reflection that it had relieved Britain 'from the insuperable difficulties of a joint negotiation'.[74]

Envoys found themselves between their home government and its ally, and this was rarely easy. A very unhappy Mitchell consoled himself in 1762 with the reflection that he had done his duty: 'I have in some measure acquired the confidence of the Hero with whom I live and he hears from me what perhaps he would not have patience to do from an other.'[75] However, to both Bute and other commentators, there was too much hero-worship of Frederick II,[76] and Mitchell was a key envoy not under adequate control.

Correspondence with ministers other than the relevant Secretary of State could be helpful to envoys, but it also risked putting them in a difficult position. Receiving letters of the type 'I only mean to give you a notion of my own way of thinking …'[77] was not always welcome.

Aside from overseeing diplomats, there was also need to control unofficial envoys. Some of these acted with authority, but not status, while others operated in a less authorized fashion, and, indeed, at times against the intentions of the government. Charles Mordaunt, 3rd Earl of Peterborough (1658–1735), had a prominent military career, being appointed commander-in-chief of the troops sent to Spain in 1705. However, he did not appreciate the wisdom of following instructions. Recalled in 1707, he instead travelled through Europe. Restored to favour, Peterborough was sent as envoy to Vienna in 1711, disobeyed orders, returned home, and was sent first to the Imperial election at Frankfurt and then to Italy in order to get him out of the country. Thereafter, Peterborough lacked any formal credentials, but that did not prevent subsequent journeys in which he sought to play an intercessionary role, including to Italy in 1717 and 1719 and to France in 1720 and 1724. In 1717, he was arrested at Bologna on suspicion of intriguing against the

Pretender. Peterborough's main effort was in 1719 when he tried to arrange a solution to the War of the Quadruple Alliance.[78] His efforts then, and on other occasions, surprised and/or embarrassed the government[79] and led to complaints from other powers.[80] In 1722, Peterborough's attempt to be made Plenipotentiary to the Italian states was unsuccessful.[81] Two years later he tried to improve Anglo-Spanish relations.[82]

Peterborough's connections and diplomatic career still await careful study; but he was far from alone among the ranks of those who sought to play a diplomatic role. Attempts to improve Anglo-French relations possibly lay behind the visit to France in 1746 of James, 14th Earl of Morton. The banker Van Neck played a role in trying to prevent the outbreak of full-scale war between Britain and France in the mid-1750s. George, 3rd Earl Cowper sought to arrange an Anglo-Austrian rapprochement in the early 1780s.

Stress on the need to control the diplomatic process reflected a strong belief in its importance, and its dangers if uncontrolled. An emphasis on the role of individual monarchs and ministers necessarily directed attention to diplomacy, both as a means to understand developments abroad and as an attempt to influence them. This sense of unpredictability, and thus the need for diplomacy, was accentuated by the emphasis throughout much of the period on an interventionist foreign policy. In addition, British diplomacy offered a means to control, or at least track and try to counter, the influence of other diplomacies. Thus, in the spring of 1733, as the death of Augustus II of Saxony–Poland threatened to unravel the peace of Europe (as it was indeed to do), Newcastle instructed Waldegrave to see the French ministers as frequently as possible:

> it would be a very great misfortune if when we have no intention to hurt France, or to give them any just cause of uneasiness, and when, if we may believe their professions, they are not disposed to break with us, yet that a rupture should be brought about between the two Crowns, by the groundless suggestions of the French ministers employed abroad, owing to misinformation, ill will, or to a desire of making their court at home, by writing what they fancy will be agreable there; so the two nations be written into a quarrel, without either of them intending or desiring it.[83]

6

The Diplomatic Life

From hunting whores and hunting play
and minding nothing else all day
and all the night too you will say.
To make grave legs in formal fetters
Converse with fops and write dull letters
To go to bed twixt eight and nine
And sleep away my precious time
In such an idle sneaking place
where vice and folly hide their face
And in a troublesome disguise
the Wife seems modest, husband wise
for pleasure here has the same fate
which does attend affairs of state.
The plague of ceremony infects,
Even in love, the softer sex
Who an essential will neglect
rather than lose the least respect.
With regular approach we storm
and never visit but in form.
That is sending to know before
At what o'clock they'll play the whore.
The nymphs are constant, gallants private
One scarce can guess who 'tis They drive at
It seems to me a scurvy fashion
who have been bred in a free nation
with Liberty of speech & passion
Yet I cannot forbear to spark it

And make the best of a bad market
Meeting with one, by chance kindhearted
Who no preliminaries started
I enter'd beyond expectation
Into a close negociation
Of which hereafter a relation
Humble to fortune not her slave
I still was pleased with what she gave
And with a firm & cheerfull mind
I steer my course with every wind
To all the ports she has designed.

Sir George Etherege, envoy to the Imperial Diet at Ratisbon
(Regensburg) 1686[1]

In December 1788, Hugh Elliot, Envoy Extraordinary in Denmark and an active self-advertiser, wrote to William Pitt the Younger. Needing to justify his recent activity, he claimed that all his negotiations were directed towards maintaining the balance of power in the North, 'which is indispensably necessary for our safety', and wrote of having spent three years in 'this dismal abode … these Northern and Gothic Regions'. Edward Finch had sought his recall from St Petersburg in 1740 with the complaint, 'believe me it is better to be dead in England than alive here'.[2] How dismal was diplomacy? As with any assessment of effectiveness, views are necessarily subjective. Nevertheless, it is important to consider what diplomats did and sought to do, not least in order better to assess their effectiveness.

Much of the difficulty in making judgements relates to the distinction between the role of the diplomat as representative of his sovereign, and as reporter and commentator. Although requirements under these two heads overlapped, they were also different. The latter functions particularly attract scholarly attention. They also invite comparisons across time.

Yet the function of royal representative was also important. It is not easy to assess, in part, because the culture and ideology of the period can appear remote and redundant. They are generally typecast with the term ceremonial, which is presented as both non-functional and anachronistic. This is very much the outsider's view. Ceremonial and protocol—and a wide range of ideas, assumptions and practices are understood by the terms—were the focus of a diplomatic world for which they served as a means of asserting and defending status and interests. It was perfect for a competitive world that wished to have an alternative to conflict. Thus, for example, William III was very anxious to be styled Majestas by the Emperor Leopold I and not Serenitas.[3] Negotiations focused the need, and provided the opportunity, for settling issues of precedence. Congresses were especially fraught occasions, and the government took great pains to maintain its position at them.[4]

The role of ceremonial had consequences in terms of diplomatic personnel and their activities. Considerations of status played a major role in the choice of diplomats and in the allocation of diplomatic rank. Both were central to precedence: to social precedence and to the precedence of office.

These factors also affected the diplomatic lifestyle. 'Being', and doing so in an appropriate fashion, was important alongside 'doing'. The terms of this 'being' were also significant: envoys lay down their stomachs for the cause of their sovereigns. In March 1687, Sir George Etherege, Ambassador to the Imperial Diet, wrote 'I hope (now there is no danger of the public peace's being broke) the ministers will no longer live in a state of war and that I may play quietly at cards with the Countess of Crecy, without giving the Austrians jealousy'. Sir Robert Sutton was a very good ombre player. Waldegrave wrote from Vienna 'play ... as necessary here for a minister as writing'.[5] For some missions, the timetable does not seem to have been too arduous. At Aranjuez in 1788, Eden recorded: 'We rise early; we breakfast before eight; we then walk till near ten ... I next write and dress from ten till a quarter before 12 at which time precisely I go every day to court.' There he was received each day by the king, the princes and the princesses.[6]

In 1793, however, Malmesbury was exhausted by the rigours of court socializing at Berlin:

> I cannot describe to you the never ending balls, dinners, suppers and operas to which I have been exposed here from the hour of my arrival. They have kept me in a dressed coat from eight in the morning till midnight and all my dispatches have been written with a sword by my side and to the great detriment of laced ruffles ... I am pressed to send away Slater [the courier] in order to be at dinner where I am sure to get nothing to eat, although I shall be three hours at table, and to sit opposite 18 or 20 Princes and Princesses who never cease to talk and ask questions.[7]

Playing at cards or being interesting and amusing at dinner were not simply useful skills, but also part of the image of gentility and pattern of behaviour held likely not only to ensure the proper representation of sovereign authority, but also the furthering of interests. Robinson wrote of his Vienna post in 1734, 'There does not pass a day without my eating, playing, or conversing at least, with one or other of the ministers. And it is from occasional hints in such discourses that I am obliged to form most of my conjectures and judgement.' Eating had other values. In 1774, Robert Murray Keith reflected, 'I love a fat ambassador ... it gives one a good opinion of the country that sends him. You know the miseries of France in the last war were never fairly laid open to the public, till the scraggy Duke de Nivernais set his tiny foot on the shore at Dover.'[8]

The strain could be considerable. Celebrations, such as the magnificent ball and dinner given in Lisbon in 1724 by the envoy to celebrate the Prince of Wales' birthday, or the party and ball given in 1726 to celebrate George I's birthday, were expensive. In 1734, Robinson complained of a lack of breaks, while, in 1721, James Scott, envoy at Dresden, wrote:

> I could wish it had been my lot to serve in a place where sobriety is fashionable, or that I were at least better able to comply with the custom here, and in Poland too; nor is it a small hardship to me that I must either avoid going into some companies or do prejudice to my health.[9]

In 1763, the 'worn-out' Titley complained, 'nor will my gouty legs any longer support me in paying court or pursuing the noble pastime of levee-hunting'.[10] The other aspects of the job could also be arduous. Macartney complained from St Petersburg in 1765, 'I have wrote so much for these three weeks past that I am almost blind'.[11]

Contemporaries were in no doubt of the importance of social rank and skills. When, in 1748, Newcastle referred to the great difficulty of filling The Hague embassy he mentioned seeking 'some person of figure and consequence'. The two were linked. That year, Legge wrote, 'if I have learned nothing else by being a foreign minister at least I have learned to give dinners, do the honours of my table and receive my guests as a gentleman ought to do'. In 1731, the French envoy in Regensburg wrote that his colleague at Cassel lacked the talent of pleasing and of gaining confidence 'et cette considération personele qui font la moitié des affaires'.[12] Hunting played a major role at many courts. Hanbury Williams complained from Dresden in 1747, 'I was obliged that very night to go fifty miles off ... to hunt with the king ... I returned ... with a violent fever'.[13]

At the same time, it was important not to allow court skills to act as a substitute for careful assessment. In 1739, Horatio Walpole, self-confessedly not the easiest of men, complained, 'Titley is amused and deceived by little outward personal civilities'.[14] Titley, himself, thought socializing important, and warned Weston in 1746 that

> the letting me want at this critical juncture my ordinary appointments are reducing me, by that means, to the low necessity of avoiding company, because I am not able to give dinners to the persons of distinction who daily arrive here, is a certain way to discourage those who might be our friends, and deprives me of the opportunity of knowing how people are inclined.[15]

Rank was the counterpart of behaviour, and both cause and consequence of it. Much diplomatic correspondence centred on the pursuit of more senior rank, while comments on the ranking of others constituted much of the ballast of private diplomatic correspondence. Not only prestige was at stake, for the enhancement of rank brought important financial benefits, and a large proportion of correspondence focused on pay and conditions.

Nevertheless, a major reason for enhancement, namely that more highly accredited diplomats were better heeded and thus more effective, captured the relationship between prestige and mission. In 1739, Tyrawly wrote from Lisbon to urge his case for promotion: 'Ambassadors must and will be heard ... dignity bears them through many things, and title [on] appearance sways much with these people.' Diplomatic 'suites' or households mirrored aristocratic households in Britain with family, secretaries, a chaplain and servants. This provided opportunities to oblige back home by making an appointment and emphasized the status of the diplomat. In Catholic countries, this was further stressed by the portable Anglicanism of a chaplain and private chapel. Other aspects of rank were also important, not least the pursuit and acquisition of honours, such as the Order of the Bath which Stanyan sought in 1725 and of the Garter which Waldegrave received in 1738, as did Essex, who had complained about not getting it five years earlier.[16]

Ceremonial was not simply of concern to diplomats and rulers. There was also a sense that it was a signifier of national prestige and honour and thus important in its own right. This was picked up by parliamentarians and by newspapers that argued the need to defend national honour.[17] In addition, honour had direct tangible consequences, for example in terms of the salute of the seas and also maritime hegemony in British territorial waters.

Diplomats' motives varied greatly. Titley wanted 'some sort of employment abroad, in which I might have an opportunity of acquainting myself with business and seeing the world'. In 1748, David Hume, later the most famous British philosopher of the century, wrote that he had been invited by Lieutenant-General James St Clair

> to attend him in his new employment at the Court of Turin, which I hope will prove an agreable, if not a profitable jaunt for me. I shall have an opportunity of seeing courts and camps … I have long had an intention, in my riper years, of composing some history; and I question not but some greater experience of the operations of the field, and the intrigues of the Cabinet will be requisite, in order to enable me to speak with judgement upon these subjects.[18]

Turin at least was warm. Hanbury Williams had sought the post in 1748 to escape the cold of northern Europe.[19] Hyndford claimed that his health had been wrecked in Russia, and Fitzherbert was 'grievously hit' by the cold there in 1783.[20] The climate in Stockholm did not suit Edward Finch in 1733.[21] Elliot sought to take part in this flight south, complaining of:

> the waste of life in dullness and infirmities in these melancholy regions … a chilling Danish fog, when the distinction between air and water seems to be lost and I only acknowledge my own existence by the intenseness of rheumatic complaints.[22]

Climate was one, although not the sole, reason why envoys such as Sir Richard Vernon did not want to go to 'that cursed country Poland'.[23] Dalrymple wrote from Warsaw in 1784:

> I have had a most uncomfortable winter of it, my health exceedingly affected by the severe cold my spirits exceedingly dejected in consequence of my illness and from the want of all amusement or rational levity … I am quite wearied of this type of existence.[24]

Nine years later, Gardiner, then in Grodno, blamed very poor health on 'this climate'.[25] Vienna offered more than Grodno, but did not please many envoys. Robinson complained in 1741:

> Society here is most dull and inanimate, few men are to be found, and though one resolves to pass time well, it all amounts at last to eating and drinking, cheering the mere animal, which is true Austrian life and I am unluckily ill calculated for it.[26]

Yet, moving further west and/or south did not always help. Having pressed for just such a transfer, Whitworth complained from Cambrai in 1724:

> this climate is absolutely ruinous to my constitution, and to my great surprise at first, much worse than any I found in Germany. We fall from one extremity to another as the wind shifts, the heats are now excessive, the colds may be so tomorrow, and I dread losing this next winter, what I have been getting up with so much pains ... I am already worn, which makes me look on abundance of things with great indifference.[27]

Spain was regarded by many envoys as distant exile, or as too hot,[28] and was 'an employment which few people seem to care for'.[29] Bubb complained in 1715 that there was insufficient food and that he could not get a cook, and in March 1716 that the court was going to Aranjuez for the summer:

> I have sent to take a house in some neighbouring village for that is not half big enough for the court; there is indeed no such thing as a country house in Spain, so I must live in a barn, and I shall be burnt, and starved to death, and were it not that I repose some hopes in the curate's niece, I should be altogether desperate.

He added that November: 'I know of no consideration that could induce me to stay a year longer.'[30]

Portugal did not please all. Dormer liked the Lisbon climate, but found the entertainment dull. Tyrawly frequently sought a move, pursuing posts in Copenhagen, Florence and The Hague.[31] Albemarle was not surprised, 'for in this world there never was so detestable a place, no company, no diversions, a little stinking town filled with bugs and vermin'.[32]

Diplomatic tasks were not all official. Diplomats were also expected to fulfil a variety of roles that can be seen as private. These included the care of visiting Britons and the local British community. Diplomats such as Colman, Keith and Mann often complained of the cost and time involved in entertaining tourists.[33] They were expected to present them at court, introduce them into local society, and fulfil a number of miscellaneous requests. Schaub was asked to help Dr Charles Bale who visited Paris in 1722 'with the design of seeing the practice of midwifery in the Hôtel-Dieu', and, the following year, the brother and son of Charles Delafaye, who was of Huguenot extraction and concerned about French laws against refugees. Waldegrave, who showed 'very great kindness' at Vienna to Chesterfield's visiting brother, was asked in 1733 to look after Sir John Shadwell, a relative of Delafaye's wife, and to ensure that medicines, chocolate and snuff for his use were not seized by the Boulogne customs.[34] Well-connected tourists could be sure of letters of recommendation from ministers to envoys. Robert Carteret, the son of Lord Carteret, then one of the leaders of the opposition, obtained recommendatory letters to the envoys at Copenhagen, Dresden, St Petersburg and Vienna. In 1793, when his sister, brother and mother proposed a journey to Naples, Charles Abbot, later 1st Lord Colchester, sought from Burges 'the customary letters of protection and introduction to our ministers abroad'.[35]

Tourists could face problems that required diplomatic assistance. Philip Thicknesse recommended tourists to call on the envoy in order to ensure protection, and noted Rochford's defence of tourists in Paris, including one defrauded by sharpers.[36] Francis Colman was involved in the seizure of a compatriot's murderer in Tuscany[37] and Waldegrave was involved in lengthy representations on behalf of a Scottish visitor involved in a duel in the Loire valley. Intercession on behalf of fellow subjects led John Methuen in 1694 to seek pardon for pirates sentenced to be hanged for piracy on the coast of Brazil.[38] Nevertheless, in general, the protection provided by diplomats was an indication of the role of personal connections in what was still essentially an elite milieu.

In addition, diplomats acted as purchasing agents for the Crown, members of the royal family and ministers. Thus, in 1725, Thomas Burnett sent seeds of fruits and vegetables for the royal kitchen gardens, and Stanyan was ordered to follow suit with seeds of Turkish plants. In 1733, Lady Suffolk asked Essex for Italian leathers for fans for the Princess Royal, while in 1755, Holdernesse instructed Hanbury Williams to buy china for him; which he did.[39] Three years earlier, the envoy sent Polish turnip seed to Henry Fox. He was also asked for the best Tokay. Claudius

Rondeau had sent plant seeds from Moscow. Newcastle asked Chesterfield for orange trees. John Methuen sent Sir John Trenchard, Secretary of State 1693–5, 'a pipe of Barra wine', James Vernon two hogsheads of wine and some snuff in 1696, and the Duke of Shrewsbury two hogsheads in 1696, while Dorset sent Carmarthen snuff from Paris. Fawkener sent Queen Caroline the sherbet she had requested, and also garden seeds for George II and Harrington. Ainslie sent coffee, drawings, antique marbles and bronzes for both George III and Carmarthen. Purchase by envoys was valuable as they were generally able to secure desired goods and to avoid customs duties and restrictions. However, the process was not free from problems. In 1696, Lexington was driven to the conclusion that Count Auersperg, the Austrian envoy in London, had kept for himself Tokay wine that Lexington had sent to William III, Blathwayt, Portland and Shrewsbury. War with France made this wine particularly valued.[40]

Diplomats also purchased items for friends and connections. Stair bought clothes and cutlery for British nobles. Davenant bought paintings for the Duke of Chandos, and Waldegrave did the same for Sir Robert Walpole. Poyntz sent truffles regularly to Newcastle, as well as a Perigord pâté. Waldegrave was asked to produce the best cook in France, burgundy, truffles and a Perigord pie for the Duke, as well as the very fine feather brushes used for cleaning the gilding of rooms for Lady Katherine Pelham. Newcastle ordered port and wine from Thomas Burnett in Lisbon, who also sent him hams, evergreen plants from James Dormer, and apricot plants from Robert Trevor, while Fitzherbert sent Spanish snuff for Earl Harcourt.[41] Tyrawly reported from Lisbon in 1733:

> I don't know that I have any other vegetable worth sending you, except tomâtoes, which is a large round fruit, as big as a small orange (of which I believe you have none in England). It is not to be eaten, by itself, yet comes within your rule of having nothing but belly timber, for if your cook scalds them first in hot water, four, or five of them, or more, or less according as you like the last, or without scalding, put them whole into your soup, provided that it stands afterwards, times enough to mitoner, it will as we think here, much mend your soup, by giving it a far more agreable tartness, than sorrel, or any other herb. It grows up to a tall shrub, with many leaves the fruit, being when ripe, as red as a cherry.[42]

In this way, embassies were points of cultural exchange. Lady Mary Wortley

Montagu brought inoculation back from Turkey and numerous Britons experienced life and artefacts from abroad via embassies.

It would be mistaken to imagine that envoys devoted themselves solely to business. In addition, they were interested in a wide range of pursuits. These were varied but, in essence, reflected the conflation of what was expected of them and the opportunities open to men of position. It is unclear, however, how best to prioritize these interests, not least because, for the majority of diplomats, we have little guide to their non-work activities. As is generally the case, there is particularly little information on the less seemly side of their interests. For example, we know little about gambling. In consequence, we may have underestimated the extent of such activities and their role in providing interest to the post.

One side of the diplomatic life that has received insufficient attention is sex. Several envoys combined their diplomatic postings with more pleasurable activities than the drafting of despatches. Stair, for example, both gambled and womanized at Paris in 1716.[43] To take simply the decade 1725–35, Abraham Stanyan (Constantinople) was described by his successor, Kinnoull, as a 'complaisant gentleman of an indolent temper ... whose life here these twelve years past, as I am informed, has been upon a sofa with the women'.[44] Kinnoull, himself, aroused the anger of the Turkey Company by the women he took with him.[45] Tyrawly (Lisbon) shared similar interests, and this was far from secret. In his *Imitations of Horace*, Alexander Pope referred to 'Kinnoull's lewd cargo, or Tyrawley's crew'.[46]

Brigadier Sutton (Cassel) had a penchant for laundry maids.[47] Sent to Turin in 1732, the Earl of Essex found the city a tedious place, but sought to compensate for this by the pursuit of feminine conquests;[48] an aim in no way dimmed, although it was complicated, by the presence of his wife. Waldegrave, a sociable widower, whose charm was acknowledged by all, led a particularly free and easy life, and was noted for his success with women, 'the King of the Belles' according to Robinson.[49] Essex, who visited Waldegrave in Paris in 1732 en route for Turin, commented enviously on his success, and Chesterfield clearly shared this envy. In 1725, journeying from Paris to Hanover, Waldegrave complained of the lack of amenable women in the hostelries of Westphalia.[50]

Three years later, Chesterfield wrote to Waldegrave from The Hague:

> If you please then, I will, for a moment lay aside the important affairs
> of Europe, and enquire a little into your private pleasures; does that

manly vigour and that noble contempt of danger, still continue? I am informed it distinguished itself at Paris; I hope it does so at Vienna too. As I know that both your rammer and balls are made for a German calibre, you may certainly attack with infinite success, and I know your fortitude too well to suppose that you will decline the combat, let the danger be ever so great. So I expect some account of your performances. As for mine they are not worth reciting; you know I never was a great hero; and in this place there are few provocations for courage, and the coldness of the enemy, even damps one's bravery; the warmest thing I have met with here between a pair of legs has been a stove; and they have not liked what I put in the place of it, half so well.

Two months later, however, he sent better news:

I pass my time here as well as I could wish and much better than I expected. I have found means to rouse them here a little into pleasures, which they now come into pretty willingly, provided it is at my expence; a snow that has lately fallen very opportunely has furnished us the pleasures of traineaux [sledges], which is a favourite diversion here, and which ends, in almost a necessity of warming one another a good deal at night.[51]

In 1731, Chesterfield had returned to his plaint, while writing of hoping to see Waldegrave,

and possibly of renewing our old acquaintance over a bottle, and a gentlewoman. A propos of gentlewomen we have one here at present of your acquaintance called L'Imperatrice. She is so handsome that I would have made her a tender of my poor services; but that I was unwilling to deceive her, of the opinion I hope she entertains, that all his Majesty's ambassadors are formed like your Lordship. So, like an honest minister, I sacrificed my private satisfaction to the reputation of my country.[52]

Chesterfield might complain, but one legacy of his diplomatic posting was a bastard and he was noted for his skill with women. In his love of display and quest for rank, such as the Order of the Garter, Chesterfield was typical of the aristocratic diplomats of the period; and, although Horatio Walpole had thought little of his diplomatic gifts, he proved to be a successful envoy at The Hague. Dorset was less so at Paris. A noted womanizer he took with his current mistress, Giovanna Zanerini, an Italian ballerina, and she performed at the Opéra, wearing the Duke's Order of the Garter.

Irrespective of their own sexual activity, envoys found themselves obliged to respond to the activity of British visitors. In 1716, Davenant wrote from Genoa to his counterpart in Paris:

> Mr. Cresswell [an ex-MP] was arrested by an order of a Deputation of the Senate, which has the inspection in cases of sodomy ... I never heard of so flagrant a delinquent, however I have some hopes of stifling the process, in regard of the nation's honour, and of the circumstances of my being here at this time to make them a compliment from His Majesty. They have been encouraged to this proceeding, by my not permitting him to visit me, but it is my opinion they would have shown more respect to His Majesty and the nation, if they had traced out one of their people for an example of severity, without fixing it on an Englishman.[53]

Diplomats sometimes colluded with the irregular life of prominent members of the royal family and others while abroad, but also had to heed the views of the monarch. Honour was crucial. In 1787, Robert Walpole stopped the peripatetic homosexual William Beckford from being introduced at court in Lisbon. Family honour was also important. George, Viscount Parker's involvement with an Italian woman and his failure to heed the instructions of his father, Lord Chancellor Macclesfield, led Macclesfield to mobilize the resources of British diplomacy to regain his son. The young James Stuart Mackenzie fell for the famous opera-dancer Barberini and arranged to marry her in Venice. This was prevented by Archibald, 3rd Duke of Argyll, who used his friend Hyndford to have Barberini brought to Berlin and Mackenzie banned from Prussia.[54]

For most envoys, there is no surviving correspondence that might supply clues about activities comparable to Chesterfield or Waldegrave. What, for example, did Woodward mean by writing 'Saxon dames, they are pretty, but cruel'?[55] In addition, there were no personnel files that could offer a secret official evaluation. As a result, it is largely the public face of the envoy that survives. The accuracy of the resulting assessments, however, are difficult to gauge. Horace Walpole might suggest in 1754 that Sir James Gray (Naples) preferred hunting to diplomacy, but Gray was an experienced diplomat who had nearly obtained the Berlin embassy in 1748 and who went on from Venice (1744–52) to Naples (1753–63) and finally Madrid (1767–9), and at the court of Charles III in Naples it would have been a major advantage to be interested in hunting. Furthermore, other commentators were more impressed than the catty Horace Walpole. A month later, the Sardinian envoy in London wrote that Gray was very wise and prudent.[56]

In December 1754, when Albemarle died in Paris, Richard Blacow reported that he was debauched and had kept a whore,[57] but there are no Albemarle papers comparable to those of Waldegrave to throw light on the issue. Anyway, it would scarcely have disqualified Albemarle in the eyes of Louis XV, who, in 1749, used the services of Joseph Yorke to obtain British condoms.[58] Horace Walpole had commented in May 1750 that Albemarle employed sixteen people in his kitchen and entertained liberally. However, six months earlier, Yorke criticized Albemarle for not keeping company with foreign ministers or at court.[59]

Again, different views can be offered of John Murray, Resident in Venice 1754–66. Lady Mary Wortley Montagu was no fan, and like other travelling literati her complaint can be found in print:

> … the British minister here. Such a scandalous fellow, in every sense of that word. He is not to be trusted to change a sequin, despised by this government for his smuggling, which was his original profession, and always surrounded with pimps and brokers, who are his privy councillors. Sir James Gray was, I am told, universally esteemed, but, alas he is at Naples. I wish the maxims of Queen Elizabeth [I] were revived, who always chose for her foreign ministers men whose birth and behaviour would make the nation respected, people being apt to look upon them as a sample of their countrymen; if those now employed are so, Lord have mercy upon us! I have seen only Mr. Villettes at Turin who knew how to support his character. How much the nation has suffered by false intelligence, I believe you are very sensible of, and how impossible it is to get truth either from a fool or a knave.[60]

Murray indeed was an aggressive and perverse womanizer,[61] as well as a smuggler; but it is worth noting that he was sufficiently competent as a diplomat to be promoted Ambassador in Constantinople in 1766 and to hold that post until his death in Venice in 1775. Anthony Storer, who was briefly first Secretary of Embassy at Paris (1783) and then Minister Plenipotentiary (1783–4) was both noted for 'the dissipated and very idle habits of his life' and an able and accomplished individual.[62] Alongside the criticism of Stanyan already cited, there was praise for his abilities, albeit from his cousin and patron.[63] Similarly, Robert Ainslie (Constantinople, 1776–93) was attacked as a stock speculator, but was also a distinguished numismatist, who built up a formidable collection of ancient coins and of antiquities. In the *North Briton* of 25 November 1769, 'Regulus' attacked the character of British envoys:

> we may say, with too much truth, of many of our Ambassadors, and still more of our travellers, that they whore, game and drink, for the disgrace of their country … Ambassadors of virtue and abilities at several foreign courts, yet have persons in that high station at some other courts, who, by the profligacy of their character, would be a disgrace to any court, or any nation.

George Cressener, Minister Plenipotentiary at Cologne, was named in the article as 'a bankrupt and a felon' as well as an unsuccessful gambler refunded out of public funds.

Seeing the sights was another, although far less controversial, personal interest. In 1725, Waldegrave was taken to see some very interesting gardens in Paris.[64] In general, however, envoys left little record of what they saw or their response to it.

Concern about remuneration was a continual feature of diplomatic life. Indeed, it can claim to be the single subject most frequently discussed in the public and private correspondence of envoys. When, in 1746, Harrington promised Burrish, then at Munich, that he would speak to Henry Pelham, the First Lord of the Treasury, about his arrears, he added 'he is under great difficulties in that respect by reason of the multitude of solicitors for the like favour, amongst which are all His Majesty's ministers abroad'. Indeed, Hyndford complained about two years of arrears.[65] In 1731, Keene was owed five quarters.[66] Guy Dickens was still pressing for his 1755 travel expenses in 1761.

The sums could be considerable. Claiming in 1744 that the cost of his journey to Russia had been near £2,000, and that he had only been given hopes of the reimbursement of £1,000, Tyrawly asked to return home in a British warship. In 1752, Keith reckoned he was £1,400 out of pocket during the course of his long career. Rochford wrote to Bute in 1767, the embassy of Spain was so very expensive that I assure your Lordship upon my honour, I spent £12,000 of my own private fortune ... at my return from Spain last year I was appointed ambassador to France and sent away almost at a minute's warning, without having the douceur that other ambassadors have had of staying some months after my appointment to prepare for the first great expense at setting out, and nothing allowed me for removing my family and effects from Madrid to Paris, added to this the embassy of Paris is by far the most expensive of all, and it will really be impossible for me to go on and continue in it, without ruining myself entirely unless the king will be pleased to restore me the pension [of £2,000 annually he had been granted after George III's accession, but that he had lost when appointed to Madrid].

In 1792, Elgin was in problems due to the debts incurred during his embassy to Leopold II, and was pressing to know if he would receive the £2,000 as 'a further sum as a sort of present or gratification from His Majesty for the additional expense which he would incur', that the Duke of Leeds had suggested.[67]

Aside from arrears, there were also deductions. In 1722, Molesworth complained that 'discount upon tallies, interest, exchange, provision, and premium, devour a very large proportion of the salary we should receive'.[68]

In effect, as diplomats had to live on 'ready money',[69] the diplomatic service relied on the personal credit of envoys. In 1722, Lord Glenorchy (Copenhagen) found his pay three quarters in arrears. Unable to raise money in Denmark he was forced to turn to his father-in-law, the Duke of Kent, for help in getting John Wace, the Chief Clerk in the Northern Office, to lend to him. Kent offered his own security to Wace. Glenorchy explained:

> All our foreign ministers have some one in London who advances their money and accepts all their Bills, for which they are allowed so much, and without that, it is impossible for us to live, we being paid so irregularly.

In 1724, St Saphorin, whose remuneration was greatly in arrears, suggested that Charles Harrison would need to be very rich to cope with this problem.[70] In 1738, Robinson claimed to be unable to live on his salary.[71] In 1775, Horace St Paul, Secretary of Embassy in Paris, was obliged 'to take up more money upon his estate', as the payment of his arrears was again put off.[72] Sir John Stepney (Dresden 1776–82, Berlin 1782–4) allegedly spent £8–10,000 of his own money on his embassies.[73] This was a matter not only of diplomats' own pay but also their expenses on government business. Thus, in 1794, Malmesbury sought reimbursement for the cost of sending his servants to carry messages from Berlin to Vienna and back, and from Berlin to The Hague.[74]

Reimbursement depended on favour, explicitly so. In 1719, Polwarth found that Craggs was unwilling to sign his bill of extraordinaries. Delafaye commented that the bill exceeded the permitted sum,

> by the expense of sending a gentleman express from Denmark with the news of the King of Sweden's death, and though it was no news when he arrived, yet I believe My Lord Polwarth will be thought to have done right in sending him.

It was not until August 1729 that the Treasury was given a warrant to pay arrears of allowances owed to several of George I's diplomats, including William Leathes and James Scott who had last served in 1724 (Scott was now dead) and James Jefferyes who had last served in 1725.[75] In 1730, Robinson, who described himself as 'an English younger brother … circumstances too generally known', received both royal approbation and £1,000.[76] In 1793, George Hammond was granted £250 for extra 'extraordinaries' quarterly, Burges noting:

> I am particularly desired by Lord Grenville to tell you that he complies with your request not as a matter of demandable claim, or as a thing which is to be drawn into precedent; but solely on the ground of his personal good opinion and esteem of you, and as an evidence of his approbation of your services in America.[77]

Such an approach simply encouraged the attempt to gain good regard, and gave it an explicitly financial turn. Envoys stressed the difficulties they were under, but, also, the detrimental consequences for British foreign policy. Thus, having complained, on 20 September 1746, that 'one quarter in nine months is but poor pay; especially after so long an arrear', Titley wrote, a week later:

> … the letting me want at this critical juncture my ordinary appoint-

ments and, reducing me, by that means, to the low necessity of avoiding company, because I am not able to give dinners to the persons of distinction who daily arrive here, is a certain way to discourage those who might be our friends, and deprives me of the opportunity of knowing how people are inclined.[78]

In 1743, Anthony Thompson warned that he could not afford to follow the court to Fontainebleau, 'nor have I the means of sending an express to Calais'. When, in 1748, Newcastle complained that Keith had taken so long to come from The Hague to Hanover, he earned the retort that Keith had 'received neither money nor credit from the public upon that occasion'.[79]

The previous year, Hyndford wrote to Chesterfield that the latter's comments about the limited chance that his arrears would be paid had led to Hyndford losing his credit.[80] In 1751, Hanbury Williams complained that salaries were more than a year in arrears.[81] Hugh Elliot took leave of absence in Switzerland in 1775 because of the debts arising from inadequate pay as Minister at Munich and Regensburg.[82]

However, a few individuals sought posts under the impression that they could make money that way; for example, having lost heavily on the South Sea Company, Richard Hampden MP applied unsuccessfully for Constantinople in 1722, while John Norris unsuccessfully applied for Naples in 1751.[83] When Edward Finch was chosen Minister Plenipotentiary to Regensburg, Tilson thought him 'a good sensible man', but added, 'I suppose it is a plan found out to give a younger brother of a noble family £3 a day'. Turin for Essex was supposed to be 'a lucky opportunity to retrieve your affairs and make your family easy'. The young Honourable Richard Leveson Gower, a fourth son, went to Aix-la-Chapelle as Joint Secretary to the Plenipotentiaries in order to try to get him to draw for fewer funds from his father Earl Gower.[84] Macartney sought Madrid in 1766 to help pay his debts.[85] Hard hit by gambling debts and concerned about the cost of maintaining Castle Howard, Frederick, 5th Earl of Carlisle, unsuccessfully sought appointment to Paris, Madrid and Turin in 1774–6.

One way to deal with costs and arrears was to seek an additional post. Thus, Stanyan, a Lord of the Admiralty when he was appointed to Vienna in 1716, held this post until 1717, and was, thereafter, Clerk in Ordinary to the Privy Council at the same time as he was envoy in Constantinople (1717–30).[86] Richard Sutton sought a regiment, as did Tyrawly.[87]

Complaints about finances throw much light on the details of diplomatic life. Stanyan responded to the appointment to mediate the war between Austria and Turkey by claiming that it would cost £1,500 'to put myself in equipage and defray my expenses to Adrianople'. Stanyan sought

> the usual equipage money and allowance of an Ambassador to be continued as long as the mediation subsists, that I may be able to undergo the charge and business of it with an easy and contented mind. I have spent £1,500 beyond the King's allowance since I have been here, without being guilty of any extravagance ... the Emperor [Charles VI] desires whoever goes to Turkey should be ordered to reside at the Grand Signior's court till the peace be made, and even follow the army into the field next summer if no peace be made this winter that he may be ready at hand to take advantage of any opportunity that may present of setting a treaty on foot, so that this circumstance will be a considerable increase of expense.

Thirteen years later, Woodward wrote from Dresden:

> I am in a post at present where my Extraordinaries seem very high and I reckon I shall be out of pocket between two and three hundred pounds for my late expedition at the camp. I don't really believe there is a court in Europe near so expensive to a foreign minister in all respects as this is; I have now actually three houses each at a considerable rent,

the last because Woodward had to follow the Saxon court to Poland, an expense that struck Hanbury Williams in 1752. The estimate of expenses for Arthur Stert MP, appointed in 1730 a commissioner for settling merchants' losses with Spain, included £800 on plate and £500 for coach, mules and equipage. The same year, Waldegrave recorded his expenses in his diary. He was paying eight servants on 'English wages' including a secretary on £100 per annum and a chaplain at £50 per annum, a total of £390, and 26 'on French money' including eight footmen, a confectioner, a cook, a maître d'hôtel, and two coachmen, a total of 5,600 livres. Other expenses included house rent, table expenses, horses, livery, candles, and, as contingencies, clothes, pocket money, postage and coach repairs. The newly arrived Robert, Lord Lexington, had to buy a 'fool's coat' for his audience with Leopold I in 1694. Whitworth explained the heavy bill of extraordinaries he sent from Berlin in 1721:

> I cannot live below my character, and the expence increases propor-
> tionably with the salary, for otherwise I cannot see any extravagancy
> I have been guilty of; a great train of useless and often disorderly
> people with some large entertainments are essentials of an embassy;
> so the world takes them, and so must I, and therefore I am not wanting.

Langlois was obliged, 'to have a pretty considerable wardrobe' at Vienna.[88]

The interest of travel was occasionally mentioned. Burges wrote to William Fawkener, en route for Russia in 1791,

> Should the weather with you be as fine as it is here, you will have
> opportunities of seeing a country, which, on so many accounts, is an
> interesting object, and which, if any can, must be worth even as long
> a journey as you have taken to see it.[89]

Alas, such interest rapidly palled.

Boredom was a major challenge for envoys. Whitworth wrote from the Imperial Diet at Regensburg in 1714:

> Since the posts of Vienna and The Hague are disposed of, I do not
> know any place in Germany, where one of my temper and education
> can subsist with pleasure in his private capacity, or he ought at least
> to have a family to take off the heavy hours of the day, otherwise
> without smoking and drinking the winter evenings will seem very
> tedious of which I have the disagreable experience at present.

He was scarcely more fond of Berlin in 1721:

> in this place, you cannot imagine how disagreably time goes away; It
> is entirely changed since you knew it, and grows still worse and worse:
> Here is neither diversion nor conversation, and people's spirits are
> under such a perpetual constraint, that there is much more formality
> and duty in our entertainments (for the King himself often enquires
> how the foreign ministers live) than satisfaction. The greatest I have
> is in playing with the good Queen at hombre, which I do every night
> there is court; but in general I am heartily glad that the day is over;
> and what is life worth at that rate?[90]

Boredom was particularly the case not only if there was little business to transact and scant of interest to report, but also if the situation elsewhere appeared of greater importance. In 1791, Francis Jackson, Secretary of Legation at Berlin, sought promotion to Warsaw:

> If sent into Spain I should be taken from the line of northern politics, which are alone likely to be of great and immediate importance to our court, and placed in one less interesting in every respect, and with the different links and holds of which I am, as yet, unacquainted.[91]

In October 1792, Thomas Walpole wrote to Burges from Munich:

> The sluggish apathy of this court is irksome to me when I see so much business of importance going on in every other court of the Empire and I can easily believe that you must attribute the baldness of my correspondence to personal inactivity which is very far from being the case.

He had not liked the Imperial Diet either: 'Ratisbon, where ceremonious visits, tedious dinners, and cards took up all my time and left me neither leisure, nor spirits to answer you'.[92] A decade earlier, Montstuart wrote to Keith from Turin: '… a regular correspondence with Turin would only be employing one's time to a great disadvantage as the return must be inadequate to the time.' The young Charles Arbuthnot was disappointed by Stockholm:

> This is a dull place and I shall not be sorry to return to England as I am not in the least fond of the foreign line though I have contrived to make my own house extremely comfortable. I am just as ignorant of what is going on in this world as if I was the inhabitant of some other … the stupidity of Stockholm.[93]

Yet, other envoys less keen on activity and promotion had a very different response. Sir William Hamilton in Naples clearly regretted the extent to which the French Revolutionary Wars led to more activity: 'As I have no assistance, public business has been rather hard upon me of late years and as one gets older, both in public and private affairs, one gets inclined to repose.'[94] The *St. James's Chronicle* of 28 December 1771 had reported:

Some persons have wondered at a noble lord accepting the post of envoy to the inferior court of Brussels, and at Mr. Hamilton's consenting to return again in that character to the court of Naples. It may not be thought amiss to put such people in mind that the appointment of envoy has annexed to it, for the splendid support of the character, £3,300 per annum, and that in those cheap places he will not spend the moiety of that sum.

Several posts were clearly not for men of business, and, in judging envoys, it is necessary to understand the variety of the profession. Essex sought appointment to Venice, 'where there could be no business at all'. He was described harshly in 1735: 'Lord Essex, in the infinite leisure of a foreign minister, in which character he has had nothing to do, but to eat, sleep, fiddle, and order his secretaries to transcribe gazettes, is grown, they say, so fat that he is hardly knowable.'[95] Gray wrote from Venice in 1747: 'I have been induced to apply to my friends to get me removed to Berlin … The transition seems to me too quick from this idle station to one so active, besides that I am sensible how much better I am qualified for a neutral republic, than the court of a powerful enterprizing prince'.[96] However, by the following January, he was determined to move: 'It is impossible to be more sensible than I am of the misery of this paultry corner, which spleen and disappointment drove me into. I am resolved at all events to leave it.'[97]

In contrast to boredom there could also be frenetic activity. This was particularly the case with negotiations in which the diplomat had to take note not only of opposing powers but also of allies. Poyntz complained in 1728, 'I am really and truly half dead with hurry and fatigue'.[98] Robinson, similarly, complained about the burden of the job in 1732.

Aside from boredom or, sometimes, an excess of business, envoys also suffered from isolation. Distant from friends and connections, many looked forward to the opportunity to return, permanently or temporarily. Isolation from the family was lessened for envoys who took members with them. This, however, could create problems[99] and was not always possible or convenient. En route for Spain in 1784, the 5th Earl of Chesterfield wrote 'the accounts we hear every day of the inconveniences we shall find in our journey from Perpignan to Madrid, particularly the bad accommodations we shall meet with everywhere make the thoughts of a Spanish journey' very unpleasant for his wife. George III gave Chesterfield permission to delay his journey at Paris because of the summer heat.[100]

As a consequence, diplomats frequently left close family members behind and were lonely as a consequence. Malmesbury wrote from Berlin in January 1794: 'It is extremely uncomfortable to be without any news of my family and if the natural bent of my mind was not towards chearfulness and never to foresee evil, I could be as fanciful and lowspirited as a nervous woman.'[101] Three years earlier, Francis Jackson had written thence: 'I am extremely desirous of seeing my father and mother in the present distressing situation of some parts of our family.'[102] Absence of family was part of the isolation of the profession: Robinson complained of having no friends with whom he could share confidences.[103]

More generally, it is depressing to note how frequently long-serving envoys bitterly complained of neglect.[104] Several who became very long-serving had earlier expressed discontent. In 1732, Robinson wrote of 'the anxieties which I have been constantly under ... exhaust both body and mind', and asked for permission to leave Vienna.[105] Envoys with less experience shared this perspective. Hedges, Envoy Extraordinary in Turin, wrote in 1727 within a year of his arrival, 'no one can wish more to keep a place than I to resign one'.[106] In 1775, Horace St Paul's wife unsuccessfully pressed for his retirement from Paris, but in 1777 he resigned the Swedish embassy before taking it up.[107] For many, diplomatic posts were indeed 'ungrateful and barren employments'. Robert Trevor noted in 1737: 'A confidential account which poor Robinson has given me of his private affairs has augmented my dread of a foreign life.'[108]

7

Diplomats and the Information Society

> You shall inform yourself as particularly as you can of the state of the
> Landgrave's country, of his revenues, and forces, and of all that may
> tend to give us a just idea of his power and influence in the present
> conjuncture.
>
> Instructions to Richard Sutton, envoy to Hesse-Cassel, 1727[1]

One approach to the diplomacy of the period is to see it as an aspect of a
developing information society. Diplomats were crucial to the state
dimension of this process, but this was not separate to other aspects of a
more general rise in the demand for information about the outer world
and also in the provision of information about it. Indeed, diplomats had
a close relationship with these other aspects. First, they were expected to
contribute to the availability of public information; secondly, to report on
the content of public information in other states; and, thirdly, at times, to
affect the content of the latter.

The rise in the information society can be seen in a number of different
lights. It is possible to focus on the mediums of information, such as the
press, but, first, it is necessary to approach the provision of information
as an aspect of a growing concern with the need for self-consciously
instructed decision-making that can be seen from the late seventeenth
century. This can be related to the drive for what was termed 'political
arithmetic', and the works produced accordingly towards the close of the
seventeenth and in the early eighteenth century. It is difficult to study (as
opposed to suggest) connections from other fields, but the notion of
instructed decision-making can be linked to the so-called Scientific
Revolution, in which Britain played a major role in the late seventeenth
century. The advances in chemistry associated with Boyle and in physics

with Newton encouraged a sense that predictable rules or laws existed in the natural world, and that these could be discovered and harnessed.

Furthermore, there was a crossover to the political world. In 1764, Sir James Porter, then Minister Plenipotentiary in Brussels, who had an interest in science and was an FRS, wrote:

> ... these various revolutions of the moral world ... I judge by analogy, and what I know and perceive in the physical world ... general laws conduct invariably the whole from the heavenly to the terrestrial creation, order and uniformity nay even of earthquakes and volcanoes are the result of them and that there are like general uniform laws varying but by the will of national agents I make no doubt.[2]

Relatively few envoys were as knowledgeable about science and David Hume, the philosopher and author, among much else, of the *Essay on Miracles* (1748) with its call for system rather than an esoteric understanding of the workings of Providence, was only a diplomat for a brief period. Dr William Aglionby, the translator from the French of *The Art of Chymistry* (1668), subsequently served at Madrid (1692, 1701), Turin (1694) and Zurich (1702–5), while Sir William Hamilton published *Observations on Mount Vesuvius, Mount Etna and other Volcanoes* (1772).

Nevertheless, scientific methods could be absorbed through much of the other literature of the period, with its preference for systemic approaches in which relationships of cause and effect were rational, clear and subject to measurement.

The centrepiece of the desire for system, as far as international relations were concerned, was the concept of the balance of power. This was a porous concept that was both associated with political arithmetic and Newtonian mechanics, and seen as the necessary protection against the imperial pretensions of other powers and, therefore, the cycle of history in which empires rose and fell. The balance brought an apparent precision to the relations between states, or at least encouraged a sense of normative behaviour.[3] The British presented their policy as designed to support the balance. For example, the Duke of Manchester reported from Venice in 1707 that he had 'proposed their entering into such alliances as will restore the balance of power in Europe, and which has been the only view the Queen [Anne] has had in engaging in this present war'. In 1739, Robinson, worried by Austrian defeats at the hands of the Turks, wrote of the need 'for a new weight, in the place of that which is lost, in the general balance of Europe against the House of Bourbon'. In 1742, Stair wrote of 'his Majesty's measures, which are principally directed to preserve the liberties of Europe by a Balance of Power'.[4] As a consequence, there was a premium on accurate information about other states. This was fostered by a lack of certainty about what was actually being measured. Different assessments of strength were based on such criteria as population, area, army, size and financial resources.

All this encouraged a drive for information. This was accentuated both by the relative absence of reliable information (certainly in comparison to the nineteenth and twentieth centuries), and by the growing provision of information in the eighteenth century, not least with the appearance of censuses. Diplomats were expected to produce information, although, in general, in a less systematic fashion than their Venetian counterparts. Nevertheless, some envoys, for example St Saphorin, produced lengthy and detailed memoranda about the states to which they were posted, although St Saphorin's were so long that they became notorious. In 1735, Waldegrave sent a state of the French revenues as requested by George II. In 1765, Edward Hay, the envoy in Lisbon, was ordered to provide full accounts of Portuguese revenues, forces and colonies, and to keep such accounts accurate by sending supplementary information. He duly delivered information on the population, finances, army and navy.[5] Copies of treaties and treaty collections were much valued from and for envoys. In 1791, Auckland obtained a recent copy of a collection of treaties printed in Göttingen for 1761–91 and recommended that the copies be obtained for the Foreign Office and for Grenville's private collection.[6]

This was not the sole form of information that was expected. Maps were increasingly employed in diplomacy. Rivers were used to delimit frontiers in the Peace of Nijmegen in 1678, and a similar policy was followed in the Peace of Rijswick in 1697. A stronger interest in precision inspired advances in mapping, which, in turn, gave the spatial aspects and pretensions of territoriality a new cartographic exactitude. A map formed part of an Anglo-Dutch treaty of 1718 that delineated the frontier between the United Provinces and the Austrian Netherlands. This owed much to the publication in 1711 of the Fricx map of the Low Countries. The frontier was fixed literally on a map, signed and sealed by plenipotentiaries as an annex to that treaty. The bill of expenses of the King's Messenger Ralph Heslop for journeys to and from Paris on 13 November and 3 December 1782 included additional expenses on the road to Paris for 'a very large case of maps' needed in conjunction with the negotiations that concluded with the signature of the Preliminary Articles between Britain and the United States in 1783.

On 23 May 1787, Sir James Harris, then envoy in The Hague, attended a Cabinet meeting in London, as the Dutch crisis reached its height, and recorded that the Duke of Richmond 'talked of military operations—called for a map of Germany—traced the marches from Cassel and Hanover, to Holland, and also from Givet to Maastricht'. The following day, Harris saw William Pitt the Younger, who 'sent for a map of Holland; made me show him the situation of the Provinces'. George III used a map to follow the Prussian invasion of France in 1792. In 1800, George Canning wrote to his successor as Under-Secretary: 'What do you think of the Italian news? And what consolation does Pitt point out after looking over the map in the corner of his room by the door?'[7]

The growing importance of maps ensured that their provision became an issue. Diplomats were expected to be active in this sphere. They procured maps both for other envoys and for the government in London. This was a reactive process. Maps were sought during wartime and during negotiations. There was no systematic attempt to build a map library. In 1735, Waldegrave obtained the maps of Italy and the Rhineland that Newcastle sought in order to follow campaigning. In response to the breakout of war between Turkey and Russia, Sir Everard Fawkener, envoy in Constantinople, wrote to Claudius Rondeau, his counterpart in St Petersburg,

> In one of your letters to His Excellency Mr. Walpole I see you had sent him maps of the Crimea. If any such things are to be had, or any new maps that are thought to be exact of any part of her Czarish Majesty's dominions, especially towards the Euxin [Black] or Caspian Seas, or the routes now used from thence to Persia or China, I shall be very glad to have them.

In 1757, George Cressener, Minister at Cologne, thanked Burrish for 'the Map of Bohemia … it appears to be a very good one, and I hope I shall have frequent occasions of looking in it this summer'.[8]

In 1762, Titley attempted to secure a map that would throw light on the 'hereditary animosity and ancient grudge', that lay behind the Holstein-Gottorp dispute. On 2 March, he wrote to Weston,

> A map of the Duchy of Holstein, wherein the Royal and Ducal posses-

sions are distinctly marked, is, I believe, one of the *Desiderata* of Geography. I do not know that there is any such map extant; but if I should happen to meet with one, you may be sure to have it. In the mean time I can send you here, in a very few lines, a list of the territories properly belonging to the Duke.

A week later, Titley wrote again:

Having found one of Homan's maps, wherein the 2 several parts of the Duchy of Holstein were distinguished with colours, though not strongly nor exactly, I have spread a shade of deep burgundy upon all the possessions, which properly belong to the Duke; and the three ducal cities (which were very obscurely exhibited) I have marked with a small black cross, that may possibly catch your eye and help you when you look them out. These possessions lie in four different parcels, entirely separated from each other by the intervention of royal or collateral territory. I am not satisfied with this part; it is blind and indistinct and the river-courses seem not always well traced; however it is right, as to the ducal dominions and may serve your purpose perhaps, till a better can be met with.

On 27 March, Titley wrote, forwarding another map:

You have herewith another map of Holstein, which is somewhat better, as being more distinct, than the first I sent you. The several territories are distinguished by colours. Green denotes the royal parts, and red the ducal. The yellow tracts belong to the Bishop and Chapter of Lubeck, and what little appears of the territory of Hanover is marked with a shade of blue. In the first map I had inadvertently put the famous baillage of Steinhorst under the same colour with ducal Holstein; but in this it is restored to its proper sovereign, and I think with interest, for there are a few villages added under the blue colour which do not really belong to it. A very accurate chart of this Duchy, I believe, is not to be had.[9]

Titley's main difficulty—and one he seems not to have fully grasped— was that in Germany, above all, single maps, as opposed to specially composed atlases of base maps all showing the same area, were not a particularly good way of expressing princely territorial rights. It was usually beyond the ingenuity of even the most skilled cartographer to indicate on one map alone areas of mixed jurisdictions, owing allegiance to various rulers for different aspects of their existence. When, on top of that, one adds the question of the interpretation of treaties, the inadequacy of single maps becomes still more apparent.

Twenty-nine years later, Sir Robert Murray Keith was concerned to obtain for the Foreign Secretary as soon as possible a copy of the map that defined the newly agreed Austro-Turkish frontier:

> The Imperialists had only three copies of the map of the frontiers of the two Empires (which is so often mentioned in the recent Convention); these they have given to the Turks, and to the Prussian Minister. But they have engaged to deliver to each of the mediating ministers, on our return to Vienna, a correct map of that kind with all the limits carefully marked out, according to this last adjustment. I shall think it my duty to send that map to your Lordship, as soon as it shall be put into my hands.[10]

Aside from information that was of direct value to the ministry, there was also an expectation that diplomats would contribute to the general pool of news that could be deployed by the government. Material for the official newspaper, the *Gazette,* was especially important in this light. The later Stuarts had attempted to maintain a monopoly in printed news for the *London Gazette* (or *Gazette* for short), although that had collapsed with the 'Glorious Revolution' of 1688–9.[11] Nevertheless, the *Gazette* was still the most widely circulated newspaper in 1705–7. Successive governments expected diplomats to provide regular reports for the benefit of the *Gazette*.[12] Diplomats obliged.[13] In 1769, Lord Weymouth, Secretary of State for the Southern Department, appealed to British diplomats to send material.[14]

Demands for information were linked to another task for diplomats, attempts to control the flow of unwelcome material. British diplomats had both to confront frequent complaints about reports concerning foreign powers in the British press, and also to seek to suppress foreign items unwelcome to the British government. As far as the first task was concerned, many of the complaints were expressed through foreign envoys in London,[15] but British envoys were also active, especially in centres of the press, most importantly the United Provinces. In 1715, Henry Worsley moved swiftly to ensure that the editor of the *Lisbon Gazette* was cautioned after he had published a favourable reference to 'James III'. In 1725, William Finch, envoy at The Hague, sent a report that has been ignored because it was dispatched not to his superior, Viscount Townshend, the Secretary of State for the Northern Department, then accompanying George I to Hanover, but to the other Secretary of State, the Duke of Newcastle, who was then handling correspondence sent to London. As a result, the letter appears at the end of the State Papers Holland in a volume that is out of the main chronological sequence. On 31 August 1725, Finch reported:

> The Burgomasters of Amsterdam have made a complaint to the Pensionary of an article in the Post-Boy from the 22 to the 24 of July. The article complained of relates to Mr. Haes late Burgomaster of Amsterdam and accuses him of having permitted, while he was in the Magistracy, that places were bought and sold like common wares in a market. His countrymen clear him intirely of that accusation, and the Pensionary has desired me to use my good offices that the writer of that paper may be obliged to retract what he has advanced and repair the fault he has been guilty of out of imprudence. I the more willingly trouble your Grace with this, because here is at present in Holland an Englishman named Forman, who has lately published a pamphlet full of impertinent reflexions on H.M.'s ministers, and though neither he nor his writings are worth complaining of in form, yet I wait only for a good opportunity of getting him mortified and hope this affair will give me one.[16]

Finch's request was clearly successful, and the *Post-Boy* published a retraction on 28 August (os) 1725, although the process by which pressure was brought to bear on the paper is unclear.

Two years later Finch moved in response to a Dutch newspaper report that the British government was abandoning its stated position on Gibraltar. The *Suite des Nouvelles d'Amsterdam du 24 Octobre 1727* reported, under a London byline, a project to settle Anglo-Spanish differences by razing the fortifications of Gibraltar. On 18 November, Finch was able to note 'The Amsterdam Gazeteer has been reprimanded for the article relating to Gibraltar'.[17]

The following year reports in the Hamburg press that George II did not oppose the Danish East India Company led to action. Townshend instructed Johann Hermann, then in charge of British interests during the absence of the Envoy Extraordinary, Lord Glenorchy, to make representations to the Danish ministry, who were believed to control the Hamburg press. He was told to wait

> on the Great Chancellor to let him know the evil tendency of printing such falsities, which, if spread here by ill-disposed persons, are enough to inflame the Parliament and the nation, as if the King were indifferent in a point which so nearly concerns the trade of his subjects, and you will leave it to his consideration whether such proceedings are not very unfriendly, when His Majesty's sense as to that company, must be very well understood at Copenhagen.[18]

In 1735, British press reports again caused problems. A Hague item in the *Daily Post-Boy* of 30 May (os) alleged corruption in the administration of Dutch justice, and the Dutch demanded action.[19] As in the case in 1725, an element of mutuality was introduced, with the instruction to Horatio Walpole, then envoy in The Hague, that action be taken against two anti-British pamphlets lately published in Holland. Walpole was unhappy with this proposal. He wrote to Lord Harrington, the Secretary of State for the Northern Department, accepting that 'these libels contain the most malicious, false, and scandalous assertions, in relation to the political conduct of England, and were certainly calculated with a view to create a diffidence and misunderstanding between the King and the State General'. However, Walpole pointed out that no printers', publishers' or authors' names had been put to the works and that they would be difficult to investigate, 'they were at first sent under blank covers, as coming from Rotterdam or Leyden, to all sorts of persons here, and were not publicly sold, although perhaps there may be some to be found in that bookseller's shops at present'. He also warned that action would provide the French envoy, Fénelon, with an opportunity for taking action against pro-British publications, and would direct attention to the works prosecuted: 'altho' the curiosity of people, lead them to read these books for a few days, yet they are at present forgotten and no more thought of or sought after; that the application in His Majesty's name to discover the author, will make them be secretly reprinted, and dispersed again'.[20]

Prosecution was widely believed to lead to greater sales.[21] However, there were other forms of influencing the press. The threat of action could disrupt the network of credit and debt within which papers operated. Intimidation and persuasion were likely to be more effective than prosecution and conviction. In 1737, covert ministerial action was taken in an attempt to discover the Dutch correspondent of a London paper. Andrew Stone, an Under-Secretary, wrote to Robert Trevor, Secretary of Embassy at The Hague:

> The inclosed is an original letter of intelligence from a novelist in some part of Holland to Mr. Van der Esch, author of the paper called The Daily Advertiser. He says, that it comes from a person, from whom he receives frequent letters of the same nature; but pretends that he neither knows the name of the correspondent, nor the place of his abode. This letter was put into my Lord Duke of Newcastle's hands by Mr. Van der Esch, with whom his Grace has lately had some conversation, on account of an impertinent paragraph, full of the grossest falsities in the Daily Advertiser of the 9th inst., which was taken literally from this letter; a recantation of which was published yesterday by Van der Esch. I am commanded by his Grace to transmit it to you, and to desire you would, in the most private manner, endeavour to discover whose the handwriting is: Mr. Walpole is inclined to think it may come from one Martiniecce (or a name like it).[22]

The interest displayed by senior ministerial figures, in this case Newcastle and Horatio Walpole, is striking. The latter was particularly interested in the public debate of foreign policy. He was active in Parliament, for example being second speaker for the government on 25 January (os) 1734 in the debate over the opposition motion for revealing Woodward's instructions. Horatio Walpole also played a role in the world of print. In 1739, he was the anonymous author of a pamphlet defending the government's foreign policy: *The Grand Question, whether war, or no war with Spain, impartially considered.*

In 1732, the diplomatic service had been used in an attempt to suppress the sale of a book deemed embarrassing for George II. His mother, Sophia Dorothea (1666–1726), had been divorced by her husband in 1694 as a result of her relationship with Philipp Christoph von Königsmarck, an officer in the Hanoverian army who had disappeared, probably murdered. The episode provided an opportunity for British anti-Hanoverian propaganda and, in particular, for the Jacobites.[23]

Histoire secrette de la Duchesse d'Hanover … appeared anonymously with a title-page announcing it was published in London by La Compagnie des Libraires.[24] The book was brought to the attention of the British government by Renard, their agent in Amsterdam,[25] who, on 13 August, wrote to James Dayrolle, Resident at The Hague, then the highest-ranking British diplomat in the United Provinces, to inform him that the 'Histoire de la Princesse de Zell' by the 'Baron de Pelnitz' (Karl Ludwig von Pöllnitz), had appeared. He claimed that in 1730, Chesterfield, then Ambassador in the United Provinces, had ordered him to stop the printing of the work, and that he had done so, but that he now found that the booksellers in Rouen had printed it.[26]

On 15 August 1732, Dayrolle wrote to Waldegrave at Paris, enclosing a copy of Renard's letter and announcing that he had spoken to the Dutch ministers on the matter.[27] On the 16th, Dayrolle sent another copy to George Tilson, the Under-Secretary, and commented that the federal structure of the United Provinces made censorship very difficult to implement.[28] Printing in Rouen shifted the centre of diplomatic attention to France. Delafaye suggested to Waldegrave that the best way to suppress the book was to buy up the entire edition.[29] Waldegrave feared that a formal approach to the French government would be ineffective, as leading ministers would welcome the chance to cause trouble:

> From my first enquiries I judged that the book had not yet appeared and being much of your mind that the only sure way of suppressing it was if it was in the press to make it worth the printers while to desist or if printed off to buy up all the copies. I therefore got Mr. Saladin to go incognito to Rouen, and have empowered him to stifle the book at any rate.[30]

Once Jean Louis Saladin d'Onex, the Hanoverian Resident in Paris, had returned, Waldegrave wrote again:

> He returned and brought three of the books with him, which he bought of two different booksellers. They told him that the book had been publicly sold there near these two months, and that those two he had were the last. One of the booksellers added, that the book was not printed at Rouen, but at Paris, and that some copies had been sent into Holland. If the book had not been out, perhaps upon applying to the ministers it might have been stopped in the press, but, as the case is, I do not know what to do, for should I make application for an *arret* to prohibit the sale of the book, and to have all the copies brought to the *Lieutenant de Police*'s office, which is the common method of suppressing of books, when once publicly sold, it would

be of service only to the booksellers who would raise the price proportionally to the instances that are made to hinder the publishing it. I send you one enclosed.[31] I confess I was surprised a good deal, for I fancied it might carry a Jacobite spirit, but it seems quite contrary. You will be best able to judge, after the perusal, what is proper to be done; so that I beg that farther orders be sent me.[32]

As far as the government was concerned, that appeared to have been the end of the matter. There is no sign or fresh instructions to Waldegrave to take action, nor of any approach to the French ministry. In 1741, it was the ministry, not the monarchy, that was at issue. On 14 March, Sir Robert Walpole wrote to Trevor, a protégé of his brother Horatio, instructing him to deal with an attempt to print opposition material. Trevor himself had contested Oxford University, unsuccessfully, for the ministry in 1737. Walpole chose to write directly, not via his usual intermediaries for dealing with the press, such as the Solicitor of the Treasury, Nicholas Paxton, nor via the Secretary of State, Harrington:

> There is a pamphlet, and by the account I have of it a pretty large one, sent over by the opponents to be printed in Holland. It is certainly a most virulent one, for the printers here, who print the worst of their scandal, would not venture upon this, but they have sent the copy over with two journeymen printers from hence, who are to have the care of it, and when it is finished are to bring it over to be published here; you know best what can be done on your side to prevent the printing of it, and even to seize the copy and the whole impression, if the government will assist you in it. Mr. Wiggs, the messenger, will explain the whole matter to you, and I really believe this is a matter that deserves attention; as such I recommend it to your prudence and management.[33]

Trevor replied by saying that he could do little without receiving reliable information from Wiggs, as general enquiries might alert the printers. He made fruitless inquiries at The Hague, Amsterdam and Rotterdam, and, with this, the incident came to an end.[34] Possibly Walpole decided that there was nothing in the reports he had received; or the pamphlet may already have returned to England. What emerges clearly, however, is the role of diplomats as part of the world of surveillance of opposition publications.

This was not a new development. Indeed, it stemmed from sixteenth-century concern about the political possibilities of print and the need by governments to counter the publication of hostile political and religious material. Jacobitism lent fresh urgency to this need from 1689. Thus, for example, in response to British requests, the French seized the entire edition of a Jacobite manifesto produced in 1728 to mark the opening of the international congress at Soissons.[35]

The role of diplomats in such issues is a reminder of their varied commitments. In part, this was simply another aspect of the obligation on diplomats to represent, to the best of their ability, their governments, but concern with the press indicates the extent to which this obligation was not confined to the world of courts. Similarly, their field of concern and sources of information were not restricted to courts. Diplomats read, commented on, and forwarded newspaper reports, and some were instructed to send newspapers. Thomas Lumley was ordered to send the *Lisbon Gazette* in 1723 and in 1727 Dormer's secretary, William White, was instructed to add the *Madrid Gazette*. At the same time, diplomats had to offer reminders of press inaccuracies. Du Bourgay wrote from Berlin in 1724:

> As to what you observe that all the newspapers will have it that I had an audience of the King of Prussia to declare the reconciliation, I must give you the same caution which Mylord Whitworth was pleased to give me some time ago in relation to the affairs at Cambrai, not to believe one word that you will find in them.[36]

Envoys travelled singularly little within the states to which they were posted. They were expected to remain with the court, and most courts travelled little other than between palaces and hunting lodges in and near the capital. Louis XVI (1774–92), for example, only left the immediate environs of Paris when he went to Rheims for his coronation (1775) and to Cherbourg to visit the harbour works (1786), and when he fled as far as Varennes (1791).

When rulers travelled further afield this could create problems, although not all monarchs wished to be accompanied by much of the court including the foreign envoys. Robinson accompanied Charles VI to Prague (1732) without too many difficulties, but the journeys of the rulers of Saxony–Poland into Poland, and even more, Lithuania, were less welcome. Woodward complained in 1729 'There is not an inn in Poland that I have yet seen fit to lodge a dog. I'll only compare them to the worst in Westphalia and leave you to judge of them'.[37] The situation became worse in wartime: Hyndford wrote from Breslau in Silesia in 1741, 'This is at present a most miserable place, everything excessive scarce and dear, and hardly a house to put one's head in, for the richest people of both parties have removed their best furniture and effects'.[38] Fortunately, Russian rulers in this period after Peter the Great did not lead their forces in person.

Such problems discouraged the acquisition of information through travel. Envoys were generally dependent for information on the states to which they were accredited on what was reported to them at court or what they could read. Foreign envoys in Britain also travelled very little within the country, in part because the monarchs did not do so. Hendrik Hop was doing well to get as far as Norfolk in 1739.[39]

The extent to which the public dimension of diplomacy was well developed varied greatly. It was most important in The Hague and Paris, the two leading courts for British diplomats and both places of great importance in the world of print. The United Provinces had the freest press in Europe, and events in Paris were much reported. After the Dutch, Britain and Germany had the most extensive and developed press, but the leading German newspaper centres, such as Hamburg, were not of great political importance.

Envoys who were book collectors focused on The Hague and Paris. Horatio Walpole returned to Britain in 1730 with a 'noble collection of books which he had collected at Paris'. Unfortunately, the ship bringing home his books and furniture caught fire off the Norfolk coast and the cargo was destroyed. In 1736, he purchased a library at Hamburg for £400.[40] John Wynne, later Bishop of Bath and Wells, spent much of his time as chaplain to Lord Pembroke in The Hague in the 1690s on book-buying from Dutch book dealers. Robert Trevor at The Hague bought on behalf of a number of collectors, including George II and Horatio Walpole,[41] and purchased both old and recently published books. In 1740, for example, Trevor sent George a pamphlet 'fattened upon the prolific brain of Abbé St. Pierre'. This pamphlet, *Idéas Pacifiques sur les demelez entre l'Espagne et l'Angleterre*, was an application of St Pierre's schemes for a pacific settlement of European disputes.[42] The same year, Waldegrave sent George a book that had been requested, adding

> … the Book you writ to me for some months ago by His Majesty's command—*Advertessement de Catholiques Anglaises* etc. I had above twenty brokers hunting for it, but could not be found till at length in

Marshal d'Estrées library and Comte d'Estrées has made me a present of it, for otherwise it was not to be had. There is not another copy of it in any library in Paris, the whole impression having been suppressed and destroyed for the dangerous doctrines it contained. I must trouble you farther with a book which Baron Swackheld wrote to one of my people for from Hanover … the book is a new play and is for his Majesty.[43]

The difficulty of gauging the 'modernity' of the British diplomatic system and of assessing effectiveness is nicely posed by such purchases. They can be treated as an extension of envoys' more general purchasing role. Thus, Waldegrave sent truffles to the Duke of Newcastle,[44] and prints to Sir Paul Methuen. Wych was involved in the purchase of horses. Newcastle used diplomats in his pursuit of tropical fruits and plants, and Sir Robert Walpole acted likewise in his quest for paintings.[45] In 1761, Wolters wrote to Weston from Rotterdam,

You will receive by the hands of our worthy friend Mr. Hampden, the catalogue of a considerable sale of drawings and prints; as I am informed that Lord Bute is a connoisseur in those things, I must beg the favour of you to present it to his lordship with my humble respects.[46]

In 1793, Burges got Whitworth to send him China tea from St Petersburg.[47] Distrustful of Wych's loyalty to the government, Robethon was dubious in 1716 about any chance of removing him, as Wych had ingratiated himself with Stanhope, not least by providing wine.[48]

In this light, the purchase of books was another instance of the diplomat as servant, a courtier dependent on whim, not a representative bounded by bureaucratic routine. Yet, at the same time, the purchase of books can be seen as another instance of the information society that was developing in Europe in this period and that increasingly affected the process of policy-making. An emphasis on information placed a premium on expertise, and also provided a set of criteria by which policies could be advanced and, both then and subsequently, judged. The extent to which policy-making and execution matched such criteria clearly varied and was frequently wanting, a point driven home by accounts of alcoholic Cabinet meetings during the North ministry.[49] Yet, the underlying requirement was for information, and, even if this material was not adequately assessed, that does not negate the extent to which the demand for information became more insistent.

The network of British representation increased, and the representatives were increasingly expected to focus on providing information, rather than looking after British interests in particular locations, not that the former function had not also been important. Diplomats as a whole became less consular. With the focus on information, it became easier to assess the effectiveness of envoys; although that remained a matter of providing confidential information, rather than what was readily available, whether in print or not. However, it was not always clear how far envoys were expected to discuss the information they provided, nor how far they could use this discussion to make comments about British policy. In 1721, Whitworth wrote to Tilson:

> I am extremely glad that His Majesty and Mylord Townshend have approved my conduct and notions about the affairs of the north … I should not have engaged so far in the discussion of them had I not thought it absolutely necessary for their service. The same object to persons in different stations shows itself in very different views; had I been in England and known the secret springs of what passes there, I don't question but I might have been of my Lord Townshend's opinion at first; and had his Lordship resided here, and seen what has been for some time, and is now acting, I am persuaded he would have fallen naturally into my way of thinking.[50]

Fourteen years later Robinson informed Tilson 'what I write today to Mr. Walpole as it is hazarding an opinion I would not presume to send it directly to Mylord',[51] i.e. the Secretary of State, Harrington.

In late 1753, the Duke of Newcastle wrote harshly (and repeatedly) to Guy Dickens in St Petersburg about the latter's failure to fulfil the essential requirement of the job:

> I cannot conceal from you the King's surprise, that at so critical a conjuncture, as the present, when letters from almost every court are full of the march of the Russian troops to the frontiers of Livonia and are assigning causes for it, you should continue your silence, either as to their numbers, their setting out, their progress, or the supposed time of their arrival in Livonia, or whether any particular general officer is appointed to command them.[52]

The provision of information by diplomats was but part of the process by which the British government acquired knowledge about the capability and intentions of foreign powers. Much of this process did not involve diplomats, but it would be mistaken to ignore it in this study, because it is necessary to understand the total information system of which diplomatic reporting formed a part. The role of the Post Office in the interception of correspondence, and the significance of Hanoverian assistance in this sphere have been demonstrated, and particular skill has been devoted to understanding the efforts made to investigate Jacobite conspiracies during the reign of George I.[53] However, this has tended to detract study from attempts to discover the plans of other states and, as a result, a misleading impression of the intentions, scope and chronology of intelligence activities during the reigns of George I and George II has been created.

The nature of the sources has made it difficult to discuss the impact of postal interception, and it is important to bear in mind the theme of the Appendix, that an understanding of diplomacy and foreign policy requires much work outside State Papers Foreign and Foreign Office papers. The two principal problems are the dispersal of many intercepts to private collections and the destruction of part of the state holdings. However, Kenneth Ellis' comment that 'diplomatic interceptions were classified as private papers, seldom kept on file', requires qualification.[54] A considerable quantity was clearly preserved in government hands, and the series State Papers 107 represents the remains of these papers. It is, however, incomplete. Much was clearly due to inadvertent destruction: 'they were thrown in a closet as papers of no consequence, and ... an immense quantity perished'.[55] The uneven nature of the series is readily apparent. For example, eleven volumes of intercepts survive for 1733, but no letters for 1735, and there are also none for the period October 1745 to October 1751.

Nevertheless, there are also intercepts in other series in the Public Record Office, although the absence of a catalogue creates serious problems for searchers. The intercepts are scattered through the diplomatic papers. In some cases, they comprise entire volumes.[56] More often, the material is occasional, sometimes intercepts sent to envoys whom it was felt would find them useful. Thus, the instructions for Count Friedrich von Seckendorf, the Austrian envoy in Berlin, sent on a special mission to Hanover in 1729, were sent to the British envoys in Paris by Townshend.[57] The following spring, Charles Hotham was sent on a special mission to Berlin in order to facilitate negotiations for a marital alliance between the ruling families of Britain and Prussia. Hotham was also instructed to secure the disgrace of the Prussian minister, General Grumbkow, and the recall of Reichenbach, the Prussian Resident in London. The government had intercepted the secret correspondence between the two men, proving that they had attempted to thwart a reconciliation. Hotham was sent copies of the intercepts in order to discredit the men. The evidence survives in State Papers Prussia and in Hotham's private papers.[58] Many other intercepts can be found in the private papers of Secretaries of State and occasionally other ministers, such as Sir Robert Walpole. For example, the papers of Charles, 3rd Earl of Sunderland, contain a large number of intercepts for the period 1716–18. This includes French, Holstein, Jacobite, Savoyard, Spanish and Swedish material, making it clear that the interception system was already well developed and successful.[59]

Foreign diplomats were certainly aware that the post was opened. This was common practice all over Europe. John Hedges, Envoy Extraordinary in Turin, noted in 1727, 'my letters are frequently stopped either here or in France for a post and I am persuaded as often opened which I don't know how to prevent'. Chesterfield was concerned about French decipherers in 1731. Robert Murray Keith commented on French and Austrian action in 1785.[60]

The crucial element in the system was not interception—the opening of letters and the copying of the contents—but the deciphering. This was a skill the British possessed in abundance, especially after the appointment of the Reverend Edward Willes, later a conscientious Bishop of Bath and Wells, as Decipherer in 1716, a post he held until his death in 1773. Earlier, in an important link with the world of science, the post had been held in 1701–3 by John Wallis, an eminent mathematician. From Willes' appointment the decipherer's office was continually staffed by members of his family until its abolition in 1844, and from 1762 onwards the entire office were members of the family. From 1701, when the office was placed on a regular basis, until 1722, the salaries were paid at the Exchequer, thereafter by the Secretary of the Post Office, out of the Secret Service money, until 1782, when the office was placed under the authority of the newly created Foreign Office.[61]

The success of the office can be gauged from its ability in the 1730s to decipher the codes of most European states, including Austria, Bavaria, Denmark, France, Naples, the Palatinate, Portugal, Prussia, Russia, Sardinia, Saxony, Spain, Sweden and the United Provinces. Evidence of a failure to decipher—either intercepts which were incompletely deciphered or not deciphered at all, or references to the problem in correspondence— is rare, although the office was constantly tested by new cipher keys. In 1731, Anthony Corbiere, one of the decipherers, informed Newcastle that the Prussians had started to employ a new key: 'the letter from Degenfeld to his master, which your Grace was pleased to send me this morning is in a cipher entirely new … consists of at least 2,000 different characters.' In 1790, Sir Francis Willes was forced to put in a lot of effort to tackle the Spanish key.[62]

Much of the strength of the British information system derived from allied co-operation, and the efforts made by ministers and diplomats in sustaining that co-operation were very important to Britain's foreign policy capability. Hanoverian co-operation began before the accession of George I, for William III was supplied with correspondence between Paris, Copenhagen and Stockholm intercepted at the Hanoverian post office in Celle.[63] The quality of Hanoverian interception remained high throughout the century, and co-operation with Britain continued. In 1750, Frederick II informed the French envoy that the Hanoverians had broken his cipher, while in 1790 Edward Willes noted that cipher keys from Hanover 'are no new thing, and have lately occurred in regard to the Danish'.[64]

Co-operation was not limited to Hanover. Particularly in the early decades of the century, the Dutch maintained, at least to a certain extent, the tradition of assistance that had developed during William III's reign. In 1730, Chesterfield provided evidence of the direct role of a high-ranking envoy in espionage when he reported:

> the postmaster at Leyden informs me that he has already sent you several copies of Count Degenfeld's correspondence; the Pensionary will do his utmost to get at those letters, but there are two difficulties; one is that the post offices belong to burgomasters who often will not do it; and the other is, that they have nobody here expert at opening and closing letters, so that the affair would immediately be discovered by their bunglings.[65]

The Dutch also co-operated in keeping an eye on British fugitives.[66]

There is no doubt that in the 1730s the Anglo-Hanoverian intelligence link was very successful. The diminution in the quantity of surviving intercepts from the mid-1740s makes it harder to gauge success thereafter. George II complained about the poor quality of postal interception in

1752.[67] However, there are indications of an important continued capability. Intercepts revealed Choiseul's plan for an invasion of Britain in 1759, in the mid-1760s and early 1770s French correspondence with Sweden was regularly deciphered, French and Prussian codes in the late 1760s were broken, and when, in 1773, Anthony Todd, who had been Foreign Secretary of the Post Office since 1752, referred to the problems facing the decipherers, he noted that three Russian ciphers as well as the Swedish cipher had been broken.[68] Ciphers caused problems for British envoys. It took time and trouble to cipher and decipher documents,[69] and there were problems when envoys did not have the same cipher. In 1784, the envoys in Dresden and Munich could not read Robert Murray Keith's cipher.[70]

Interceptions were useful for a number of reasons, including the political one of strengthening the ministry by discrediting its opponents. This last was an extension of the task that ministers attributed to diplomats, namely strengthening the government. If this was given a marked political slant when it was a question of discrediting opponents then this was not completely separate from the tasks of a diplomatic service that, from 1689, faced in the 'Pretender' a rival claimant to the throne.

Intercepts also threw much light on the foreign perception of British politics. Horace Walpole recorded an event that allegedly occurred soon after the death of Queen Caroline in 1737: 'the King reading with Sir Robert some intercepted letters from Germany, which said that, now the Queen was gone, Sir Robert would have no protection.' George II was not above intercepting his family's correspondence, certainly that of his son Frederick, Prince of Wales. It was possible to gain information from intercepts on the impression created by parliamentary debates, and on the extent to which foreign envoys were influenced by domestic British politics. It was hardly surprising that the government sought the recall of Broglie, the French envoy in 1731, when they were made aware by their intercepts of his increasing criticism of British policy, culminating in his suggestion that, in response to the new Anglo-Austrian alliance, France need only turn to the Pretender in order to harm Britain.[71]

Evidence of intrigues between diplomats and the opposition was more serious. Thanks to intercepts, the ministry was well aware of the hostile intrigues of envoys such as the Austrians Starhemberg (1725), Palm (1726–7), Kinsky (1728–30) and Strickland (1734–5), the French Broglie (1730–1) and Chavigny (1732–6), the Prussian Reichenbach (1726–30), the Spaniards Monteléon (1718), Pozobueno (1726) and Montijo (1733–5), and the Swedes Gyllenborg (1716–17) and Sparre (mid-1730s).

In 1736, an intercept revealed a Prussian effort to develop links with the Prince of Wales.[72]

These revelations were of political value to successive ministries as opponents could be presented as treasonable. This was a variant of the traditional Whig identification of the Tories with Jacobitism, but was more useful politically as it could implicate domestic Whig opponents, such as William Pulteney, the leader of the opposition Whigs in the Commons from 1725 to 1742. He was revealed as in negotiation with the Austrian envoy Palm in 1726–7.

Furthermore, the intercepts referred directly to issues of foreign policy and were thus of great interest to the king. It is known that the monarchs took a close interest in the intercepts, and they appear to have read them regularly. Intercepts were sent from London to Hanover when the king went there. In addition, royal instructions were sought on the best way in which to use them. In 1730, Newcastle wrote to George II: 'Doctor Willes has this moment deciphered the letters. Though Grumbkow's to Reichenbach is a very extraordinary one, I most humbly submit it to your Majesty whether the original should be stopped.' Newcastle was opposed to the idea, arguing that the intercepts were useful for the discovery of Prussian intentions. George agreed in his appended reply: 'Gromkow's letter must be sent to Reichenbach to keep up the correspondence; very likely the next will be more curious and fitter to be sent to Berlin.'[73]

The intercepts served to compromise opposition politicians in royal eyes. The Earl of Strafford, a former diplomat who was Tory leader in the Lords, was playing with fire in his intrigues with Reichenbach, for George II was more concerned about relations with Prussia than with any other power. In 1730, the ministry intercepted letters from Reichenbach seeking information about the Hotham mission which he claimed the opposition had asked him for, and he sent Berlin supposed opposition advice to reject Hotham's terms and thus gain concessions.[74]

The intercepts provided a basis for criticizing opposition intrigues. In 1734, Horatio Walpole accused the opposition of links with foreign powers, and his brother attacked 'those gentlemen, who may perhaps have hearkened to every little whisper of some of the foreign ministers at this court, which is, I believe, the only foundation they have for what they have asserted'.[75]

Intercepts were also of value in understanding the diplomatic policies of other powers. The surviving intercepts suggest that the British were able to benefit from a mass of information and opinion in assessing these policies, although their value was limited by measures taken to avoid interception.

The use of couriers increased the importance of intercepting messages at their points of departure or arrival rather than en route. There is no evidence of individuals on the staffs of foreign envoys in London being suborned, although there were doubtless attempts, but British diplomats clearly sought agents. In 1735, Waldegrave recruited François de Bussy, a senior member of the French Foreign Ministry. Waldegrave was less successful when he tried to recruit Chauvelin, the French Foreign Minister.[76] Further evidence of British espionage within France comes in an interrogation of an Englishman detained in Calais in 1738 who claimed that George Robinson, a former MP, who had fled Britain in 1732 when his frauds had been discovered, had been able to gain copies of French diplomatic correspondence at Paris and to send them to Newcastle, and that that process had been going on for about three years. In 1786, Eden obtained a secret source on French finances.[77]

Espionage abroad was not simply devoted to gaining copies of diplomatic correspondence that had evaded British postal interception. For most of the period, Britain was threatened by the Bourbons and the central problem for British intelligence was to ascertain their capabilities and intentions. This was not a problem that could be solved by postal interception. Instead, there was a requirement for more active intelligence operations, HUMIT (human intelligence) rather than SIGNIT (signals intelligence) to employ modern terms, designed, in particular, to discover Bourbon naval strength and preparedness. The latter was seen as a sign of political intentions.

As most warships were not kept prepared for sailing let alone action, but, instead, were left without masts and rigging up, cannon on board, or sailors at hand, it was possible to focus on steps taken to prepare them. However, the time British preparations took ensured that it was crucial for the British to be kept fully informed of Bourbon moves. Much effort was devoted to assessing the naval strength, preparedness and intentions of France and Spain, although, in 1734, Sir Charles Wager, the First Lord of the Admiralty, complained, 'though we have an ambassador in France, I don't find that he sends any account of the motion of the ships; though he has been writ to about it'.[78]

Agents were sent from the embassies, especially from Paris, to the ports, and envoys also sought to gain information from French officials. In 1731, at a time of tension, Newcastle ordered Waldegrave to send spies to the naval bases at Brest, Port Louis, Rochefort and Toulon. Waldegrave's assurances about French intentions and the limited state of their preparations, however, were not believed. Two years later, Waldegrave reported, 'I am in a fair way to settle a correspondence in the sea ports'.[79] In 1749, Albemarle forwarded from Paris a report of the state of the French navy at Brest and Rochefort that had cost 300 louis d'or to obtain. Albemarle also read the report: 'Your Grace will observe in the inclosed paper, that notwithstanding all the noise made in England, of our workmen having been debauched into this service, that there are none in any of the principal docks of this kingdom.'[80]

In Spain, in peacetime, more reliance could be placed on the Consuls; there was no comparable system in France. Certain Consuls were of particular importance. William Cayley reported regularly from Cadiz in the 1720s and 1730s,[81] and was, for example, a crucial source for the armada of 1732 which, in fact, captured Oran; while Ferrol was covered from Corunna by John Parker; in 1716, as Consul at Faro, he had sent reports on French warships off the Algarve possibly linked to Jacobite plans.

In addition, a number of informants and officials, ranging from captains of warships and merchantmen, to Robert Wolters, the Consul in Rotterdam, who forwarded reports from Dutch merchantmen, were used in order to build up a reliable picture, not least by permitting the checking of individual reports. During the 'cold war' between Britain and France in the early 1740s, Anthony Thompson, then in charge of affairs in Paris, sent regular reports and ran agents, including one in Brest.[82] During the Nootka Sound crisis in 1790, the government was fully informed of the build-up of a large Spanish fleet at Cadiz. Information from Spain was supplemented from Lisbon by Robert Walpole. His dispatch of 26 May included details of Spanish preparations transmitted by the Portuguese government. Earlier, another envoy in Lisbon, Henry Worsley, had spent £337 15 shilling on obtaining intelligence about Jacobite-Spanish plans in 1719–20.[83]

In wartime, diplomatic sources became less satisfactory. Diplomats and Consuls were withdrawn or subject to surveillance. This did not prevent them from providing useful information. In the Anglo-Spanish War of Jenkins' Ear (1739–48), Parker withdrew from Corunna to Oporto in neutral Portugal, but still retained local agents in Corunna and sent regular reports on Spanish naval activities to London. David Jackson, Consul in Oporto, had sent reports in 1719. Diplomatic agents in other neutral ports also became more important. For example, in early 1744, the sources of naval intelligence included Consul Goldsworthy at Leghorn and Renard, the agent in Amsterdam.[84] Increased reliance had to be placed in wartime on reports from British warships and merchantmen and from foreign ships. Diplomats and Consuls played a role in passing on such information. In 1744, Abraham Castres, the Consul in Lisbon, reported to the Admiralty that a British merchantman had arrived in Lisbon having seen the Brest fleet sailing towards the Mediterranean,[85] information that was in fact inaccurate. The effective Wolters agency was continued by his widow and the chief clerk, Hake, after Wolters died in 1770. During the French Revolutionary and Napoleonic Wars the provision of military information again became important. Thus in 1798 Thomas Jackson Secretary of Legation in Turin, reported on the movement of French troops to Genoa, indicating that a major amphibious operation was planned.[86]

The quality of the information gathered varied. The French and Spaniards took steps to hinder espionage. Worsley's intelligence network in Spain was broken in 1719. In February 1741, Thompson reported 'I have not heard a word from any of our private correspondents. I fancy my Toulon friend has unconscionably dropped us. The man I sent to the other coast [Brest] I am afraid is lost.' The hanging of a Mr Gordon, for naval espionage in 1769, made it difficult for Harcourt to recruit new agents.[87] On occasions, the British were surprised by French moves. Nevertheless, in general, the British were fairly well informed about the state of the Bourbon navies. Lists of ships detailing their condition can be found frequently in the British archives, and the major problem was not in establishing the strength of Bourbon forces, but was, rather, one of assessing their probable moves.[88]

A similar problem affected the gathering of information concerning the French army. During peacetime, occasional reports were sent by the envoy in Paris, usually concerning the size of the army or projected summer manoeuvres. The apparent approach of war led to the employment of agents who could provide more detailed information. Fears about French troop moves towards the Channel in 1731 led Thomas Pelham, Secretary of the Embassy in Paris, whom Waldegrave suspected of spying on him, to turn to 'S', possibly John Sample, for information on French plans. The former diplomat Stephen Poyntz blamed the panic of that summer partly on such agents: 'we have had secret intelligencers who, if I don't mistake, had been infusing jealousies of us into the Cardinal [Fleury], and afterwards had been playing the same game here with regard to us.'[89] Similarly, in the winter of 1792–3, the government used agents like Gideon Duncan to report on French military moves and plans in the Low Countries. For example, on 17 November, he wrote from Ostend that the French were to send warships up the Scheldt and were likely to attack the Dutch.[90]

When Britain itself became a combatant, then it was in turn more important for diplomats to report on military matters and harder for them to do so. Neutral posts, such as Lisbon in the Nine Years' War (1689–97), the War of the Austrian Succession (Britain at conflict 1743–8), and the Seven Years' War (1756–63), and those in Switzerland, became important listening stations.[91] In 1742, Onslow Burrish was ordered to report on French moves from the then neutral Austrian Netherlands.[92] During the War of the Austrian Succession and the Seven Years' War, the British relied heavily on George Cressener, Resident in Liège from 1747 to 1755, then Minister in Cologne until expelled by the French in 1759, when he moved to Maastricht and was given credentials as chargé d'affaires in the United Provinces to provide some protection. Cressener not only maintained agents in parts of the Austrian Netherlands, but also a regular source of intelligence in Paris. The quality of his reports was high, and they included information concerning French intentions.[93] The outbreak of the Seven Years' War also led to reliance on information sources in the neutral United Provinces.[94]

The use of spies was clearly valuable, but a concentration on this form of espionage is as misplaced as one on postal interception. Given the constant nature from 1689 of the Jacobite challenge, and from 1689 to 1716 and, again, from 1731 of the Bourbon threat, the crucial problem was the assessment of the intentions of the French government, rather than their military capability. This was a field in which spies were of limited value. Most agents were men of relatively humble birth engaging in espionage in return for payment. Such men might serve to count warships or steal documents, but, in general, they lacked any point of access to the courts of the age.

Foreign policy in most European states, including France, was not a matter of bureaucratic routine and discrete independent chancelleries. Instead, policy was made in the courts by a small group of individuals who knew each other, many of whom lacked any formal competence or responsibility in the conduct of diplomacy. The inchoate, usually secretive nature of policy-making created difficulties for those who wished to ascertain what was going on, whether they were diplomats, spies or newspapers. The role of personal diplomacy, either by rulers, such as Louis XV and his *secret du roi*, or by ministers, such as the Austrian Prince Eugène, created particular problems.[95]

141

Faced with this situation, it was not satisfactory to rely on bribing minor officials or intercepting correspondence. Instead, the most satisfactory method for obtaining information, and one that has received relatively little attention, was the attempt to develop links with courtiers, ministers and diplomats. Sometimes, these 'agents of influence' were rewarded financially, but, in general, they cannot be regarded as spies gained by bribery. The willingness of courtiers and ministers to provide information reflected the nature of politics. Far from states being monoliths, it is clear that policy options were debated and discussed within each country, wherever the constitutional responsibility for foreign policy might lie. These debates were intertwined with struggles over power, patronage and domestic factional considerations, making it possible for foreign diplomats to find allies in divided courts and ministries.

In some cases, this process was pushed very far and diplomats intervened actively in domestic politics. British, French and Russian diplomats in Sweden, British, French, Austrian and Prussian diplomats in Russia, and British and French envoys at The Hague all played a very active role, subsidizing politicians and seeking to provoke changes in government.[96] More frequently, diplomats took a less active role, but the factious nature of court politics still provided them with significant sources of information. In France, in 1716–18, the British were close to the Regent, the Duke of Orléans and his confidant Dubois, who followed a policy in opposition to that of the Duke of Huxelles, the head of the Council for Foreign Affairs.[97] In Prussia, in the late 1720s, the British envoy was close to one ministerial group led by Ilgen and Knyphausen, his Austrian counterpart to their rival Grumbkow.

Although some attempts to develop links failed, the divided nature of most governments ensured that there were usually individuals keen to further British interests. Information from favourable ministers is usually found in the reports of envoys. Thus, rather than there being any sharp break between diplomatic and intelligence material, the two were closely intertwined, a situation that owed much to the absence, with the exception of the deciphering office, of any espionage institutions or establishment.

Due to the absence of such an institution and because the funding of spies was handled on an *ad hoc* basis, it is difficult to gain a complete picture of espionage activities. Horn concluded in 1961 that 'the extent and importance of the British secret service organization in the eighteenth century has been exaggerated'.[98] This assessment was substantially based on the situation in the second half of the century, and may be less appropriate prior to 1760, when concern about Jacobitism, especially when combined with Britain's more vulnerable international situation after the collapse of the Anglo-French alliance in 1731, led to greater ministerial interest in the gathering of information. This was a prime responsibility for diplomats,[99] and it is possible that the recovery of more sources will throw greater light on the process. Thus, the deposit in 1986 of two hitherto inaccessible volumes of the papers of Horatio Walpole improved the existing knowledge of the relationship between diplomacy and espionage in the mid-1720s. They reveal that Horatio, then envoy at Paris, had been informed of Jacobite agents in Britain, including a clerk in the Secretary of State's office, that an Italian agent planted by Horatio at Boulogne had been revealed, because the Jacobites had gained access to Horatio's correspondence, and that Horatio was spending heavily to obtain details of possible Jacobite invasion plans, including the payment of £400 to one informant.[100]

Horn's conclusion also begs the question of what resources it was reasonable to expect that an eighteenth-century state would devote to espionage given the nature of diplomatic activity and the limited resources of most governments. Although some agents produced low-grade material,[101] by the standards of the age British information gathering was reasonably successful. In 1755, Frederick II, a ruler very sensitive to issues of secrecy and espionage, wrote to his envoy in Paris, Baron Knyphausen:

> I have received letters from London that, to my great surprise, contain all the details of what has happened between France and me since the time of the Anglo-French rupture in America. They are so well informed that they know my very phrases. Clearly there is either no secrecy in the French Council or a leak. You are to press Rouillé [French Foreign Minister] on the need for France to take better arrangements in order to ensure that secrecy is maintained. Tell him that unless this happens I will be unable to confide in France, as secrecy is crucial to me.[102]

The role of espionage in information gathering and the prominent part of diplomats in this process is a reminder of the need to present both such gathering, and diplomacy in general, in the context of the severe challenges facing Britain and its government. The acquisition of information, and skill and success in negotiation, were therefore not part of a process in which advantage was sought but without great danger if things went wrong.

Instead, success was crucial. This elides what might otherwise have been a more substantial gap between diplomacy and espionage.

The situation varied by post, period and individual. Certain diplomats were particularly prominent and trusted in this field. Several had personal links with leading ministers, which serves to underline both the sensitivity of the task and the extent to which the diplomatic service was both pervaded and animated by such relationships. Horatio Walpole and Robert Trevor are obvious examples. Another is Thomas Pelham MP, both second cousin to, and political client of, Newcastle, and used by the latter, when Secretary of Embassy in Paris from 1730 to 1736, both to direct espionage activities in France and to keep an eye on Waldegrave, whose Jacobite family connections aroused Newcastle's suspicion.

In this case, the use of second-level diplomats to keep an eye on their colleagues had a definite espionage dimension. More generally, it was part of a surveillance process that could be directed towards other British diplomats, their connections, and the policies they proposed. Information within systems was not simply for the transmission of material obtained from outside, and comments thereon.

This is a reminder of the mistake of thinking of states as coherent blocks with diplomatic services that were separate and competing. Instead, the intertwining of diplomatic service and domestic politics was matched by an inter-penetration of states and, more specifically, of these diplomatic/political nexuses. Thus, individual British diplomats linked to particular British and foreign ministers, and advocating a specific alignment and a resulting policy, could find themselves opposed by foreign diplomats with links to rival foreign ministers and to different British ministers and/or sections of the British opposition. As an addition, or an alternative, this opposition could be mounted by other British diplomats. This was seen in the early and mid-1720s with differences over links with France, the attitude towards French factional politics, and policy towards Austria; and in 1786–7, when William Eden's support for better relations with France was well received by Pitt the Younger, but encountered hostility from both Dorset, the Ambassador, and Carmarthen, the Foreign Secretary.[103] During such struggles, diplomatic appointments and promotions could serve to record and advance the situation in factional struggles within both Britain and other states. Thus, in 1723, Townshend greeted the appointment of Horatio Walpole to Paris:

the King's putting so near a relation of ours over Schaub's head in a court where the whole sense of affairs centres at present in Lord Carteret's Province, and in the strength and heart of his interest will be such a publication to the world of the superiority of our credit, that I think a stronger neither can nor ought at present to be desired.[104]

Good news of this type was publicized, and politicians were adept at the eighteenth-century equivalent of 'spin doctoring'. In addition, information was important in such struggles. It was not separate from opinion. Indeed, opinion about the policies of other powers was central to the search for information. The evaluation of such information was not conducted in some impartial fashion, in so far as such a process is indeed possible. Instead, it was partisan, particularly being geared to the interests of the dominant minister.

Thus we return to the themes of several of the other chapters and see their interconnectedness. The partisan nature and/or consequences of information flows accentuated the need to choose diplomats carefully, and emphasized the issue of control. It also made the subsequent task of assessment more difficult, not least because it is unclear how best to distinguish the interests of a particular ministry from those of the state or indeed the country. Such categories can appear nebulous and the distinctions can seem artificial; but the issue cuts to the heart of the problem of judging the formulation and execution of foreign policy.

8

Diplomacy and British Foreign Policy

> It is astonishing that our ministry don't take more notice of their
> ministers abroad, they seem to think no more of us as soon as we have
> left the kingdom.
>
> Charles, Earl of Northampton, Ambassador in Venice, 1762[1]

During the period as a whole, diplomats became more necessary. Until
the mid-1750s, a considerable amount of diplomatic activity had been
handled by the monarchs or by ministers who travelled on the Continent.
William III had spent much of his reign in the Low Countries, while George
I had visited Hanover in 1716, 1719, 1723 and 1725 and died at Osnabrück
en route in 1727. George II had journeyed to his native Electorate in 1729,
1732, 1735, 1736, 1740, 1741, 1743, 1748, 1750, 1752 and 1755. Most of
these visits were lengthy. They gave the monarch an opportunity to conduct negotiations in person, as, for example, George II did in 1729 when
he sought to arrange an alliance with the Wittelsbachs. In addition, British
diplomats could be summoned to Hanover, while the Secretary of State
who accompanied the king benefited from a much shorter turn-round
time in his correspondence with most envoys. Queen Anne (1702–14) did
not go to the Continent, but, for much of her reign, John, Earl, and later
Duke, of Marlborough, acted as the co-ordinator of the Grand Alliance
while commanding the British forces in the Low Countries.

However, during the Seven Years' War (1756–63) the elderly George
II did not visit war-torn Germany, and, although imminent visits by
George III (1760–1820) to Hanover were reported on a number of
occasions,[2] he never went. Nor could his eldest son, George, Prince of
Wales, serve as a surrogate. As a consequence of George III's attitudes
and behaviour, foreign policy centred on Britain, rather than Britain–

Hanover, and its management was pushed back to London.[3] This altered the nature of control over British diplomats, not least because the links with the Hanoverian system that had fed information and opinion directly to George II and Newcastle via Gerlach Adolf von Münchhausen[4] were significantly weakened.[5] The greater marginality of the Hanoverian system under George III also owed something to the rise of trans-oceanic issues in British foreign policy, and thus the focus on relations with France, Spain and, in the 1780s, the Dutch, and, in particular, on extra-European relations with them. In contrast, developments in the Empire came to be of lesser importance. This was helped not only by George III's down-playing of Hanoverian expansionism but also by the neutrality Hanover was able to enjoy during the War of American Independence.

An even greater role and independence was therefore thrust on British diplomats. Furthermore, the chains of command and influence were simplified by the reduction in the Hanoverian concerns of the monarch. The focus was far more clearly on instructions received from the Secretaries of State and, from 1782, the Foreign Secretary. This was to culminate during the century with the powerful position of William, Lord Grenville, Foreign Secretary from 1791. He was an effective and energetic minister who wielded a powerful position in Cabinet, and was not greatly hindered by George III, but one who had limited diplomatic experience and stayed in London and thus did not circumvent his diplomats.[6]

These specific changes interacted with a more general shift in government. Despite George III's growing popularity from the 1783–4 political crisis on, the role of the monarch was declining, and becoming increasingly symbolic.[7] The growth of business and the increased scope of government lessened the ability of any individual to master the situation and encouraged the development of the Cabinet. Collective responsibility and loyalty to the leading minister increased, and the formulation of policy came to be more under ministerial control.

Royal influence and patronage declined with the abolition of sinecures, the diminishing influence of court favourites and the growing accountability of Parliament. Greater Cabinet cohesion and influence was more a feature of the 1790s than the 1780s, in part because of George III's illness in 1788–9, and the subsequent slackening of his grip.[8]

In this light, George III's active role in the mid-1780s can be seen as becoming less marked subsequently, not least because he accepted that Pitt was the effective head of the ministry.[9] The way was prepared for the far less energetic role that was to be played by George IV, a monarch who was short on duty and diligence, but also understood that the Crown could not dispense with Cabinet and the exigencies flowing from Parliament's role.[10]

This long-term shift away from personal rule improved the prospect for more regular administrative practices, but it did not ensure them. Indeed, in one respect, it made the situation less predictable, because ministries were now better able to insist on the dismissal of envoys. The Earl of Hardwicke pointed out in 1782 that diplomats were 'servants of the *state* at large, rather than of *any particular ministry*',[11] but uncertainty and changes in the diplomatic corps in 1782–3 and again at the time of the Regency Crisis in 1788–9 indicated the extent to which ministerial power posed a challenge to diplomatic continuity. The role of diplomats as advocates as well as implementers of policy was such that ministers wished to be certain of key envoys, thus explaining the controversies over representation in Paris in 1723 and 1786–7. Diplomatic posts were not yet clearly administrative, rather than political, in character.[12]

The assessment of how far the consequent arrangements were deficient is far from clear-cut. For example, clashes between envoys, as they advanced different interpretations of the international system and suggested clashing policies, were not necessarily harmful. They ensured that the government was offered various options and that policy was not therefore controlled by the diplomats. It would have been a different question if policy had been undermined by diplomats, but there was little sign of that. Individual diplomats, such as Auckland in early 1791, criticized the direction of policy, but they did not try to undermine it, although that was not how the situation always appeared to critics.[13]

This chapter considers two of the tasks of British diplomats, by way of indicating the multifaceted character of foreign policy. It then attempts to evaluate the ability of the diplomats to further foreign policy objectives, before concluding by examining the conduct of policy as an aspect of Britain's great power status, and assessing the extent of 'modernity' that can be discerned. The impact of the French Revolution and British representation outside Europe are also both discussed.

The multifaceted character of foreign policy can be covered thematically, although that risks suggesting a ready categorization that was in practice absent. The same individuals had to cover a multitude of tasks, frequently in the same interview with ministers of the state to which they were accredited. Thereafter, the envoys reported on their tasks in dispatches sent to the same Secretary of State. The extent to which diplomats distinguished between these tasks is unclear; so also is the way in which they prioritized their commitments. Clearly, the situation varied by envoy, posting, issue and conjuncture. It is necessary to be aware of this tension when judging envoys and their effectiveness.

The prime commitments—reporting and negotiation—have been discussed in earlier chapters. Before offering an overview assessment it is necessary to turn also to other commitments. The defence of economic interests was an important task. The intensity of this goal varied both by posting and by envoy, but it was an issue for all diplomats, even for those where there was an option of consular support. In such cases, diplomats could turn to consuls for advice.[14] The legacy can readily be seen among diplomats' papers. Aside from the general pursuit of interests, there was also the role of advocate in specific cases and for particular merchants. Thus, amongst the papers of Sir William Trumbull (Constantinople 1687–9), there is an entry book of his business as Ambassador chiefly relating to the Levant Company, including copies of merchants' petitions, depositions, appeals and sworn statements. In Constantinople the envoy's salary was paid by the Company, and the Company paid more regularly than the Crown. This, however, posed problems as the Company essentially sought a commercial representative and was unwilling to pay for political services.[15] Trumbull's secretary, Thomas Coke, was also Chancellor of the English Factory at Constantinople in 1680–95, while, in addition, the Levant Company appointed to the Consulship of Aleppo.

Constantinople might seem a special case because of the role of the Levant Company. However, other embassies were also greatly encumbered by mercantile disputes, although these may be under-reported in the documents. Wych reported in 1734:

> the ordinary business of my station, such as the affairs of shipping
> and trade, keep me generally employed … the adjusting of differences
> betwixt merchants, masters of ships and sailors are such disagreeable
> occupations, that I believe your lordship will willingly dispense with
> my troubling you with accounts of such matters.[16]

This was not solely the case for envoys accredited to courts in port cities, such as Copenhagen, Naples and Stockholm. In addition, the role of imperial jurisdiction ensured that disputes over Hamburg's trade were pursued in Vienna, while, at Paris in 1722, Schaub was embroiled in a 'quantité de petites affaires marchandes'.[17]

This was an irritation to many diplomats. This was especially so where merchant communities were well entrenched. In 1728, Tyrawly complained that the British merchants in Lisbon claimed excessive privileges, adding the following year: 'excepting Mr. Stert, and some 4, or 5, more, they are a parcel of the greatest jackanapes I ever met with, fops, beaux, drunkards, gamesters, and prodigiously ignorant even in their own business'. Keene wrote in 1736, 'if ever I have another commission in my days it shall be in a country where there are no sea ports'. William Cayley, the Consul in Cadiz, was another critic.[18] Furthermore, envoys were less than diligent in sending news of economic circumstances and developments. In 1765, Sandwich, then a Secretary of State, wrote:

> The Board of Trade having represented to me that the orders which, in consequence of a proposal from that Board in 1715, were sent to all the King's Ministers, and Consuls, in foreign parts, to transmit, under certain regulations, states of the British commerce within their respective departments, have not been executed for several years, by which the great public advantages proposed thereby have been entirely frustrated.[19]

Nevertheless, the support of commerce was an automatic response for most envoys. In 1734, Essex wrote that he 'ever looked upon it as one of the most essential parts of my duty to protect as much as possible His Majesty's trading subjects'.[20] In 1755, Burrish noted, 'although I have never received any immediate commands upon this subject, yet as the utility of the thing was self-evident, I have continued my endeavours to introduce the use of our tobacco into this Electorate, and I have now succeeded'. He followed this up by pressing for the import of sugar from the British West Indies.[21]

Other envoys were less satisfactory. In January 1754, the Attorney-General, Sir Dudley Ryder, had to listen to mercantile complaints about the situation in Portugal:

> he says our present consul Crowle is ignorant of mercantile affairs and has taken part with the Portuguese against his own country. And he thinks this disturbance must at last be attended with his being recalled. He says our minister there [Castres] is a very good sort of man, but not of weight enough either at court for want of a title or with our own factories there. But that Lord Tyrawly being sent over lately [1752] to settle the affair relating to the exportation of gold and silver which the

King of Portugal had disputed, he very soon settled to our satisfaction.

George Crowle had possibly obtained the Consulship to escape his creditors.[22]

The negotiation of commercial agreements was a particular facet of the representation of trade that called for the abilities of a diplomat and the quality of an envoy. Trade treaties could not be entrusted to Consuls. The importance of such negotiations varied by posting and period. They were especially significant after major wars when attempts were made to settle differences and to cement new relations with improved trade links. Thus, in 1715, an effort was made to improve trade relations with Spain by the commercial treaty negotiated on the British side by George Bubb, better known by his later name, Dodington. However, in 1718–20 and 1725–9, confrontation and conflict interrupted trade and the issue had to be addressed afresh. Keene was responsible for the 1750 commercial treaty.[23] Some negotiations failed, such as the lengthy attempt in mid-century to develop trade with Austria and the Austrian Netherlands. The complexity of the task encouraged the appointment of particular individuals. James Porter acted as Commissary in Vienna, while in Antwerp commissioners under Colonel Bladen were responsible for the negotiations. In 1784, George Crawford was sent as a Commissary to Paris to settle African boundaries and to negotiate commercial differences. William Eden was subsequently sent, in 1786, to settle the latter.[24] Porter, who had a City background, went on to Constantinople.

A particular effort to improve trade through commercial treaties was made after 1783.[25] The considerable effort that was made, however, had few consequences. The most important was the Eden Treaty with France (1786), but the political benefits were slight in the short term, and outweighed in the long run by the adverse impact on French public opinion. Political developments ensured that the commercial potential of the treaty was not realized.

Aside from being instructed to negotiate agreements, envoys were also ordered to ensure that they were enforced. Such action could arise from the pressure of traders on the envoys themselves, but, in general, major interventions stemmed from pressure on the ministry in London. This left a clear trail in the archives, as State Papers Foreign were especially appropriate for recording the challenge and response dynamic of instructions and reports. For example, in 1731, Newcastle responded to reports of a new Venetian duty on British fish exports by firmly instructing the

Resident, Colonel Elizeus Burges, to have it removed. Three years later, Bristol and London sugar merchants and refiners petitioned George II against a new Venetian duty on imports of British refined sugar. Again, instructions were sent to Burges.[26]

A discussion of commercial issues focuses attention on the extent to which, as Britain became more self-consciously mercantile and maritime in its political presentation,[27] there was a change in ideas about diplomatic representation. In short, was there a diplomatic counterpart to 'blue water' notions of British behaviour? Public discussion by the second half of the century certainly assumed the need for a knowledge of commercial interests. The *Monitor*, a London paper that advocated colonial and commercial expansionism, called on 5 January 1760 for the negotiation of the forthcoming peace with France to be handled not by diplomats appointed thanks to royal favour, but instead by those

> who have given proofs that they are capable of conducting, with ability and dexterity, that important business of negotiation with the most subtle and tenacious enemy ... they, (who besides a perfect knowledge of the interests, pretensions and connections of the several European states; a well-grounded skill in the principles of public law, with a capacity to apply them on every particular occasion; a thorough acquaintance with the commerce, the colonies, and the manufactures of their own country; and a clear apprehension of the rights, pre-eminences and just claims of their own sovereign; and being well instructed in all the instances of infraction of former treaties, which provoked Britain to take up arms) are men of such rank and consequence amongst ourselves, as may command respect and procure them authority amongst our enemies; and who with every other qualification shall be endowed with a sagacity to discover the finesses and artifices of the other public ministers; with fidelity, probity and disinterestedness, to execute punctually all the articles of their invitations, so as not to be biased by any view whatever.

This was a social politics of diplomacy still firmly expressed in traditional terms. There was no demand for embourgeoisement in the reference to men of 'rank and consequence', although it could be argued that this was a porous concept capable of multiple interpretations and that the understanding of both rank and consequence was more flexible than might appear.

Diplomacy provided another example of how Britain developed as a commercial and, later, industrial, power without overturning its social or political systems.[28] Compared to the two following centuries, this was a period of marked continuity in diplomatic composition, organization and ethos. Proposals for change, such as that of Stanyan in 1713, or the creation of the Regius Chairs in 1724, were not followed up or had little impact. There was at least one proposal for improved consular representation, but no major changes. In 1766, Rochford pressed Shelburne

> that a Consul General here [Paris] would not only be useful but absolutely necessary, as well as Consuls in all the French sea ports ... redress can only be obtained at this court for any grievances in matters of trade which the British Factories of Bordeaux, Marseilles, Sette, Boulogne or Dunkirk may labour under, as the most essential business in all the affairs of France is transacted by the first Clerks in office, who have an immense influence upon the ministers in commercial affairs of the greatest importance, and are a set of people a foreign minister, particularly an Ambassador cannot apply to.

Rochford added that a Consul-General would provide information on trade, and that the innovation had been useful in Spain, but his idea was not followed up.[29]

The protection of co-religionists was another important task of British envoys, particularly prior to 1725. This was irrespective of diplomatic alignments. For example, despite his conviction that Huguenot (French Protestant) refugees had played a role in the Monmouth rising of 1685,[30] and French complaints, the Catholic James II (1685–8) was firm on his royal dignity. Trumbull's pressure on behalf of the Huguenot wives of James' subjects and his own Huguenot servants was supported. The legalistic Trumbull was himself well aware of recent precedents. His papers included a volume containing memorials and petitions addressed to Louis XIV and his government on behalf of British residents in France and their affairs during the embassies of Henry Savile and Lord Preston in 1681–5.[31] Envoys had to intervene on behalf of co-religionists. Many, like Waldegrave in 1738 and Horace St Paul in 1775, found themselves acting 'in regard to an English girl unjustly confined in a convent'. Protection of the property of those who died abroad was also an issue, although, at times, envoys were asked to defend very difficult positions. Sir William Godolphin, formerly Charles II's envoy in Spain, died a Catholic in Madrid leaving his soul his heir, but this was contested by an Act of Parliament on behalf of the family in England, which envoys were required to support.[32]

More generally, great concern was shown about the position in Poland[33] and the Empire,[34] where Protestantism was on the defensive, and in Savoy-Piedmont, where the British acted as protectors of the Waldensians.[35] Concern about confessional disputes led to Edward Finch being known as the 'Protestant envoy' or 'Protestant thing'.[36] Some envoys revealed contempt for aspects of Catholicism. Elliot, no friend to 'bigotry and superstition', and Liston tried to make a miracle-working priest drunk in 1775.[37]

An itemization of foreign policy objectives does not clarify the ability of diplomats to further them. In part, envoys could contribute by providing information and advice that assisted in the setting of realistic goals, or in the moderation of objectives once set. That, however, is a benign account of what was a less mechanistic procedure and also one to which most envoys contributed singularly little. As with other states, the essential drive behind instructions came from the government and policy was set with only limited reference to advice from diplomats. Indeed, diplomats were most influential when, in formulating policy towards other states, they represented the views of Britain's allies, as, for example, did Mitchell during the Seven Years' War. More generally, diplomats were possibly most effective in forwarding goals in the case of Britain's alliances. Such links required representation, and a presence that was at once advisory, intercessionary and symbolic. The absence of such links left diplomats with less to do under all three headings. It ensured that negotiations were more *ad hoc*, and reporting more that of an outsider. Both functions were still important, but they were less central to the objectives of British foreign policy than when an alliance was at stake.

As a consequence, at one level the effectiveness of British diplomacy was, in part, a consequence of the degree to which foreign policy was focused on the search for alliances. This was indicative of the extent to which the basic stance, in terms of European power politics, was 'interventionist', or more 'isolationist'. Thus, for example, diplomacy was less important to British foreign policy in *c.* 1767–75 or in early and mid-1792[38] than in years when more active goals were being pursued. When it was less important, then dispatches became fewer[39] and representation became less prominent as envoys were given leave or withdrawn and not replaced. Furthermore, fewer instructions were sent.

This process could be true of British diplomacy as a whole or of areas of representation that no longer seemed so important. Thus, for example,

Turin had been a key posting during the wars with France between 1689 and 1748.[40] From 1764, the situation changed. George Pitt, the envoy in Turin since March 1762, left on leave in April 1764 and did not return. He refused to do so unless made a peer or promoted Ambassador.[41] Pitt's revocation was not issued until September 1768, when Sir William Lynch was appointed his successor. Lynch served in Turin from 1769 until 1776, but, after leaving, was not replaced as envoy until John, Viscount Mountstuart was appointed in 1779. He left in November 1782 but was not replaced at that rank until John Trevor arrived in October 1783. Trevor himself also had long periods of leave including July–October 1785, February 1787–October 1788, and July–October 1789. In the last case, poor health was the grounds for an absence of leave in Switzerland. The Sardinian envoy suggested in 1771 that George III could reproach most of his envoys 'lesquels passent pour le moins autant de tems à Londres qu'à leurs residences'.[42] William Norton, Minister in Berne from 1765 to 1783, served there from 1765 until 1768 and in 1769, returning only for a few days in 1776. Morton Eden was absent from Dresden in June–August 1785, August 1786 to November 1787, and May 1788 to May 1789.

Such gaps threw the burden of representation on chargés d'affaires and secretaries. Thus Mackenzie's secretary, Lewis Dutens, was in charge between Mackenzie's departure and George Pitt's arrival, again in 1764–5, and again in Mountstuart's absence in 1781. Lynch's secretary, William Deane Poyntz, was in charge between Lynch's departure in 1776 and Mountstuart's arrival in 1779. Norton's secretary, Jean Gabriel Catt, was in charge in his absence until his (Catt's) death in 1776. He had earlier been Robert Colebrooke's secretary and had been in charge between Colebrooke's departure in 1764 and Norton's arrival. Louis Braun was appointed by Norton to succeed Catt as representative and acted as Chargé d'Affaires until he died in 1792. Travelling through Europe in 1787, Thomas Brand reported:

> Mr. Walpole, the English minister at Munich was gone into England and we found only a Molloy, his secretary and a chargé d'affaires in his absence. It is wonderful how England is represented in the present moment at Turin and Munich. Of all the Laurentian Boars I ever saw this man is the greatest.

To turn to a more important example, William Eden left Madrid on 2 June 1789 in order to visit his ill wife in England. He never returned, although his recredentials were not sent until July 1790. Charles Fraser was appointed Secretary of Embassy and Minister Plenipotentiary to Spain in July 1789, but his instructions were not drawn up until the following February, and he did not reach Madrid until May 1790. In the meantime, the Consul, Anthony Merry, took charge of affairs.[43]

Such gaps in high-level representation are commonly neglected, but, in total, were very considerable. In mid-century, Hanbury Williams suggested that envoys should not leave until their replacements arrived, but such a system was never adopted. Elliot complained in 1776:

> The Germans, Russians and French in general fix secretarys of legation at the most considerable posts, whose duty it is to give a new Minister every information he requires, and this constant residence and experience in business enables them to do much more effectually than the most voluminous collections in writing.
>
> It is also common for foreigners to have resided some time without character at a post they are destined to fill.
>
> In England the original establishment for foreign missions does not seem to have been founded with so much caution as on the continent. An English minister often arrives at his station with no better assistance than what a private secretary of his predecessors can give him, that is copying papers, cyphering etc. Information from home may be worded with the greatest clearness. It can no more convey an adequate idea of the situation of a court and of its principal inhabitants, than a map can of the high and low grounds of a country. Ten days conversation upon the spot with his predecessor would forward a newcomer at least a twelve month in his knowledge of men and things and enable him to take up the thread of intelligence where it had been left.[44]

There was a distinctly episodic character to British representation, and this was punctuated by reliance on envoys of inferior rank. The latter frequently had considerable experience, but they lacked the rank to take a significant role in representation or negotiation. As a consequence, they were essentially reporters.

Possibly there was a certain decline in quality from the 1760s. Earlier, interventionist policies and foreign-born rulers had ensured that ministers and diplomats were generally forced to take a close interest in foreign policy and in the views of other powers. Alliances helped in the development of personal links and of habits of co-operation. The close interest of the monarchs in foreign policy led some diplomats to win favour. After 1760 most diplomats, however competent, were less close to the centre of the political storm. Shelburne, a former Secretary of State, complained in the Lords in 1779 that 'the business of the northern courts had been so ill-conducted by the ignorant persons to whom it had been entrusted of late years, that we had not a friend among them'.[45] Nevertheless, a diplomatic corps that could boast Goodricke, Grantham, Harris, Keith, Rochford, Stormont and Yorke was not without men of activity and talent.

The problem of absences or gaps in high-level representation was addressed in the 1780s by the creation of a new rank, Secretary of Legation. These royal-appointed and paid officials appeared first in Berlin (1785: Ewart), St Petersburg (1787: Charles Fraser), and Vienna (1789: Alexander Straton after Robert Murray Keith had had George Hammond replaced). They were seen as improving the structure of the foreign service, and can be presented as evidence of the ability of the British to introduce reform without having to adopt it in response to a crisis. Hammond noted in 1790:

> the Duke of Leeds has determined in my case and in that of all others, not to allow to the Secretaries of Legation the pay of chargés d'affaires during the absence of the Ministers ... that his object in instituting the office was to prevent the contingent necessity of appointing chargés d'affaires, and as he considers the Secretaries of Legation, to be in a state of progressive advancement, that circumstance ought to counterbalance the difference in emolument.[46]

Alongside such a sign of systematization, there was much that cannot so readily be located in terms of an analysis, or even teleology, of professionalization and modernity. To take the 1780s, it is difficult to see Dorset's appointment or conduct in such a light. The same is even more true of a curious episode in 1783 when John Strange, Resident in Venice, negotiated with Colonel, the Hon. Charles Stuart MP about the latter succeeding him in return for an annual payment out of the income. The proposal was not pursued and the government not approached.[47] Strange left Venice in 1786 in order to return home and follow his antiquarian interests, but he did not resign until 1789.

Aside from personnel, there was also a failure of control over the diplomatic system in both 1786–7 and, more clearly, the Ochakov crisis of

1790–1, with envoys advocating contradictory policies and obstructing colleagues. Grenville's reliance on close connections can also be seen as symptomatic of an administrative ethos reliant on personal links and happy to use them. His brother Thomas was sent to Vienna in 1794 and to Berlin in 1799, his friend William Wickham to Switzerland in 1795, and his brother-in-law, John, Earl of Carysfort, to Berlin in 1800. Auckland's sponsorship of his brother, Morton Eden, again reflects an ethos more typical of the *ancien régime* than of a latter age; although care is needed on this point, as Auckland advanced utilitarian notions within the parameters of the system.

The 'mechanics' of the system were bureaucratic, but not in what would later be seen as a particularly advanced fashion. In 1789, Burges received the congratulations of Edward Mason on becoming joint Under-Secretary in the Foreign Office, as well as the offer of a key item built in 1750:

> I have got a piece of *secretarial* furniture of mahogony [sic], which was of the greatest use to me, when I was in office … It consists of *48* pigeon holes, or two sets of alphabet, the one for letters, placed in them according to the initial letters of the names of the writers of them. The other alphabet for miscellaneous papers, according to the subject matter. There are besides drawers for writing paper, pen and ink etc. There is a large flap, with a lock and key, which shuts up safe all the papers in the pigeon holes, and lets down *ad libitum*, as a pretty large table (with green cloth) to sit to and write upon.[48]

Criticism of Grenville's 'system', or at least methods, is not anachronistic, as doubts were expressed at the time. These are worth considering, as the selection of envoys is a crucial indicator of the extent to which a bureaucratic system can be discerned and is also a vital guide to the prevailing ethos. James Craufurd was to become Resident at Hamburg and subsequently Minister Plenipotentiary at Copenhagen, but in 1795 he wrote from Copenhagen to Burges. The latter had told Craufurd's father

> that the present situation of affairs in Europe had thrown so many diplomatic people out of employment, that you did not think I had any chance of succeeding to this mission … and that you did not remember that it had ever happened that a Secretary of Legation did succeed at once to such an office; and that the usual mode was for the Secretaries of Legation first to pass through that of Secretary of Embassy.

Craufurd accepted the first, but not the second:

> there are many instances of gentlemen going at once from the office
> of Secretary of Legation to that of Minister; full as many, since the
> creation of the employment of Secretary of Legation, as of those who
> have first gone through the employment of Secretary of Embassy. Mr.
> Ewart, from being Secretary of Legation at Berlin, was made Envoy
> Extraordinary and Minister Plenipotentiary if I mistake not at that
> court; Mr. Lindsay, from being Secretary of Legation at Petersburg,
> was appointed Minister at Venice; he indeed gave up that place for
> that of Secretary of Embassy at Paris, but that was his own choice.
> Mr. Drake, from being Secretary of Legation and Chargé d'Affaires
> here, as I am, was sent Minister to Genoa, after having been named
> to Venice. It has, as you know, been very usual for people to get the
> appointment of Envoy or Minister, who have never been in the line
> at all. Now surely there can be no reason why a Secretary of Legation
> should not get one of these appointments as well as these gentlemen;
> they are not, it is to be hoped, more eligible than those who have
> already served in diplomatic capacities; it would be hard if the circum-
> stance of a man's having served as Secretary of Legation were to be
> considered as an obstacle to his getting any particular appointment,
> to which a person who has never been in the line is eligible. As to all
> the Secretaries of Legation going through the office of Secretary of
> Embassy, before they rise to a superior employment, I have only
> farther to observe that, if such a rule were laid down, it would be
> almost shutting the door altogether against us, as even in time of peace,
> supposing that Holland were recovered, and that we sent an embassy
> there and to Paris, we have only three embassies; now there is only
> one, that to Spain. What a time then may a man have to wait before
> he arrives at a mission.

Craufurd was soon to discover that waiting times varied. Hailes was
succeeded at Copenhagen by Lord Robert Fitzgerald, who had been
Minister to Switzerland, but what really struck Craufurd was the appointment of William Wickham as Minister to Switzerland:

> When Lord Grenville laid down the rule of all persons beginning their
> diplomatic career as Secretary of Legation I was not so ignorant of
> these matters as not to know that now and then, when great family

interest intervened, this rule must give way; but I did not think we should be so hardly treated as to have it broken through in favour of an obscure individual, without either interest or services to recommend him ... I should be infinitely obliged to you if you would inform me what I have to expect. All idea of rising by any sort of rotation is now quite out of the question, and is removed to too great a distance, by this constant intrusion of new people, that it requires more patience than I find myself master of, to wait for it.

Wickham had been at Christ Church with Grenville, but he had much more to recommend him, not least having studied in Geneva and being married to a local woman, as well as his recent role as a Swiss-based spymaster. Wickham continued his activities, helping finance the election of royalist deputies in the French elections of 1797.[49]

The use of unofficial agents can also be seen as a qualification of any ready depiction of modernity, although, again, states in the twentieth century frequently employed such agents. The range of unofficial British envoys during the century extended from unaccredited agents of the British Crown to British agents opposed to the British government. The first category included foreigners acting on behalf of the Crown without formal authority. Thus, for example, in 1728 George II considered secretly approaching the Austrians via the Saxons, while General Diemar, the Hesse–Cassel envoy in London, was later employed as a secret conduit for talks with Vienna.[50]

Unofficial agents were more usually British. Some were erstwhile diplomats being used without credentials, while others came from the world of projectors whose prose recurs so often in the papers of eighteenth-century ministers. For example, in 1790, when Britain and Spain seemed close to war in the Nootka Sound Crisis over Pacific trade and settlement, the government sought unofficial links with politicians in the National Assembly in order to dissuade the French from fulfilling their treaty commitments to Spain. William Augustus Miles was sent to Paris in July, Hugh Elliot, formerly envoy in Copenhagen, and a friend of Mirabeau, following in late October. Miles made approaches to Talleyrand, Mirabeau and Lafayette, was elected a member of the Jacobin Club, and seems to have succeeded in lessening suspicion of Britain among the popular politicians. Elliot worked to the same end and, as a more distinguished, though still unofficial, agent appears to have had more success. Elliot's discussions with high-ranking French politicians were carried out with the full knowledge and approval of the envoy, Earl Gower. They enabled the government to follow what Leeds termed 'a double negotiation; *official* with the court, and *private* with the leaders of the Assembly'. This seemed a necessary response to the complexities of a situation of divided authority. Pitt warned Elliot:

> whatever confidential communications may take place with the Diplomatic Committee for the sake of bringing them to promote our views, no ostensible intercourse can be admitted but through the medium of accredited Ministers or the Secretary of State for Foreign Affairs, and that in the name of the King.[51]

Despite the commonplace assertion that the French Revolution transformed diplomacy, this process (like much else in the Revolutionary period) was not in fact a novelty. Instead, the use of unofficial agents, in response to divided authority structures and competing centres of power, had been frequent. Examples can be seen in systems with representative assemblies, such as Poland, Sweden and the United Provinces, as well as in states that lacked them. The role of unofficial agents could be accentuated if the British government was itself divided.

Other agents reflected far deeper divides within the British political structure. The most important was the Jacobite diplomatic net, which developed from 1689 and left an extensive archive in the Stuart Papers in Windsor Castle. Furthermore, the actual or potential appointment of Jacobites as envoys by other powers created difficulties, although when Yorke complained to the French foreign minister about the new Prussian envoy, George Keith, the 10th Earl Marischal of Scotland, the latter responded 'how all courts employed foreigners, that we had French refugiées'. Frederick II claimed to see him as his own subject and one who had ceased to be British.[52]

In addition, it is worth noting representatives of British Jacobitism who travelled abroad to make representations, not only to the Jacobite court, but also to sympathetic rulers and ministers. However, the absence of a closely-knit and united Jacobite group in Britain ensured that most Jacobites who went abroad did so as representatives of themselves or of only some British Jacobites. This was the case, for example, with the missions of Henry Hyde, Viscount Cornbury to Rome to see the Pretender in 1731 and to Paris to seek French military assistance in 1733. Furthermore, others on the fringes of Jacobitism also found it expedient to make such visits. In 1740, Sir William Wyndham, the Tory leader in the Commons, went to Paris to see the Jacobite envoy and the French first minister. Foreign support for Jacobitism posed considerable problems for British envoys and they were instructed to keep an eye on Jacobites.[53]

Such activities did not end with the collapse of Jacobitism. Indeed, the search for foreign support by the American Patriots can be seen in this light. Again, it caused problems for British envoys. Furthermore, in 1791, the envoy in St Petersburg, William Fawkener, found his attempt to persuade Catherine II to heed British views over the Balkans complicated by the arrival of Robert Adair, an agent of the Whig opposition. Burges described Adair as 'sent Ambassador from Burlington House to Petersburg'. Fawkener had a humiliating reception, while Adair was received very well by Catherine, unsurprisingly so as he argued that Pitt was unable to coerce Russia.[54] Not all Fox's allies approved, however, Frederick, 5th Earl of Carlisle, writing: 'It was an egregrious folly in Fox sending a Mr. Adair ... to counteract Mr. Fawkener'.[55]

As the Americans were rebelling against Britain, the British did not face the challenge of deciding how best to respond diplomatically to a new revolutionary state, although unsuccessful attempts were made to negotiate a settlement. In 1776, the military commanders, the Howe brothers, were given authority to treat, and in 1778, Frederick, 5th Earl of Carlisle, was sent as head of a commission 'to treat, consult, and agree upon the means of quieting the disorders'.[56] There were, however, no negotiations as the Americans were intent on independence.

Opposition in the Austrian Netherlands in 1787 which led in 1789 to a declaration of independence posed the challenge of whether to acknowledge a revolutionary state. It was part of a widespread process of disorder in the late 1780s and early 1790s of which the French Revolution was the most important episode. Diplomats were affected. Travelling to The Hague in 1787, Grenville had to give in his name at one town commanded by Free Corps. Leaving Brussels for Warsaw in 1792, William Gardiner observed, 'It seems to be my destiny to reside in countries where anarchy prevails'.[57] Despite pressure from Britain's ally Prussia, which was keen to see Austria weakened, the government adopted a cautious response to the rebellion in the Austrian Netherlands. The Lord Chancellor, Lord Thurlow, pointed out that it was difficult to decide whom to negotiate with in a revolutionary system, and the government was primarily concerned to restore the situation prior to the crisis. The government was willing to talk to Belgian agents in London, and to urge the Belgians to send envoys to negotiate at The Hague on the terms of a return of Habsburg authority, but not to send an envoy.[58]

Jacobitism had tested the identity and coherence of the British state, a fundamental challenge to the loyalty and thus to the monopolistication of representation that diplomacy seeks. This challenge was to be repeated with the French Revolution, although here the issue was social, rather than dynastic, politics. Thus, links between ministers and French *émigrés* were an issue, as were those between British radicals and the French government. Efforts to align Britain under the banners of counter-revolution or the rights of man, especially the latter, represented an attempt to infringe the autonomy and authority of governmental control over the diplomatic process.

The French Revolution also created a crisis in diplomacy, not only because it led, in 1792, to a major war (the first in Western Europe since 1748), in which Britain became involved the following year, but also because the Revolutionaries deliberately rejected the established conventions of diplomatic behaviour.[59] From the outset, suspicion of British intentions harmed relations. Dorset's known attachment to Marie Antoinette and to courtiers opposed to reform posed a problem,[60] but this was exacerbated by the publicity given to an intercepted letter from Dorset to the Count d'Artois, Louis XVI's brother and the leading opponent of reform, congratulating him on his escape from France. Dorset argued that he had written nothing that was incriminating, but, as he pointed out, 'it was sufficient the being spread abroad that I had written to the Comte d'Artois to make me an object of public attention'.[61] The Duke was inaccurately accused of distributing large sums of money in order to foment disturbances; and, in response to criticism in the National Assembly, Dorset, concerned about his own safety and that of his compatriots, wrote to Montmorin, the French Foreign Minister, in order to refute the accusations made against him and to state that Britain favoured good relations. Montmorin communicated the letter to the President of the National Assembly, who read it out publicly.[62] Dorset, who had already sought permission to take a leave of absence already granted him, left Paris on 8 August 1789, never to return.

Dorset was replaced not by the experienced William Eden, who sought the post, but by Lord Robert Fitzgerald, a nephew of the Duke of Richmond who lacked diplomatic experience. Richmond had made it clear to Pitt that Fitzgerald was inexperienced and suggested that it was best if he acquired the diplomatic 'trade' by serving in a court without 'very important business'. Fitzgerald's mission as Minister Plenipotentiary was undistinguished. When his relationship with a married woman ended with her death, he left without leave. He had earlier received very few instructions. One of the few ordered Fitzgerald to destroy all 'the ciphers and deciphers in your Lordship's possessions which might be endangered upon any sudden commotion arising at Paris'. All the enciphered letters Fitzgerald received from any other British envoy were to be sent to London to be deciphered.[63] In effect, the embassy was to be a listening post, not a base for negotiations.

No diplomat of any experience was sent to Paris to succeed Fitzgerald. Instead, in 1790, George, Earl Gower (1758–1833), the eldest son of the Marquess of Stafford, was sent. He had travelled widely and was an MP but had no diplomatic experience.[64]

The challenge posed by the Revolution was made concrete in August 1792 when the violent overthrow of the monarchy led to a breach of diplomatic representation in Paris and to fears about the safety of British diplomats there, not least Gower. The removal of executive power from Louis XVI ensured that diplomatic credentials were no longer valid. It was unclear who was now wielding authority in Paris and what the effect of the Duke of Brunswick's advance on the city would be. The British, Danish, Dutch, Polish, Spanish, Swedish, Swiss and Venetian envoys all left. The Cabinet met on 17 August and decided to recall Gower, in part because of the danger to his life: his Swiss guard had been killed. The government had been horrified by the accounts it had received from Paris. That from Gower's messenger, Morley, was more grisly than the Earl's dispatch. It referred, in the storming of the Tuileries Palace on 10 August, to the mob 'industriously' disfiguring the faces of its victims 'by roasting them' in fires and to an indiscriminate massacre without distinction or age or sex. The Cabinet met twice and sent two agents to Paris to acquire information, but it was Gower's recall that was seen as crucial.[65] Despite concern that he had been stopped en route for the Channel, Gower reached London on 1 September. Burges recorded the end of the panic:

> Lord Gower is at length arrived at one o'clock today, having taken nearly five days to perform his journey from Paris, and not having announced his approach by a single line to anyone. The obstinate sangfroid of this young man perfectly gets to the bottom of my temper. It took me a quarter of an hour to argue with him the propriety of going to Weymouth[66] and of writing to his father and Lord Grenville.

With much ado he was at last convinced that the first was an indispensable duty, and he talks of doing it in a day or two.[67]

The Secretary of Embassy, William Lindsay, arrived a week later, after his threat to leave anyway and let the French take the consequences if he was detained or killed, led to his finally receiving his passport.[68] As the British government refused to acknowledge the new republican government, no replacement was dispatched. The opposition *Morning Chronicle* in its issue of 26 December referred to itself as having a reputation as the 'English Ambassador at Paris'. Had this situation lasted for long then there would have been pressure to end the impasse, but the outbreak of war early in 1793 ensured that the issue of recognition for a *de facto* government was shelved.

The Revolutionary Crisis and the subsequent conflict also thrust foreign policy and diplomacy forward in governmental and public attention. This created opportunities for diplomats. Congratulating William Eliot in 1793 on his appointment to The Hague, Burges wrote:

> You probably will remain for some time without an ambassador; and you must have bad luck, if, in the present distracted state of Europe, some opportunity of distinguishing yourself does not occur. Your predecessor, Lord Henry Spencer, had several, and he availed himself of them so well, as to establish a reputation for ability and good judgement, at a period of life when few young men are supposed to have any. I make no doubt of your succeeding to him in this respect as well as in political situation.[69]

Many missions were focused on military preparations. In 1794, the Earl of Yarmouth was instructed to further Austro-Prussian co-operation, while, in 1795, Colonel Craufurd was sent on a mission to the *émigré* Prince of Condé in order to improve the readiness of his army, and also to get the Austrians to be more active.[70]

However, as the armies of Revolutionary France advanced, so British diplomats had to flee. A sense of the frenetic pace of the latter can be gained from Ralph Heathcote's report of August 1796 from Leipzig. Due to French advances, he had left Mergentheim with the Elector of Cologne, to whom he was accredited, for Nuremberg,

> but I had scarcely reached the latter place when the accounts of the uninterrupted success of the enemy, both on the Upper and Lower

Rhine, became from day to day so alarming, that every hope, of finding a place of security either in that Imperial City or in any other southern place of Germany was necessarily given up entirely.

The Elector left for Leipzig, followed by Heathcote, but 'it was impossible for me to take the direct road ... partly on account of the absolute want of posthorses, and partly because the road was entirely covered as it were by baggage waggons belonging to the Austrian armies ... being then in full retreat'. As a result, Heathcote had to travel via the Upper Palatinate and Bohemia, 'a journey both extremely fatiguing and expensive'. Once in Leipzig, he had to think of fleeing to Hamburg.[71]

The period closed with a sense not only of national danger, but also of a threat to civilized values. In 1799, Grenville wrote to Sir Charles Whitworth about the need for Anglo-Russian co-operation 'for the cause of religion and morality, and for the maintenance of civilized society'.[72]

Yet that had also been the situation at the outset of the period, with the combination of French aggression, Counter-Reformation Catholicism, and a war for Jacobite *revanche* challenging the Revolution Settlement. It is as appropriate, and more so in the long term, to search for change in the need to respond to the developing trans-oceanic situation, specifically the creation of the first independent state of European provenance outside Europe, the United States, and also increased pressure to define acceptable relations with distant non-European states, in the 1790s China and in the 1800s Persia. In 1785, Pitt received a letter from the ever-busy William Miles:

> I have met a Mr. Bingham ... a native of America ... He speaks in the highest terms of admiration of Sir James Harris and laments that a minister of his manners and capacity has not been sent to America. He assured me that the people of property and weight in the United States wish very much for a cordial and permanent reconciliation with Great Britain and that all ranks of people were dissatisfied at the appointment of a man for Consul General who was universally reprobated and detested ... He also assured me that unless some measures were speedily adopted by government, that resolutions would be taken by all the provinces, fatal to our commerce with America.[73]

Thus, Britain was having to come to terms with the problems of decolonization, and to define a diplomacy with the newly independent, as she had not done before. It took time for American political practice and theory to define a response to the conduct and contents of international relations. Thus, as a result of the Longchamps affair in 1784, in which a French diplomat was attacked, the Supreme Court was given jurisdiction over international law and the authority of the individual states subordinated.[74] In 1796, the disclosure of diplomatic papers relating to Anglo-American relations became an issue in the House of Representatives.[75]

George Hammond, the first British Minister Plenipotentiary to the United States, arrived in Philadelphia in October 1791. Early British envoys were not terribly sympathetic to American political culture. However, many of their complaints echoed those of earlier foreign commentators on British politics, for they focused on the difficulties created by both public discussion and governmental change. In 1796, Edward Thornton, Secretary of Legation in the USA, noted support for Britain, but added 'an opinion so fickle and inconstant is scarcely to be relied upon for any length of time'.[76]

There was a legacy of disputes left over from the War of Independence, for example over debts owed to Loyalists. Hammond found the suspicions, indeed hostility, towards British policy of Thomas Jefferson, the American Secretary of State, hindered the progress of negotiations.[77] In addition, there was the issue of British recognition of American sovereignty. This was qualified both by the encouragement of frontier separatists, especially in Vermont[78] and, to a lesser extent, Kentucky, and by continued support for Native Americans in the 'Old North-West'. However, this was primarily a case of policy being set by officials on the ground, especially military commanders in Canada, rather than by the Foreign Secretary and the diplomatic system. The role of frontier disputes and the issue of the Native Americans was such that relations with the United States provided the best example of the potential clash between formal diplomacy and other agencies of the British state. Prior to the establishment of formal representation, there was also the issue of informal diplomacy. In 1790, during the Nootka Sound Crisis, George Beckwith, a British agent in New York, although not an accredited envoy, explored the possibilities of better relations in discussions with Alexander Hamilton, the Secretary of the Treasury, although different views about the fate of any conquests from Spain prevented these talks from being taken further.[79]

In the case of the USA, there was a common language, and a background in the Western diplomatic tradition: the USA followed the Swiss Confederation and the United Provinces in rising from rebellion to assured sovereign status. The situation was less clear elsewhere, although, in the case of the Ottoman Empire and the Barbary States of North Africa, relations had been defined through frequent contact in the seventeenth century. Indeed, the latter were happy to accept bilateral agreements that conformed to established European diplomatic practice.[80]

Elsewhere, there was not such a tradition of regular contact and established practice. The need to create one interacted with the problems created as the diplomacy of imperialism gathered pace. War with France in North America, Africa and India accentuated the interacting pressures of fear and opportunity that helped to drive forward Britain's diplomatic engagements with the non-European world. Much of this represented a continuation of the diplomacy of periods of peace, and this was the case with the opening to China. Yet, the process was pushed forward in wartime with greater urgency and with more of a sense of denying the resources of the extra-European world to France and her allies and, instead, employing them to Britain's ends.[81] This sense of potential was captured by George Staunton when he wrote from China in November 1793 about the Macartney mission: 'there is a foundation laid for a great deal more in time'.[82] This was not, in fact, to be the case, but reflected the interest in long-term benefit.

Diplomacy with non-European powers involved a number of problems. These included arriving at a shared understanding of the meaning and content of representations and agreements. Overlapping with, and in addition to this process, the British sought to project the values of European diplomacy. This was far from easy, not least because diplomatic practices elsewhere frequently were very different. After a meeting with the Grand Vizier in 1736, Fawkener reported from Constantinople in 1736:

> I hope your Grace will not think I have taken too much upon myself; it has been a constant principle with me to avoid laying myself under any engagements ... Forms and modes are not indeed much to be insisted on here, and allowance must be made to manners, custom and education; and on these considerations I flatter myself His Majesty will not think his great and sacred character has been made too free with in the frequent direct address of a subject; this court follows their old forms, and matters of ceremony in the commerce between His Majesty's Crown and them have never been closely attended to.

In North America,

diplomacy could not be a matter of technical agreements secretly contrived by a few leaders. To be effective the process must culminate in public, participatory, and consensual rituals involving diverse constituents not only rhetorically but economically, through the exchange of goods ... Alliances ... required periodic collective affirmation.[83]

In North America, the British sought to create a practice of agreement with those who they hoped could direct their people, but this entailed moulding native politics, as such leaders were frequently not in evidence. Nevertheless, 'kings' were required in order to validate treaties and thus agree land transfer. Thus in 1718, Olumapies, whom the British treated as 'king' of the Unami Delawares, agreed a treaty confirming Delaware land sales to the British.[84]

Diplomacy towards the American Natives was both extensive and complex. This was in part because the chain of command in dealing with the Natives was less than clear, and the individual colonies, Superintendents for Indian Affairs,[85] the military, the Board of Trade, the ministry etc. had different, and often competing, agendas. Individual colonies launched offensives, as in 1724 when Governor Shute of Massachusetts sent an expedition into modern Maine to destroy the mission of the French Jesuit Sebastian Râle at Norridgewock, and thus French influence among the eastern Abenakis. There were also less official intermediaries, especially Indian traders, such as Lachlan McGillivray, who served as an intermediary with the Creeks. His place and power rested on the ability to act on behalf of two worlds.[86] The extension of trading networks had consequences in terms of relations with Natives. For example, in the 1720s, merchants established temporary posts on the upper Ohio and on an eastern tributary of the Wabash. Further complicating the issue was the diversity of relations the Crown and each colony had with the various tribes, as well as the enormous range of knowledge the competing groups had of the Natives.

As contemporaries in Britain widely recognized, the Natives were hardly one people with the potential for unification. Even when they were most united against the British in 1763, several tribes remained on the British side through diplomacy. That year, the British state found itself involved in war as a consequence essentially of tensions arising from the actions of individuals that it had been unable to control. British American merchants acted in an arbitrary fashion and settlers moved into Native lands, breaking agreements.[87]

Recent work has advanced the thesis that Europeans living in North America and Natives had to create a new culture that drew from both sides in order to co-exist, creating a 'middle group'. Trade and criminal justice were part of this relationship and diplomacy was interwoven with both.[88] Older studies offer much on the detail of links, but less on cultural issues and they do not portray the Native perspective well.[89] Alongside the British–Native relationship, there was the context and issues created by the role of rival European powers and, from 1775, the Americans.[90]

In West Africa, the British posts were not held by sovereign right but by agreement with local powers. Rent or tribute was paid for several posts. The Royal African Company and, from 1750, its successor, the Company of Merchants Trading to Africa, had a role similar to that of the East India Company in the early eighteenth century. As in the situation in India, limited sovereignty did not prevent active intervention in local politics. The interaction between the companies and the African states depended upon the ability of the companies' officials to maintain a beneficial relationship with numerous local *caboceers* (leaders) and *penyins* (elders) through an elaborate, and costly, system of presents, dashees and jobs. The British distinguished between presents, which they gave, and dashees, which the Africans demanded. The companies served both private interests (through the slave and African trade), and public (by representing Britain in West Africa).[91] However, Senegambia, the area conquered from the French in the Seven Years' War, was organized as a Crown colony. The Sierra Leone Company was chartered in 1791 to organize and expand the British presence around Freetown, but it did not become a colony until 1807.

In India, European and native practice in diplomacy seems to have been converging, and Europeans had little difficulty in adjusting to what seems to have been an established system of *vakils* (agents) at courts. At Bombay, Calcutta and Madras the Company received *vakils* who dealt personally with the Governor or Governor General. They, in turn, appointed Residents at Indian courts, who dealt with ministers, rather than directly with the ruler. The official language on both sides was Persian. Knowledge of Persian and Indian courtly etiquette led to the promotion of John Kennaway. William Kirkpatrick, Resident to the Maratha Prince Sindia in 1786–7 and to the Nizam of Hyderabad in 1794–7, was regarded as excellent in Persian and had also learned Indian languages.[92]

Prior to Lord North's Regulating Act (1773), the three presidencies—Bombay, Calcutta and Madras—each received *vakils* and conducted their own relations with the Indian princes, with the Company's *ad hoc* Secret

Committee of the East India Company and the Court of Directors providing distant supervision. After the Regulating Act, Calcutta was given a vaguely defined supervisory authority over the foreign relations of Bombay and Madras, and the Company was required to show despatches and consult the Cabinet on matters regarding war, peace and other crucial issues. This led to problems, not only when the Cabinet, which was especially distracted by other imperial concerns after 1773, knew little and cared less about Indian affairs, but also when Bombay and Madras failed to accept Calcutta's supervision and appealed to London. The origins, course and settlement of both the first Maratha War (1778–82) and the second Mysore war (1780–4) show instances of Madras and Bombay conducting their relations with the Indian princes independent of Calcutta. Also, in the late 1770s, Calcutta and Madras each had their own representatives at Hyderabad.

After Pitt's India Act (1784), a clear chain of authority was established whereby the Governor-General was legally responsible for Company relations with the Indian princes. The Governor-General in turn reported to the now statutory Secret Committee of the East India Company which wrote despatches dealing with war and peace and relations with other powers at the behest of the Board of Control, a committee linked through overlapping personnel with the Cabinet.

After 1784, within India all matters regarding relations with the Indian princes were channelled to Calcutta and the Residents posted to the major powers of India, the Peshwa of Pune/Poona, the Nizam of Hyderabad and Sindia, received their instructions from the Governor-General. In the late eighteenth century (and later) routine affairs with minor powers, most notably those between Madras, and both Arcot and Tanjore, and between Bombay and the Malabar chieftains, were handled by the Governors under the supervision of Governors-General. In such dealings, Madras and Bombay received and negotiated with *vakils* and instructed Residents.

In 1770, George Paterson, secretary to Commodore Sir John Lindsay, Commander-in-Chief in the East Indies, noted in his diary problems between the East India Company's Bombay Council and the ruler of Mysore, Haider Ali:

> Hyder threatened to detain the two Bombay gentlemen sent to negotiate with him unless they should conclude such a treaty with him as the Governor and Council of Madras had done. The Council have represented strongly against this measure; and told him of the sacred

character of ambassadors: but he minds this little and has told them that it is for such reasons he desired two gentlemen to be sent to him.[93]

Sir John Shore, Governor-General in India in 1793–8, observed of the ministers of the Maratha 'paramount government' in Pune/Poona: 'they trust to delay and procrastination as the safest rules of political conduct; jealousy and suspicion form an essential part of their character.' Negotiations with the Marathas were also affected by differences in diplomatic method. For example, Kirkpatrick found Sindia offensive and the Maharaja thought him haughty, while, in November 1803, Arthur Wellesley was unwilling to negotiate with Jaswant Rao Ghorpade, the *vakil* from Sindia, unless he produced full powers, i.e. satisfactory credentials. However, the envoy claimed that it was not customary for members of the nobility to carry letters.[94]

There was also the need to define the position of the British, and other Indian powers, with reference to the Mughal Emperor. Sir William Norris, sent to the Emperor Aurangzeb as King's Commissioner in order to obtain support for the New East India Company, offended the Chief Vizier in 1701 by refusing to visit him unless he was received in the European style, a request that was rejected. Norris' lack of diplomatic skills and the deficiencies of his interpreter also contributed to the poor impression he made. In theory, all powers, including the East India Company, which was granted the Diwani of Bengal by the Treaty of Allahbad in 1765, were subject to the Emperor. The fluid state of Indian politics, in which the power of the Emperor greatly declined from the early decades of the eighteenth century, entailed problems in determining how best to define legal settlements with Indian rulers. Sovereignty was an issue for the British, as they sought to interpret and extend conditional and limited grants and other rights.

Racialism does not appear to have been a hallmark of diplomatic relations in the late eighteenth century. Residents, including the Anderson brothers, John Collins, John Kennaway, the Kirkpatrick brothers, Charles Malet and William Palmer, cannot be described as providing examples of British racialism in anything like the way that might be employed to describe the Wellesleys. While the exclusion of Indians from the upper echelons of the Company-state's administration started under Cornwallis in the mid-1780s, it picked up pace under Wellesley in the 1800s. The Wellesley brothers were not old India hands.

However, differences of method rather than racialism itself may well have been the issue. In the specific case of 1803, Jaswant Rao Ghorpade was using delay and procrastination at a time when Arthur Wellesley needed a rapid settlement of victory or peace with Sindia before he could turn against Holkar. He could not allow Sindia to stay in the field inhabiting a nether-world between peace and war with the Company whilst keeping his options open through negotiations with the other Maratha princes.

Power and sovereignty were both asserted by military and diplomatic means and the two were closely intertwined. As the British relied on Indian resources, both military and political, diplomacy played a major role in securing power at the same time as it advanced claims and commitments that entailed the fresh display, and maintenance, of power. British strength in large part depended on an ability to secure support within India, and to prevent hostile leagues, and that required diplomatic skills not only in negotiation, but also in reporting on a fast-changing situation. Thus, Charles Malet, Resident at Pune/Poona since 1785, was made a baronet in 1791 for his success the previous year in winning Maratha co-operation against Tipu Sultan. His successors, Colonel William Palmer and Adjutant-General Barry Close, had a military background. Close had also carried out frontier negotiations with Mysore in the 1780s and was Resident in Mysore in 1799–1801 before serving at Pune in 1801–11. Close's replacement, Mountstuart Elphinstone, had fought in the Maratha war in 1803, before becoming Resident at the court of Raguji Bhonsle II, Maharaja of Berar, at Nagpur, and then in 1808 being appointed envoy to the ruler of Afghanistan.[95] John Collins, Resident at the court of Sindia from 1799 to 1803, had been an officer in the East India Company army. In 1799, Collins was sent to secure the alleged murderer of George Cherry, Resident at Benares. Kirkpatrick was also an officer in the East India Company army. Aside from his Residencies, he led a short mission to Nepal in 1792. This brief extension of the diplomatic network was sent in response to conflict between China and Nepal. At the same time as Malet was made a baronet, Kennaway was made one for engaging in the similarly delicate task of negotiating the Treaty of Pangal, which secured the Nizam's assistance in the war against Tipu Sultan.

At times, British policy involved a particularly blunt conflation of diplomacy and force. The successful resolution of the Dutch crisis in 1787 led Earl Cornwallis, Governor-General and Commander-in-Chief in India, to press the East India Company's claim, under a 1768 treaty with the Nizam of Hyderabad, to the circar or fief of Guntoor (Guntur). Certain that the Nizam, bereft of external support, would be compliant, Cornwallis was nevertheless determined to act firmly. He sent Kennaway, then his aide-de-camp, 'who is perfectly master of the languages, and who has already some knowledge of the Courts of Hindoostan', to Hyderabad as a temporary Resident, but also took pre-emptive action:

> it will be most expedient that our troops should march into the Circar on Captain Kennaway's arrival at Masulipatam; and that our present Resident Meer Hussein should about ten days before inform the Nizam of our intention giving the most positive assurances that our design was entirely limited to the taking possession of the Circar as our undoubted right by treaty and that Captain Kennaway had orders to settle the account in the most fair manner.

The Nizam complied without resistance, and Britain's domination of India's eastern coast was strengthened.[96] In 1792, Kennaway even more clearly benefited from force when he negotiated the Treaty of Seringapatam with the defeated Tipu: Cornwallis' forces were encamped outside Tipu's capital.

In India, the East India Company's presence as a native power was given direction by British assumptions and requirements. There, as elsewhere, representation acted as a focus for different drives and requirements.

Issues of rank had to be negotiated anew outside Europe. In some respects, the situation was similar: diplomatic rank was often seen as dependent on, and necessarily flowing from, social rank. However, it was difficult to circumvent the issue by dispatching high-ranking envoys. With his experience as a colonial administrator, in both India and the West Indies, Macartney could be appointed to the China embassy, but this was not intended as a long posting, and, in general, high-ranking potential diplomats were very reluctant to leave Europe. This created problems. In 1804, the Dey of Algiers took the 'low degree' of the new Consul at Algiers as an insult and refused to receive him. His predecessor

> had been an officer, but was more a country gentleman than anything else. A very honest, honourable man, but very little qualified for that or any other employment; he was appointed to it by the interest of the Egertons with the Duke of Portland. The Dey was much flattered at being told he was a man of family, and that his brother was in Parliament: he liked him, and imputed every thing he disliked to Mr.

174

Falcon his Secretary, to whom he took a great dislike. When Mr. Master was appointed Governor of Tobago: Mr. Falcon was by the same interest appointed to succeed him. I really think it was very impolitic to send a man whom the Dey knows as a Secretary at £100 a year, and whom he looked upon as a man of low degree, as Consul, to the place where he was before an humble Secretary. The Dey looked upon it as an insult ... Mr. Falcon is not much a gentleman, but a man of pretty good abilities, and a man of business. I believe he has conducted himself very well ... he should not have been sent there. A subaltern officer would have been more respected, and would therefore have been better. The prejudices of the ignorant must be attended a little to.[97]

This was not the only instance of pressure for enhanced social or diplomatic representation. Indeed, two months later, Samuel Manesty, the Resident at Basra, sought promotion to become Envoy to Persia, arguing that such a mark of royal favour would be beneficial to British interests in the Near East. Equally, Manesty's request indicated the role of turf wars, careerism and jealousy in British representation, and, specifically, the possible tensions arising from representation and its control at a distance. On the spot, and away from authority, Manesty volunteered to go to Tehran when Wellesley's envoy, Jonathan Lovett, having reached Bushire, relinquished his post due to failing health. Manesty assembled a sizeable entourage, but, fearing reprisals from Wellesley for doing so without permission and with big ideas about the shape Anglo-Persian relations should take, he thought that royal credentials would protect him from the Governor-General's wrath. While Wellesley sent Lovett on a modest mission to deliver a letter of condolence to the Shah concerning the death of a Persian diplomat at Bombay two years previously, Manesty had other ideas. He travelled to Tehran in style, spent money lavishly on gifts and entertainments and, upon delivering Wellesley's letter, at which point his mission ought to have ended, he, without any authorization, talked with the Persian government about Britain's great and vital interests in the Gulf and the Caucasus and how he would travel to St Petersburg via London and act as a mediator between Russia and Persia over differences over Georgia and Azerbaijan. Wellesley condemned Manesty's unauthorized conduct and refused to pay his bills: £105,000 spent in less than a year. Unable to pay his creditors, Manesty left Tehran in a hurry.[98]

Diplomacy outside Europe created problems, but the extension of the range of British diplomacy was an aspect of a newly gained great power status. For Britain, this was also a facet of modernity, although that term has to be employed without suggesting a teleology, or even more a beneficient disposition, that would be inappropriate. In conclusion, it is necessary to consider whether the quality and operation of diplomacy helped or hindered this great power status. Such an approach takes on greater weight if it is argued that the powers of this period owed success and failure not so much to structural factors, such as resources and economic capability, as to the play of contingency in particular conjunctures. More specifically, military success and diplomatic combination interacted.[99] Such an approach necessarily directs attention to the factors that affected military and diplomatic actions. As the role of choice is emphasized, so emphasis is directed to individual qualities, to the ability to appreciate and direct, or at least influence, events. Thus, the quality of diplomacy is at issue. This does not have to mean that British diplomats were better than those elsewhere, but rather that they operated effectively in terms of British interests as they were presented to them by governments. This process was not without problems, not least because perceptions of interests, and of how best to further them, varied.

Yet, allowing for a stress on variety, the reader has a right to anticipate a conclusion in the shape of an overall impression. The nature of the diplomatic organization did not conform to the bureaucratic assumptions entailed by the term diplomatic service in the late Victorian period, and by 1800 there had been only limited development in specialization of function, the creation of a system of promotion by merit and seniority, bureaucratic professionalization (as opposed to learning on the job and long service), and an infrastructure of, for example, buildings and staff.[100]

However, accepting these limitations, and the inchoate processes involved in recruitment, pay and, to an extent, control, there were many envoys who acquired considerable experience through long service and thus became professionals,[101] and most diplomats operated effectively. Partly because of that, there was little pressure for new methods, either from within or, even more, outside the diplomatic sense. Furthermore, although there were shifts in emphasis, such as the decline in the role of Hanover under George III, it is continuity rather than change that is most apparent. The system was 'fit for purpose', in terms of a combination of regular reporting and *ad hoc* negotiating. Alongside deficiencies and failures, there was a steady competence.

Appendix

Sources

Your idea of bringing England and France to be peaceful neighbours, without jealousy, rivalship or mutual inveteracy is a perfectly just one—but as impossible in execution as the Republic of Plato—If ever we cease to suspect France of being our enemy, if ever we suffer it (when it is in our power to prevent it,) to increase its riches, its influence and strength, and if we ever omit an opportunity for sinking, distressing, and keeping it under, we should be guilty of the highest political folly, and the minister who advises such measures, will deserve something more than dismission.

Sir James Harris to Hugh Elliot, 17 January 1786

An understanding of the nature of diplomacy and the role of diplomats requires an appreciation of the available sources. More particularly, it requires moving away from the formal records of foreign policy in the Public Record Office in London and, instead, searching for informal records. Harris' letter cited above is instructive because it reflects the disquiet of an experienced diplomat about the government's policy of improving relations with France. The letter survives in volume 12999 of the Elliot papers in the National Library of Scotland.

More generally, probably as a result of the absence of revolution or violent political change since the eighteenth century, numerous collections of manuscripts survive in the British Isles that were originally private, although many of them have been deposited in public archives. It is thus possible to supplement and qualify the state records. This is a crucial process because it is clear that too narrow a concentration on official diplomatic correspondence can be misleading. The Foreign Secretary, Lord Grenville explained to one diplomat, Thomas, 7th Earl of Elgin in 1792, 'that my constant practice is to consider *private* letters as really such, and that they never find their way into the office, or into official circulation'.[1]

Attempts to acquire sensitive diplomatic material were sometimes made for political ends. Seeking evidence against the previous, Tory, ministry, the Whigs in 1715 sought the papers of Matthew Prior, Plenipotentiary in France in 1712–15.[2] In 1792, the papers of Joseph Ewart became involved in the politics of justification, as politicians sought to make political capital out of the Ochakov crisis or to avoid condemnation. Ewart had complained that Morton Eden had refused to let him have documents he wished to keep. Ewart's brother returned to Burges the letters he had written Ewart, and whose return Burges had sought. Eden, however, was still concerned. He informed Auckland that the opposition had sought to purchase the papers from Ewart's widow, and suggested that the government should seek to obtain them. Auckland was less concerned, and the papers remained within the family. Today, they are held at Williamwood by a direct descendant.[3]

The following chapter rests on over twenty years of searching for such papers. A note on organization is required at the outset. It might seem that the obvious task would be a listing of diplomats and their papers. This, however, is not appropriate for two reasons. First, and most significantly, the papers of an individual largely consist of their 'in' correspondence. Relatively few diplomats kept copies of their 'out' correspondence. They would use a secretary to keep an office copy of their official reports, but private correspondence was a different matter. As a consequence, an attempt to record the 'out' correspondence of diplomats would necessitate a listing and discussion of the enormous range of receiving sources. This is not possible for the second reason, that of space. This book is not a finding-list, a task best handled elsewhere,[4] and the section on sources is constrained for that reason. However, it has been made more necessary by the 1994 decision of the Royal Commission on Historical Manuscripts to abandon their proposed guide to the papers of British statesmen and politicians for the period 1660–1782. This chapter focuses on the types of sources that contain the correspondence of diplomats. This is designed to indicate the range of material that has to be consulted. At once, this throws light on the subject of this book, as well as the foreign policy of the period, provides guidance to future scholars, and highlights the limitation of much of the available scholarship. The organization is as follows:

Public Record Office
British Library

Other British National Archives
County Record Offices
Other Public Collections Outside London
Private Collections
Foreign Material.

Public Record Office

The Public Record Office holds, most obviously, State Papers Foreign and the Foreign Office series. These have been worked on extensively, but it is often the case that readers do not appreciate that letters from a given diplomat may appear in a series other than that of the court to which he was accredited. In addition, even if study is restricted to bilateral diplomatic relations, it is necessary to look at more than the correspondence with the relevant envoys, because much contact between states could occur through other channels, not least in other locations.

Anglo-Russian relations in the 1720s and 1730s provides an example. Thus, Chesterfield reported from The Hague in 1732 about an approach for an alliance from the Russian envoy, Count Golovkin.[5] Similarly, that year, there is material in State Papers, Germany (Emperor) about contacts in Vienna in 1732 between Robinson and the Tsarina's favourite and envoy, Count Levenwold.[6] A major underrated source for Russia in these years is State Papers, Hamburg. This was not so much because of the important commercial links, but rather the bustling, self-important figure of Sir Cyril Wych, who represented Britain in the Hanse towns from 1713 until 1741, when he was posted to Russia, where he served from 1742 until 1744. Wych was of importance because he had very close links with the court of Holstein-Gottorp, which was then in Russia: in 1724 the Duke, Charles Frederick, had married Peter the Great's elder daughter by his second wife. In seeking appointment as British envoy to Russia in 1725, Wych stressed his close links, and other commentators noted the same. In 1735, the British government gave Wych permission to accept the Duke's offer of the Order of St Anne.[7] Much of Wych's information derived from the Holstein connection,[8] and this made his reports valuable, as British diplomats in Russia, such as Claudius Rondeau, tended to have poor relations with the Holstein court. State Papers Saxony–Poland throw light on another attempt to create Anglo-Russian links, in this case an unsuccessful British approach in 1725.[9]

Aside from State Papers Foreign, it is also important not to forget the very important material in State Papers Regencies. Furthermore, although State Papers Confidential (107), the product of British success at postal interception and deciphering,[10] largely refers to the situation in Britain, and negotiations there, there are also references to British diplomats.

PRO. 30 (Gifts and Deposits) includes a number of relevant collections in which diplomatic correspondence appears, such as Chatham, Cornwallis, Egremont, Gower and Neville-Aldworth papers. The papers of William Pitt the Elder and the Younger in the first, especially those of Pitt the Younger, contain much useful material for their periods in high office. For example, PRO. 30/8/110 consists of letters from William Eden to Pitt the Younger. They are especially valuable for his negotiation of the trade treaty with France in 1786, and, in some respects, throw more light on this negotiation than Eden's reports to the Foreign Secretary, the Marquis of Carmarthen, in PRO. FO. 7/19–20. Similarly, there are crucial letters from Joseph Ewart in Berlin in 1790–1 in PRO. 30/8/133. The Cornwallis Papers offer insights into the character of East India Company diplomacy in India in the late 1780s and early 1790s when Cornwallis was Governor-General. Charles, 2nd Earl of Egremont was a Secretary of State (1761–3), Richard Aldworth Neville an Under-Secretary (1748–51), and George, Earl Gower, Envoy in Paris (1790–2).

The PRO also contains the papers of individual diplomats. PRO. SP. 110/6–8 contains those of Onslow Burrish, an active, but low-ranking, diplomat in the 1740s and 1750s. His correspondents included most of the British diplomats of the day: Albemarle, Chesterfield, Cope, Cressener, Dayrolle, Dickens, Gray, Hanbury Williams, Holdernesse, Keith, Robinson, Sandwich, Trevor, Villettes, Villiers and Yorke.

The correspondence of John Augustus, Lord Hervey, envoy in Florence 1787–94, was presented to the Foreign Office in 1952 and is now held in the PRO as FO. 528. Additional material (as well as copies of FO. 528) are held as part of the Hervey Collection in the West Suffolk Record Office. The Jackson Papers (FO. 353) are a valuable source for the 1790s and 1800s. Francis Jackson, the eldest son of Thomas Jackson, the former tutor of the Foreign Secretary, served as Secretary of Legation at Berlin (1789–91) and then at Madrid, before becoming Ambassador at Constantinople in 1796. His papers include important private correspondence with such diplomats as Hailes and Liston.

British Library

This has numerous relevant holdings, including, in the Additional Manuscripts series, the Althorp, Auckland, Blakeney, Blathwayt, Drake, Dropmore, Essex, Fox, Grantham, Grenville, Hardwicke, Hill, Holland House, Keene, Keith, Liverpool, Lynch, Mitchell, Mountstuart, Newcastle, Norris, Paget, Raby, Robinson, Shirley, Skinner, Stepney, Townshend, Trumbull, Tyrawly, Weston and Whitworth papers; in the Egerton series, Gunning, Holdernesse, Leeds, Titley, Townshend and Vernon material; and, in the Stowe series, the papers of James Craggs, Richard Phelps, Jean de Robethon and Alexander Stanhope. This is by no means an exhaustive list. There is also, for example, the correspondence of Henry Davenant in the Birch papers (Add. 4740–7, 4291), and many of Schaub's letters (Add. 35837 for example). For unofficial diplomatic activity, there are the papers of Nathaniel Forth for the 1770s (Add. 65145–52).

Aside from the papers of diplomats it is important to consider those of Secretaries of State. For example, the Fox Papers contain relevant material for 1782–3, including letters from Fitzherbert, Thomas Grenville, Harris, Manchester, Stepney and Thomas Walpole. The Dropmore papers include the papers of Lord Grenville, who became Foreign Secretary in 1791. Letters from a number of diplomats, including Auckland, Drake, Elgin, Ewart, Gardiner, Hailes, Hammond and Lindsay, can be found in this collection. As is usually the case, the printed version is less extensive.[11] This directs attention to the need to consult manuscript sources even when printed material is available.

The relevant holdings are growing appreciably, the three most important recent accessions being the Blenheim, Althorp and Wolterton papers. The former has now appeared in a microfilm edition, while the British Library has also published a catalogue. Aside from the correspondence of diplomats with John, 1st Duke of Marlborough, the collection also includes the papers of his son-in-law, Charles Spencer, 3rd Earl of Sunderland, who was a Secretary of State in 1706–10 and 1717–18. This is doubly valuable, as problems for the State Papers for this period were noted as early as 1789 by the then Foreign Secretary, Francis, 5th Duke of Leeds:

> I have been looking into the Vienna Correspondence of 1705 and 6. I heartily wish it contained less Latin, and that Lord Sunderland and Stepney had been supplied with better ink; many of their dispatches

being scarcely legible, and apparently written in dirty water or lemon juice at most.[12]

Among the interesting information provided by the Blenheim collection is that relating to rivalry and tension in the diplomatic corps. These are topics that are all too elusive in the official correspondence, but that are of great importance, both as indicators of overall effectiveness and for the light they throw on particular negotiations. In 1717, Abraham Stanyan wrote from Vienna about his counterpart in Constantinople, Edward Wortley-Montagu, with whom he was supposed to be co-operating in order to arrange a mediated settlement of the Austro-Turkish war:

> I did not think it hitherto proper for me to let your Lordship know how little the ministers of this court are satisfied with Mr. Wortley's conduct, lest my information might be thought to proceed from ill will, or a desire to supplant him; but having now reason to believe your Lordship will be fully informed of that matter both from hence and at London, I think myself at liberty to acquaint you that the ministers have made no scruples of saying they can repose no confidence in him, nor rely upon the informations he may send them; so that the King seems to be reduced to the necessity of employing another minister for that business, or of losing the honour of the mediation, as well as the advantages it may bring to his affairs both here and in Turkey.[13]

The Althorp collection includes the papers of Stephen Poyntz, whose daughter Georgina married John, 1st Earl Spencer. Poyntz was envoy in Stockholm (1724–7), and subsequently a Plenipotentiary at the Congress of Soissons and one of the British envoys at Paris (1728–30). The Wolterton collection, acquired by Private Treaty Sale in 1993, includes the papers of Horatio Walpole, the younger brother of Sir Robert. Secretary to James Stanhope in Spain in 1706–7, he was Secretary of Embassy at The Hague in 1709–11 and senior envoy there in 1715–16, 1722, 1734–7 and 1739, as well as being at Paris in 1723–30. Though Archdeacon William Coxe employed these papers for his *Memoirs of Horatio, Lord Walpole* (1802), this used only a fraction of the then available correspondence. The collection also includes letters from St Saphorin to Queen Caroline, from Robert Trevor to Walpole (1736–46), from Couraud, Weston and Stone (1746), correspondence between Vanneck and Thomas Walpole in 1755–6 concerning Anglo-French relations, the papers of Sir Everard Fawkener, envoy in Constantinople 1735–42, and those of William Fawkener for 1791 when he was sent to St Petersburg to find an acceptable retreat from the Ochakov crisis. The latter include originals and copies of letters to Fawkener from Auckland, Burges, Ewart and Jackson, from Whitworth and Fawkener to Ainslie, Grenville and Keith, and from Elgin to Grenville.

Other recently acquired collections include the Trumbull papers, which contain a wealth of material for the 1680s and 1690s when Sir William Trumbull was envoy in Paris and Constantinople, additional Stepney material, comprising letters sent him in 1691–1706 (Add. 71171), and the papers of Thomas Hopkins, which include letters from Stanyan from Zurich and Berne in 1705–6 (Add. 64928). The Portland Loan, which has now been permanently allocated to the British Library, contains much material in the papers of Robert Harley for the diplomatic history of Anne's reign. There are his letter-books as Secretary of State, 1704–8, papers relating to the Treaty of Utrecht of 1713, general correspondence, and the diplomatic papers of William Greg, Secretary in Copenhagen, who was placed in charge of affairs there in 1704. Material from Bowood throws light on William, 2nd Earl of Shelburne's period as Secretary of State for the Southern Department, 1766–8. To indicate the rate and variety of new deposits, collections added in the late 1990s included not only material from Bowood, but also letters from Henry St John, Viscount Bolingbroke to Thomas Wentworth, 1st Earl of Strafford for 1711–13 when Strafford was at The Hague and Plenipotentiary at the peace negotiations in The Hague,[14] and also letters from Lord Grenville to Sir Morton Eden (Vienna) for 1798–9.[15]

The collections in the British Library include much material on the problems of being a diplomat. Inadequate and late pay were frequent topics of complaint. Whitworth argued in 1714 that 'in any employment abroad I am to consider three things, the place, the business, and the salary'.[16] Rank was also important, Titley, for example, being most concerned to become an Envoy Extraordinary in 1739. Not all diplomats were dissatisfied, the muscular Hugh Elliot writing from Regensburg, where he was Minister in 1776:

> I am content, pleased and honoured with my situation; there is scarcely any in the foreign department more agreable or better adapted to one so unexperienced in business as myself ... There is little of the hurry or dissipation of what is called pleasure in large capitals; but, on the

other hand, regular hours, health, and leisure make more than amends for the want of it.[17]

Other British National Archives

The range of material available is indicated by the Sandwich papers in the National Maritime Museum. John, 4th Earl was not only Secretary of State for the Northern Department in 1763–5, but also an important diplomat in 1746–9: Minister Plenipotentiary at The Hague and at the peace conferences of Breda (1746) and Aix-la-Chapelle (1748). Much of his correspondence at the NMM consists of original letters to Sandwich that are unobtainable elsewhere. This includes letters from other diplomats, including Burrish, Dayrolle, Hyndford, Keith, Legge, Villettes and Hanbury Williams. There is also private correspondence for diplomats for his period as a Secretary of State. In contrast, the Cadogan papers in the House of Lords contain nothing of value for the diplomatic career of the 1st Earl.

The National Library of Scotland has relevant material in the Elliot and Liston papers. Hugh Elliot (1752–1830) served at Munich, a post that included representation at the Imperial Diet at Regensburg (1774–6), Berlin (1777–83), Copenhagen (1783–9), Dresden and Naples. Elliot was recalled from Naples after trying to prevent Lieutenant-General Sir James Henry Craig from withdrawing his force from vulnerable Naples to Sicily in 1806. While at Copenhagen, Elliot played a role in the Danish coup of 1784, which brought Crown Prince Frederick to power, and was largely responsible for ending the Dano-Swedish war of 1788. He also went on a secret mission to Paris in late 1790, designed to prevent France from supporting Spain during the Nootka crisis: correspondence about this survives in his papers. These papers also throw much light on the views of other diplomats. For example, volume 12966 contains letters from James Harris in 1774–82 during his missions to Berlin and St Petersburg. Only five of these were printed in the 1844 edition of Harris' diaries and correspondence, although that contains two other letters from Harris to Elliot of 1782, neither of which are in this volume. Another box contains a valuable series of letters from Joseph Ewart in Berlin in 1788–9.

Liston was private secretary to Elliot on his missions to Munich, Regensburg and Berlin, taking charge in Elliot's absences, for example from Berlin in May 1779 to April 1780. Liston served at Madrid as Minister Plenipotentiary in 1783–8, then at Stockholm as Envoy Extraordinary in

1788–92, before going on to Constantinople (1794–6), Washington (1796–1802), The Hague (1802–4) and Constantinople (1812–21). His papers include personal correspondence from other diplomats. For example, William Eden's letters in 1787–8 offer an interesting insight on the development of his views.

The papers of the Earl of Crawford and Balcarres have been deposited in the National Library of Scotland, having previously been in the John Rylands Library in Manchester. This collection includes the correspondence and papers of Robert Keith and his son, Sir Robert Murray Keith. The latter include details of his dispute with the Duke of Leeds as Foreign Secretary in 1788–9, arising from Keith's bitter complaint that he was being ignored, and also interesting letters concerning international developments in 1791, not least those from Auckland.

The Scottish Record Office holds a mass of under-utilized material relating to the Paris embassy of the 2nd Earl of Stair in 1715–20. Most of this was not printed by John Murray Graham in his *Annals and Correspondence of the Viscount and First and Second Earls of Stair* (2 vols, 1875). The archive also holds the papers of John Viscount Dalrymple, later 6th Earl of Stair, envoy in Warsaw 1782–4 and Berlin 1785–7, but these simply duplicate his reports to the Foreign Secretary and his letters to Keith. The only relevant papers in the National Library of Wales are those of Thomas Lewes. This includes Hanbury Williams' account of the court of Dresden in 1747, but is otherwise unimportant.

Material in the Public Record Office of Northern Ireland include letters from James, 2nd Lord Tyrawly as envoy to Portugal in 1739 and 1762; letters to Sir Robert Murray Keith in 1776–7, including from Stormont, Ainslie, Elliot and Morton Eden; the papers of Francis Wilson, Chargé d'Affaires at Brussels (1790–2), including Torrington's comments on the Declaration of Pillnitz; and Lord Macartney's correspondence relating to his mission to Louis XVIII at Verona in 1795–6.

County Record Offices

The most important collections are as follows. The Buckingham office (Aylesbury) contains the papers of Robert Trevor, 4th Lord Trevor and 1st Viscount Hampden, envoy at The Hague 1736–47. Much of interest was omitted from the Historical Manuscripts Commission edition of the correspondence, published in Report 14 Appendix IX (1895), and the edition also omitted sections from many letters that were published. The archive does not, however, hold the papers of Trevor's second son, John, 3rd Viscount Hampden, envoy at Munich (1780–3) and Turin (1783–98).

The Bedfordshire office (Bedford) contains, in the Lucas collection, the papers of Lord Glenorchy, envoy in Copenhagen 1720–9, and Thomas Robinson, 2nd Lord Grantham, envoy in Madrid 1771–9 and Foreign Secretary 1782–3. The West Suffolk office (Bury St Edmunds) contains the papers of Augustus, 3rd Duke of Grafton, Secretary of State 1765–6, and diplomatic material in the Hervey papers, including the correspondence of the 2nd Earl of Bristol, envoy in Turin (1755–8) and Madrid (1758–61).

The Essex office (Chelmsford) holds the papers of William Mildmay as Commissioner at Paris after the Treaty of Aix-la-Chapelle for negotiations over American colonial frontiers and prizes. The Devon office (Exeter) includes material relevant to the embassy of Francis Drake at Copenhagen in the early 1790s. Diplomatic correspondents included Daniel Hailes, George Hammond and Sir William Hamilton.

The Gloucestershire Office (Gloucester) holds the papers of Guy Dickens, envoy in Berlin (1730–41), Stockholm (1742–8), and St Petersburg (1749–55), although the collection is a somewhat disappointing one. Light is cast on relations outside Europe by the papers of Sir Harford Jones Brydges in the Herefordshire Office (Hereford). As Harford Jones, he was assistant and factor for the East India Company in Basra, 1783–94. He was subsequently its Resident in Bagdad (1798–1806) and British envoy in Tehran (1809–11).

The Panshanger collection (D/EP.) in the Hertfordshire Office (Hertford) contain material in the papers of the 1st and 3rd Earls Cowper, although neither was a diplomat. The papers of the first, a prominent Whig politician, include diplomatic correspondence, especially letters from John Wich, Resident in Hamburg 1706–12. George, the 3rd Earl, lived most of the time from 1759 until his death in 1789 in Florence. His papers throw light on unofficial diplomacy, as they include a bundle relating to his negotiations on behalf of the government.[18] In 1780–1 he attempted, at the request of Sir Horace Mann, envoy in Florence, to persuade Austria to negotiate with Spain on Britain's behalf, and in 1784 Cowper attempted, unsuccessfully, during a visit of Joseph II to Tuscany, to negotiate an Anglo-Austrian *rapprochement*. There is also relevant correspondence concerning the latter among the letters from the Foreign Secretary, the Marquess of Carmarthen, in the collection. The letters from Mann, John Strange, Minister in Venice, and John Udney, Consul in Leghorn, are mainly social in content. The archive also contains a letter-book and some original letters of Charles, 2nd Viscount Townshend, when Ambassador at The Hague, 1709–11; and some letters in the Delme–Radcliffe papers relating to the consulship at Aleppo in the early and mid-eighteenth century.

The former Huntingdonshire office at Huntingdon, now one of the two country record offices in Cambridgeshire, includes, in the Manchester papers, material relating to George, the 4th Duke's embassy to Paris in 1783. The East Suffolk office (Ipswich) contains correspondence to and from William Leathes, envoy in Brussels 1715–22, although the printed catalogue underrates the amount of diplomatic material. The collection of the Keppel family, Earls of Albemarle, includes a few papers of William, 2nd Earl as Ambassador to France, 1749–54. There is also the correspondence of Alexander Straton, who served at Vienna from 1782, as secretary to his kinsman Sir Robert Murray Keith, and then as Secretary to the Legation. Straton was subsequently at Constantinople (1801–6) and in 1807 was appointed to Stockholm. His papers at Ipswich include correspondence from other diplomats such as Auckland, Elgin, Ewart, Jackson, Robert Murray Keith and Whitworth.

The Finch papers in the Leicestershire office (Leicester) contain material relevant to the career of Edward Finch, but no records of his embassies at Stockholm and St Petersburg, nor that of his elder brother William at The Hague. The Worsley papers in the Lincolnshire office (Lincoln) include the papers of Henry Worsley (Lisbon 1714–22) and Sir Richard Worsley (Venice 1793–7). The Greater London Record Office holds the Jersey family papers. These include the correspondence of Edward Villiers, 1st Earl of Jersey, who was Ambassador-Extraordinary in Paris 1698–9, and Secretary of State for the Southern Department, 1699–1700, and who played a role in Anglo-French negotiations at the end of the War of the Spanish Succession. The collection includes letters to Jersey from Matthew Prior, Secretary of Embassy in Paris, 1698–9.

The Kent office (Maidstone) holds the Sackville, Stanhope and Sydney Papers. The Stanhope collection includes the papers of Alexander Stanhope, envoy at Florence, Madrid and The Hague (1689–1706), as well as James Stanhope. The Stanhope collection also includes a number of special collections mainly acquired by the 5th Earl. Aside from material in the Pitt papers, there is also the correspondence and other papers of Henry Grenville, Ambassador at Constantinople, 1762–5. The Sackville collection includes Whitworth papers, but, more extensively, those of the 3rd

Duke of Dorset as Ambassador in Paris 1784–9. Much of the material duplicates correspondence in PRO. FO. 27 though U269 C172, which corresponds to Dorset's dispatches for 1787, includes number 66, later withdrawn from the series of official dispatches at the request of Carmarthen, because it contained a complaint from Dorset that he did not feel he had the full confidence of the British government. Material of which there are not always duplicates at Kew includes correspondence with envoys and personal or confidential correspondence with Carmarthen.

The Derbyshire office (Matlock) holds the papers of Alleyne Fitzherbert, among which are some very important letters of Joseph Ewart, envoy in Berlin 1784–91. The Northumberland office (Newcastle) holds the papers of Horace St Paul, envoy in Paris 1772–7.[19] The Northamptonshire office (Northampton) holds, in the Finch-Hatton collection, the Earl of Nottingham's letter-books as Secretary of State, 1702–4. It also holds the papers of Morton Eden, Lord Henley, but these are disappointing, and mostly restricted to Eden's instructions on successive appointments. There is nothing equivalent to the extensive correspondence of his brother William Eden, Lord Auckland, held in the Auckland papers in the British Library.

The Norfolk office (Norwich) holds, in the Bradfer Lawrence collection, material from the period of Charles, 2nd Viscount Townshend's career as Secretary of State, although much Townshend material remains at the family seat of Raynham. There are also, in the Lothian collection, the papers of John Hobart, Earl of Buckinghamshire, Ambassador in Russia 1762–5. These include letters from Hyndford, Mitchell and Yorke. The Walsingham papers include letters to the 2nd Lord Walsingham about his proposed appointment as Ambassador to Spain in 1786, as well as copies and translations of Anglo-Spanish diplomatic material. The Berkshire office (Reading) indicates the potential transience of listings. The papers of David Hartley, part of the Hartley Russell collection, have been withdrawn by the private owner, although microfilm of some of them are held in the office. The Trumbull papers, also held in Reading, went to the British Library.

The Shropshire office (Shrewsbury) holds the bulk of the personal papers of Richard Hill, envoy in Brussels (1696–9) and Turin (1699, 1704–5). The Staffordshire office (Stafford) holds the papers of John Chetwynd, who represented Queen Anne in Turin, although not always as envoy, in 1704–13. There is also material from the embassies of William Paget at Vienna (1689–92) and Constantinople (1693–1702). The Dartmouth papers include rough notes on diplomatic news in 1770, apparently abstracts from the reports of British envoys. There are also some papers of Viscount Torrington, envoy in Brussels 1783–9, held in the Bradford family collection, although the letter-books relating to his embassy have been retained at the family seat of Weston Park.

The Warwickshire office (Warwick) holds no relevant British material, although there are the papers of the noted Dutch diplomat of the late seventeenth century, Everard de Weede, Baron de Dyckvelt. Dyckvelt was related to Isabella de Yonge, wife of the 5th Earl of Denbigh, and his papers are preserved in the Denbigh collection. Many have been reported upon in the HMC's printed reports.

The Hampshire office (Winchester) holds the papers of Hans Stanley, who was sent to Paris in 1761 on an unsuccessful mission to negotiate peace with France. There is also a substantial collection of the papers of James Harris, 1st Earl of Malmesbury (1746–1820), although some material still remains with the family.[20] The collection in the Winchester office includes thirty letter-books containing private correspondence 1760–1800. These include correspondence from other envoys, such as Robert Murray Keith, Stepney and Torrington.

The West Yorkshire Archive Service has a number of archives. That in Leeds has relevant material in the Vyner collection. The papers of Thomas Robinson, 1st Lord Grantham, contain diplomatic correspondence, both from his period as envoy in Vienna (1730–48), and from that as Secretary of State (1754–5). A number of offices, including those at Barrow, Cambridge, Cardiff, Carlisle, Chichester, Guildford, Halifax, Kendal, Lewes, Lowestoft, Northallerton, Nottingham, Preston, Taunton, Trowbridge, Truro and Worcester, appear to have no relevant material.

Other Public Collections Outside London

University libraries of Cambridge, Oxford, Hull, Manchester and Nottingham hold a wealth of material. In Cambridge, the papers of Sir Robert Walpole in the Cholmondeley Houghton collection contains much material of value for foreign policy. The Bodleian Library in Oxford has a wider range of relevant holdings. There are state papers relating to foreign affairs 1686–1702,[21] letters to Richard Hill,[22] letters to Horatio Walpole and Charles, 2nd Viscount Townshend from J. Laws in Brussels (1709), J. Wich in Hamburg (1709), Francis Palmes in Turin and Vienna (1709–11), Daniel Pulteney in Copenhagen (1710–11), and Thomas Wentworth, Lord

Raby in Berlin (1711),[23] correspondence concerning the peace negotiations of 1709–10,[24] papers relating to the Peace of Utrecht,[25] correspondence of and to John Rawlinson, one of the Plenipotentiaries at Utrecht in 1711–14,[26] and a letter-book of Thomas Lumley, later 3rd Earl of Scarborough as envoy in Lisbon, 1722–3.[27]

The diplomatic correspondence of William, 4th Earl of Rochford during his Turin embassy (1749–55) includes Rochford's drafts, as well as letters from Consuls in the Italian state.[28] However, the main body of Rochford's diplomatic papers, sold at Sotheby's in 1930, has been scattered. The Bodleian also holds Rochford's notebook from his Spanish embassy, 1763–6, although this relates chiefly to ceremonial.[29] The Bodleian also holds the papers of Sir John Goodricke, envoy in Stockholm 1764–73,[30] and letters from Buckinghamshire throwing light on Anglo-Russian negotiations in 1763.[31]

The Bland Burges papers are a major collection held in the Bodleian, although the permission of the depositor, Richard Head, is required before copies can be made. Sir James Bland Burges, Under-Secretary at the Foreign Office 1789–95, had a confidential correspondence with most of the British diplomats of the period, and his papers include some important letters from Auckland. There are also valuable letters from America, both from George Hammond, who was appointed in 1791 to be the first minister accredited to the United States, and his secretary Edward Thornton who, in 1793, became Vice-Consul in Maryland.[32] The only relevant material in the archives of the Oxbridge colleges are some letters of Sir James Harris to his sister held in Merton College, Oxford.

Hull University Library holds the papers of Sir Charles Hotham, 5th Bt., who went to Berlin in 1730 in an unsuccessful attempt to improve Anglo-Prussian relations. There are also letters from the Earl of Buckinghamshire, envoy in Russia 1762–5, to Sir Charles Hotham, 8th Bt. The John Rylands Library in Manchester includes material on the War of the Austrian Succession, especially details of Anglo-Dutch negotiations in 1745, as well as a volume of the correspondence of Benjamin Keene after 1751, letters addressed to William Deane Poyntz, Chargé d'Affaires at Turin 1776–9, mostly sent by successive Consuls at Nice, and the correspondence of John, Viscount Mountstuart, envoy at Turin 1779–83, mostly sent by diplomats in Mediterranean Europe, especially Genoa and Nice. The letters of Henry Legge in the John Rylands Library do not contain any material from 1748, when he was sent to Berlin.

The Clumber collection in Nottingham University Library includes the correspondence of diplomats with Henry Pelham, most interestingly from Legge during his 1748 mission to Berlin. Legge's critical attitude towards Newcastle is readily apparent. The collection also includes letters from James, 2nd Lord Tyrawly, envoy in Moscow 1743–5, and papers concerning Ambassadors' allowances and payments to Russia. The Portland collection in the same library includes the papers of William Bentinck, friend and advisor to William III, and his envoy in Paris 1697–1700. These papers include correspondence from diplomats, friends and spies. The collection also includes some of the papers of Robert Harley, 1st Earl of Oxford, Secretary of State 1704–8, and, as Lord Treasurer, head of the 1710–14 Tory ministry. Among his correspondence preserved at Nottingham can be found letters from envoys such as Charles Whitworth at St Petersburg and Robert Jackson at Stockholm. Southampton University Library does not hold any significant groups of papers for diplomats of this period, although it does contain a series of six letter-books of Sir William Temple concerned with his negotiations with the Dutch, 1674–8, and another containing official correspondence, 1665–81.

Private Collections

A number of private collections contain correspondence or other papers of eighteenth-century diplomats, a product of the distinguished, or at least established, social background of most diplomats, especially at the senior level, and of the fact that those from a less exalted background were sometimes able to establish themselves socially. Four of the most important collections based on the papers of an individual diplomat yet remaining in private hands are the Waldegrave, Granard, Stormont and Ewart collections. James, 1st Earl Waldegrave was envoy in Vienna 1728–30 and Paris 1730–40. His papers are held in the family collection at Chewton Hall, and belong to Earl Waldegrave. They are most extensive, comprising his correspondence with other diplomats,[33] with ministers in London and, most valuably, with the Under-Secretaries. Only a small sample was used by Coxe in his invaluable *Memoirs of the Life and Administration of Sir Robert Walpole, Earl of Orford* (1798). The most interesting single document is Waldegrave's detailed journal of his period in Paris in late 1727 and early 1728 as he waited for Anglo-Austrian relations to improve sufficiently for him to set out for Vienna.

The papers of the Earl of Granard at Castle Forbes, County Longford, include the papers of George, Lord Forbes, later 3rd Earl of Granard,

Minister Plenipotentiary in Russia 1733–4. The papers include a large bundle of documents relating to Anglo-Russian trade, as well as the diary kept by Forbes while in Russia, and the correspondence between Forbes and the envoys in Constantinople, Copenhagen, Stockholm, Vienna and Warsaw.

The Stormont papers in Scone Palace have been ably used by Hamish Scott in order to throw light on the process of decision-making during the North ministry. Stormont was envoy to Augustus III (1756–63), before being posted to Vienna (1763–72) and Paris (1772–6), and becoming a Secretary of State (1779–82). Scott also used the Cathcart papers in the possession of Earl Cathcart: Charles, Lord Cathcart was Ambassador in St Petersburg, 1768–72.[34] The papers of Benjamin Langlois, who was Secretary of Embassy during Stormont's embassy at Vienna, survive in the possession of Jeffrey Lefroy of Carrigglas Manor, County Longford.

The major collections for the last years of the period remaining in private hands are the papers of Joseph Ewart, envoy in Berlin, 1784–91, held by a descendant, Sir Hector Monro, as part of the Monro of Williamwood papers in Williamwood House at Williamwood near Kirtlebridge, Dumfriesshire, and those of Thomas, 7th Earl of Elgin in the family archive in Broomhall, Fife. For example, to appreciate the firm response of Ewart and Elliot to the Danish attack on Sweden in 1788 it is necessary to consult Elliot's letters in Williamwood, as well as Ewart's in Edinburgh.[35] This very need to turn to private collections throws light on the character of British foreign policy, not least of the role of individual initiatives and the importance of links between envoys.

Elgin's early diplomatic career comprised a mission to the Emperor Leopold II in 1791 and a posting to Brussels in 1791–2. A recent study of the family offers no real information on these missions, or on the nature of the surviving material,[36] but the collection is a very rich one. It includes Elgin's drafts and some of his own letters, as well as correspondence he received from a number of diplomats, including Auckland, Morton Eden, Ewart, Jackson, Straton and Trevor. Typical of the insights into individual views is a letter from Auckland in August 1792:

> If the affairs of France could be separated from the interests of other countries, I should earnestly turn my attention from all French news which I have long ceased to regard otherwise than with horror and disgust:—but the fate of Europe and of mankind may be connected with the French catastrophe.[37]

Aside from the private papers of diplomats, there are also those of Secretaries of State which include correspondence with diplomats. For example, despite the major dispersals of 1911 and 1924 and other losses to collectors, much still remains at Raynham.[38] Aside from being Secretary of State for the Northern Department, 1714–16 and 1721–30, Charles, 2nd Viscount Townshend was Ambassador Extraordinary and Plenipotentiary to the United Provinces (1709–11); Horatio Walpole serving as his Secretary of Embassy. Raynham material includes the correspondence of both. Letters from diplomats include that from Daniel Pulteney at Copenhagen 1709–10 and John Lawes, Secretary at Brussels, 1709–11. The papers of Thomas, 3rd Viscount, who served as an Under-Secretary in 1724–9, are also in the collection. Other holdings of Townshend diplomatic material include the British Library and the National Library of Australia.

Other Secretaries of State whose papers are in private hands include Bedford (1748–51), Bute[39] (1761–2) and Weymouth (1768–70, 1775–9). The papers of Edward Weston, some of which remain in private hands, held by a descendant, John Weston-Underwood,[40] are the leading example of the papers of an Under-Secretary in private hands.

As far as other governmental figures are concerned, the most significant were members of the royal family. The Cumberland papers in the Royal Archives at Windsor Castle contain some very important correspondence on peace negotiations and relations with allies at the end of the War of the Austrian Succession. Although the correspondence of George III has been substantially published, the Royal Archives still yield unpublished material for the foreign policy of his reign, not least with reference to the influence of Frederick, Duke of York on the diplomacy of the mid-1780s.[41]

Foreign Material

Most of the papers of British diplomats that are abroad are held in American archives, although there are also important holdings elsewhere. The St Saphorin papers are held in Switzerland, and this is possibly the reason why they have not been studied adequately. François Louis de Pesmes, seigneur of St Saphorin, represented George I at Vienna from 1716 until 1727. His papers are held by a descendaent in the Pesmes-St Saphorin archive, but access to them is far from automatic. There is also some useful correspondence for the period among the papers of George

I's minister Friedrich Wilhelm von Görtz, held in the Hessisches Staatsarchiv in Darmstadt. These provide a basis for assessing the influence of Hanoverian considerations on British policy. For example, for early 1720, the despatches of Charles Whitworth, envoy in Berlin, survives in the PRO, while his correspondence with Görtz, then effectively Regent of Hanover, survives in Darmstadt. Whitworth received instructions from three separate sources: the Secretary of State in London, James Stanhope, George I and the Hanoverian Chancery in London, and the Regency in Hanover, and it is important not to view these in isolation. The Niedersächsisches Hauptstaatsarchiv in Hanover similarly holds letters from a number of British diplomats including Hanbury Williams. There is material from Horatio Walpole and Townshend in the Heinsius, Hoornbeek and Slingelandt collections in the Algemeen Rijksarchief in The Hague.

For the second half of the century, Cork University College Library has two volumes of instructions and letters sent to Sir George, later Lord, Macartney, as Envoy Extraordinary to Russia, 1765–6. One volume largely consists of instructions from Sandwich, Grafton and others, relating, in particular, to the negotiation of the Anglo-Russian Treaty of Commerce of 1766, although it also includes some private letters from them, as well as correspondence from Stormont and Langlois at Vienna. The other volume contains a series of letters to Macartney from his fellow diplomats, including Burnet, Goodricke, Gunning, Stanhope, Woodford, Wroughton and Yorke.[42] Uppsala University Library has a collection of the correspondence of Sir John Goodricke, envoy in Stockholm 1764–73, that includes a bitter complaint of 1766 by Macartney about his treatment by the British government.

The most important American collections are the Beinecke Library in New Haven, the Huntington Library in San Marino, California, the Lewis Walpole Library in Farmington, and the New York Public Library. The largest relevant collection in the Beinecke is material in the Osborn collection from the late seventeenth and early eighteenth centuries. This centres on the Blathwayt papers, the correspondence of William Blathwayt, who was not only Secretary-at-War, but also acting Secretary of State when he accompanied William III to the Continent. This and related collections include papers of diplomats of the period, such as Richard Hill, Edward Poley and George Stepney. From the same period, the Beinecke also has the papers of Charles, 4th Earl and later 1st Duke of Manchester, envoy in Venice 1697–8 and 1707–8 and in Paris in 1699–1701, the last a crucial period as Anglo-French relations deteriorated on the eve of the War of Spanish Succession. From the same period, the Sterling Memorial Library in New Haven holds Townshend diplomatic papers from 1709.

The Beinecke also holds twelve letters written by Robert Trevor, envoy in The Hague, that make clear his concern with the direction of British policy in 1744–5, a series dealing with Anglo-Portuguese relations in 1759–62, including letters from Edward Hay, Envoy Extraordinary in Lisbon, Macartney papers for 1764–7, and the unbuttoned letters of John, 3rd Duke of Dorset, envoy in Paris 1784–9, to Nathaniel Wraxall MP.

The Stowe papers in the Huntington Library include material on Thomas Grenville's diplomatic missions of 1794 and 1799, to Vienna and Berlin respectively. The Library also contains a letter-book from Sir Robert Murray Keith, envoy in Vienna 1772–92, to his cousin, Frances Murray. This is full of valuable details about diplomatic life and is also characterized by a strong sense of neglect. In 1783, he wrote, 'there is something so dark and *enigmatical* in the conduct of my superiors, and their tiresome reserve upon many points equally interesting to the *public* and to myself'. Keith also complained about changes in the office in London, and about the distracting impact of domestic political commitments.[43]

The Lewis Walpole Library at Farmington has the largest collection of the papers of Edward Weston, one of the often shadowy and generally ignored bureaucrats on whom the government of Hanoverian Britain depended.[44] He was a long-serving Under-Secretary (1729–45, 1761–4), and much of his correspondence was devoted to diplomatic matters, and of value precisely because of its often confidential and private nature. A portion of it was printed in *Report Ten Appendix 1* of the Royal Commission on Historical Manuscripts (1885) when it belonged to Charles Fleetwood Weston Underwood. Of the twelve volumes calendared in that report, ten belong to the Lewis Walpole Library; the other two are in the British Library.

Farmington also holds the collection substantially printed in *The Grenville Papers* edited by W.J. Smith (4 vols, 1862–3), but there are differences of omission and inclusion. In addition, there are also over 6,000 separate items in the Hanbury Williams collection. There are Hanbury Williams papers in the Holland House (Fox) collection in the British Library and in Newport Public Library, South Wales, but the largest holding is in Farmington.[45] This includes much of the correspondence of George Woodward, envoy to Saxony–Poland in 1728–75, but most of it consists of correspondence to and, to a lesser extent, from Hanbury Williams, envoy to Augustus III of Saxony-Poland (1747–55), Frederick II (1750–1), and Elizabeth I of Russia (1755–7). Envoys represented include Albemarle, Burrish, Dickens, Hyndford, Keene, Keith, Rochford, Titley, Villettes and Yorke.[46]

The New York Public Library holds the Montague collection, which includes papers on the Peace of Utrecht, and the Hardwicke collection, which includes the papers of Sir Luke Schaub, who represented George I in Vienna in 1715–16 and 1718, Paris in 1718 and 1721–4, and Madrid in 1720, and George II in Dresden and Warsaw in 1730–1.[47] This is a very extensive collection, including correspondence to Schaub from fellow diplomats, such as Dodington, Stair, Walpole and Whitworth, from Secretaries of State, such as Stanhope, and from others, such as the French Foreign Minister Dubois, as well as drafts of letters by Schaub. It is a most important series for the diplomatic history of the reign of George I, and, although used by Philip Yorke, 2nd Earl of Hardwicke, in his *Miscellaneous State Papers ... 1501 to 1726* (1778), has been largely neglected by modern scholars. Other volumes in the Hardwicke collection include one of letters of Charles Whitworth from Berlin, 1719–20, and one of letters and papers of Whitworth and Lord Polwarth as Plenipotentiaries at the Congress of Cambrai, 1722–3.

There are other American libraries with collections of note. The William Clements Library in Ann Arbor, Michigan holds a number of important collections, most obviously much of the Shelburne material. This includes secret and private correspondence not in the Public Record Office, for example sensitive correspondence between Shelburne, then Secretary of State for the Southern Department, and William, 4th Earl of Rochford, Ambassador at Madrid, over the Manila Ransom and the Falklands.[48] The collection includes Macartney's manuscript 'Account of Russia, 1767', while the Library also has a small collection of letters to and from Macartney. The Augustan manuscript collection in the Lilly Library of the University of Indiana at Bloomington, includes eleven letters from George Stepney, then envoy in Vienna from 1705. Letters to Stepney from Richard Hill in 1704 can be found in the McLennan Library in McGill University, Montreal. There is Blathwayt correspondence in the Boston Public Library, while the Kenneth Spencer Research Library at the University of Kansas includes the correspondence of John Methuen, envoy in Lisbon 1702–6 with Sir William Simpson, as well as the papers of Arthur Moore, one of the members of the Board of Trade 1710–14, who played a major role in the negotiation of the abortive trade treaty with France of 1713 as well as in commercial negotiations with Spain. There are also the letters and reports of Colonel John Armstrong, the British expert on the demolition of the works that prevented the silting up of the strategic harbour of Dunkirk, as well as of the fortifications there, as demanded by the Treaties of Utrecht (1713) and The Hague (1717). There is also Armstrong's diplomatic notebook while at Paris in 1727–30. Furthermore, the Spencer Library holds some confidential letters from diplomats received by Weston in 1743.

Coverage

There are, however, ministers and diplomats whose private papers appear to have disappeared. Possibly the most serious case is that of William Stanhope, Lord Harrington, envoy in Spain in 1717–18, 1720–27 and 1729, and at Paris in 1719, Plenipotentiary at the Congress of Soissons and, subsequently, in Paris in 1728–30, and Secretary of State in 1730–42 and 1744–6. His role, particularly as Secretary, but also at Soissons, is obscure, and the discovery of his private papers would be of the utmost importance.

An indication of the number and range of archives that have to be consulted if a comprehensive account of any particular period is to be attempted can be provided by considering the period 1727–39. Britain was then at peace and diplomatic representation was therefore extensive. There were three Secretaries of State in the period: Townshend, whose papers are in Raynham, the British Library, Norfolk Record Office and the Australian National Library; Newcastle, whose papers are in the British Library, and Harrington, whose private papers do not appear to have survived. Harrington earlier was one of the three Plenipotentiaries at Soissons who also represented Britain at Paris for all or part of 1727–30. The papers of the other two, Stephen Poyntz and Horatio Walpole, have recently been transferred from private archives to the British Library. Thereafter, Waldegrave was the envoy in Paris and his papers are still held at Chewton. Waldegrave (1728–30) and then Thomas Robinson (1730–48) were envoys at Vienna. The latter's papers are in the British Library, as are those of the 3rd Earl of Essex (Turin, 1732–6), Benjamin Keene (Spain throughout), Brinsley Skinner (Consul at Leghorn/Livorno, in charge of affairs in Florence, 1731 and 1733–4), Lord Tyrawly (Lisbon, 1728–41), and Walter Titley (Copenhagen, 1729–68). The papers of George Woodward, envoy at Dresden and Warsaw 1728–35, survive in the Lewis

Walpole Library at Farmington, those of Luke Schaub (Dresden and Warsaw, 1730–1) in the New York Public Library. There are also at Farmington a few letters of Thomas Villiers, who became Envoy Extraordinary to Augustus III of Saxony–Poland in 1738. The papers of Sir Charles Hotham (Berlin, 1730) survive in Hull University Library. The papers of his successor, Guy Dickens (Berlin, 1730–41), in the County Record Office in Gloucester are very sparse. This is not so of those of his counterpart at The Hague in 1736–47, Robert Trevor, in the Buckinghamshire County Record Office in Aylesbury. The papers of Lord Forbes (St Petersburg, 1733–4) survive in family hands, being still part of the collection of the Earls of Granard at Castle Forbes. The private papers of Charles Du Bourgay (Berlin, 1724–30), Charles Fane (Florence, 1734–8), Edward Finch (Stockholm, 1728–39), William Finch (The Hague, 1733–4), George, Earl of Kinnoull (Constantinople, 1730–6), Claudius Rondeau (St Petersburg, 1730–9), Richard Sutton (Cassel, 1727–31), Arthur Villettes (Turin, 1734–49), Thomas Ward (Russia, 1728–30) and Cyril Wych (Hansa towns, 1713–42) do not appear to have survived, either at all or, if so, in any appreciable quantity.

This survey is inevitably incomplete, but suggests the range of material that survives from the period. This is an important aspect of any account of the diplomats and diplomacy of the century. Without a comprehensive assessment of the private papers of the diplomats, it is impossible to produce authoritative accounts. The official records alone will not suffice. However, an instructive warning about any paper chase is offered by a private letter of Holdernesse to Joseph Yorke of 1754:

> You receive, by this post, leave for a short expedition to England, when I hope to receive from you, by word of mouth, a more ample account of the state of affairs in Holland, than could possibly be conveyed upon paper.[49]

Notes

1 Introduction: The Diplomacy of a Rising World Power

1. Robinson to Titley, 1 Apr. 1739, BL. Eg. 2685.
2. Hailes to Francis Jackson, Secretary of Legation at Berlin, 24 Sept. 1790, PRO. 353/66.
3. M. Lee Jr., 'The Jacobean Diplomatic Service', *American Historical Review*, 72 (1966–7), pp. 1276–80.
4. Dorset to Sir Nathaniel Wraxall, 22 Feb. 1787, Beinecke, Osborn Files, Dorset.
5. Elliot to Philip Yorke, 3rd Earl of Hardwicke, 1 Mar. 1781, PRONI. Caledon papers.
6. J.M. Black, *Britain as a Military Power 1688–1815* (1999).
7. G.M. Bell, *A Handlist of British Diplomatic Representatives 1509–1688* (London, 1990), p. 11.
8. Lee, 'Jacobean Diplomatic Service', p. 1282.
9. Huntington Library, HM. 18940, p. 344, letter amongst 1785 papers.
10. Keith, 'Observations', in *An Essay on the Education of a Young British Nobleman* (1730), p. 167.
11. C.-G. Picavet, *La Diplomatie Française au temps de Louis XIV, 1661–1715: institutions, moeurs et coutumes* (Paris, 1930); W. Roosen, *The Age of Louis XIV. The Rise of Modern Diplomacy* (Cambridge, Mass., 1976) and J. Baillou (ed.), *Les Affaires Étrangères et Le Corps Diplomatique Français I. De l'ancien régime au second Empire* (Paris, 1984).
12. Gordon to the Earl of Sandwich, 2 Aug. 1764, PRO. SP. 81/107.
13. W. Coxe, *Memoirs of Horatio, Lord Walpole* (1802).
14. D.B. Horn, *The British Diplomatic Service 1689–1789* (Oxford, 1961), p. 10. Horn also compiled a valuable listing, *British Diplomatic Representatives, 1689–1789* (1932). The sequel, covering 1789–1852, edited by S. Bindoff, E.F. Malcolm Smith and C.K. Webster (1934).
15. D. Goffman, *Britons in the Ottoman Empire, 1642–1660* (Seattle, 1998); A.C. Wood, *A History of the Levant Company* (1935), p. 133; Sir Everard Fawkener,

envoy in Constantinople, to Horatio Walpole, 29 Nov. 1736, Fawkener to Sir Robert Walpole, 24 Jan. 1737, BL. Add. 74072.

16. M.S. Anderson, 'Great Britain and the Barbary States in the Eighteenth Century', *Bulletin of the Institute of Historical Research*, 29 (1956), pp. 87–107; Captain John Blankett RN to Shelburne, 9 Feb. 1784, Bowood vol. 11. For letters to the Duke of Newcastle from Consuls in Tripoli, Tunis and Algiers, see the recently deposited BL. Add. 73990.

17. Delaval to Lord Dartmouth, Secretary of State, 15 Apr. 1713, PRO. SP. 89/22; Keppel to Anson, 15 July 1750, T. Keppel, *The Life of Augustus Viscount Keppel* (2 vols, 1842) I, 180.

18. R. Bonney, *Kedah 1771–1821. The Search for Security and Independence* (Oxford, 1971), vi, pp. 52–101, 110; D.K. Bassett, *British Trade and Policy in Indonesia and Malaysia in the Late Eighteenth Century* (Hull, 1971), pp. 73–96.

19. J. Meares, *Voyages made in the Years 1788 and 1789, from China to the North West Coast of America* (1790); P. Nightingale, *Trade and Empire in Western India, 1784–1806* (Cambridge, 1970), ix, pp. 240–2; E. Stokes, 'The First Century of British Rule in India', *Past and Present*, 58 (1973), pp. 136–60; P.J. Marshall, 'British Expansion in India in the Eighteenth Century: A Historical Revision', *History*, 60 (1975), pp. 28–43.

20. W.S. Sorsby, 'The British Superintendency of the Mosquito Shore 1749–1787' (Ph.D. London, 1969); F.G. Dawson, 'William Pitt's Settlement at Black River on the Mosquito Shore: A Challenge to Spain in Central America, 1732–87', *Hispanic American Historical Review*, 63 (1983); R.A. Naylor, *Penny Ante Imperialism: The Mosquito Shore and the Bay of Honduras, 1600–1914. A Case Study in British Informal Empire* (1989).

21. L. Joré, *Les Établissements français sur la Côte Occidentale d'Afrique de 1758 à 1809* (Paris, 1965), pp. 114–17.

22. Grenville to Lord Thurlow, the Lord Chancellor, 15 July 1789, BL. Add. 58938 fols 3–4.

23. E.H. Pritchard, *The Crucial Years of Early Anglo-Chinese Relations 1750–1800* (Pullman, Washington, 1936), pp. 236–311; J.L. Cranmer-Byng, 'Lord Macartney's Embassy to Peking in 1793, from Official Chinese Documents', *Journal of Oriental Studies*, 4 (1957–8), pp. 117–87, and *An Embassy to China … the Journal Kept by Lord Macartney* (1962); P. Roebuck (ed.), *Macartney of Lisanoure 1737–1806* (Belfast, 1983), pp. 216–43; A. Singer, *The Lion and the Dragon: The Story of the First British Embassy to the Court of the Emperor Qianlong in Peking, 1792–94* (1992); A. Peyrefitte, *The Collision of Two Civilisations: The British Expedition to China, 1792–4* (1993).

24. M. Roberts, *Macartney in Russia* (1974).

25. W.E. Washburn, 'The Moral and Legal Justifications for Dispossessing the Indians', in J.M. Smith (ed.), *Seventeenth Century America: Essays in Colonial History* (Chapel Hill, 1959), pp. 24–32; A. Frost, 'New South Wales as *terra nullius*: The British Denial of Aboriginal Land Rights', *Historical Studies*, 19 (1981), pp. 513–23.

26. J.L. Wright, *Britain and the American Frontier 1783–1815* (Athens, Georgia, 1975), pp. 3, 38; F. Merk, *The Oregon Question* (Cambridge, Mass., 1967), pp. 1–5.

27. G. Vancouver, *A Voyage of Discovery to the North Pacific Ocean, and Round the World* (3 vols, 1798); R. Fisher, *Vancouver's Voyage: Charting the Northwest Coast* (Seattle, 1992).

28. Marshall, *Bengal: The British Bridgehead. Eastern India 1740–1828* (Cambridge, 1987), pp. 96–7; C.A. Bayly, 'The British Military–Fiscal State and Indigenous Resistance. India 1750–1820', in L. Stone (ed.), *An Imperial State at War. Britain from 1689 to 1815* (1994), pp. 322–54.

29. Black, 'The Theory of the Balance of Power in the First Half of the Eighteenth Century: A Note on Sources', *Review of International Studies*, 9 (1983), pp. 55–61.

30. W. Robertson, *The History of the Reign of the Emperor Charles V* (1769; 1782 ed.), I, 134–5.

31. E. Gibbon, *The History of the Decline and Fall of the Roman Empire*, ed. J.B. Bury (1896–1900), IV, 163–6. See, more generally, Black, 'Empire and Enlightenment in Edward Gibbon's Treatment of International Relations', *International History Review*, 27 (1995), pp. 441–58.

32. Black, *The Rise of the European Powers 1679–1793* (1990).

33. For more conventional accounts of diplomats, Horn, *British Diplomatic Service*; P.S. Lachs, *The Diplomatic Corps under Charles II and James II* (New Brunswick, 1965); Black, *British Foreign Policy in the Age of Walpole* (Edinburgh, 1985), pp. 66–70, *A System of Ambition? British Foreign Policy 1660–1793* (Harlow, 1991), pp. 59–68 and *British Foreign Policy in an Age of Revolutions 1783–1793* (Cambridge, 1994), pp. 480–8; H.M. Scott, *British Foreign Policy in the Age of the American Revolution* (Oxford, 1990), pp. 23–7. Keith Hamilton and Richard Langhorne, *The Practice of Diplomacy. Its Evolution, Theory and Administration* (1994) is weak for the period prior to 1815. For one post, R. Przezdziecki, *Diplomatic Ventures and Adventures: Some Experiences of British Envoys at the Court of Poland* (1953). Doctoral theses devoting attention to diplomats include P.F. Doran, 'Andrew Mitchell and Anglo-Prussian Diplomatic relations during the Seven Years' War' (London, 1972); G.W. Rice, 'An Aspect of European Diplomacy in the Mid-Eighteenth Century: The Diplomatic Career of the Fourth Earl of Rochford at Turin, Madrid and Paris, 1759–1768' (University of Canterbury, New Zealand, 1973); A.I. Bagis, 'The Embassy of Sir Robert Ainslie at Istanbul' (London, 1974); Scott, 'Anglo-Austrian Relations after the Seven Years' War: Lord Stormont in Vienna, 1763–1772' (London, 1977).

2 The Choice of Envoys

1. Wallace to Burrish, 27 June 1748, PRO. SP. 110/16.

2. A.C. Carter, *The Dutch Republic in Europe in the Seven Years War* (1971).
3. The best guide for this period is H.M. Scott, *British Foreign Policy in the Age of the American Revolution* (Oxford, 1990).
4. There is need for a detailed study of this period.
5. Newcastle to Dickens, 27 Feb. (os) 1750, *Sbornik*, 148 (1916), p. 12.
6. Tilson to Delafaye, 28 Aug. 1725, Wych to Weston, 2 Dec. 1740, PRO. SP. 43/6, 82/61.
7. Wych to Tilson, 23 Mar., Wych to Townshend, 30 Mar. 1725, Chesterfield to Townshend, 31 Dec. 1728, Wych to Weston, 19 Dec. 1741, PRO. SP. 82/42, 84/302, 82/63.
8. Trevor to Grenville, 28 Sept. 1792, BL. Add. 59025.
9. Allen to Newcastle, 9 Aug. 1732, PRO. SP. 92/34.
10. Yorke to Duke of Cumberland, 22 Mar. 1749, RA. CP. 43/144.
11. Richmond to Newcastle, 18 Dec. 1748, BL. Add. 32717.
12. Bedford to Keene, 2 Mar. (os) 1749, PRO. SP. 94/135.
13. Bedford to Villettes, 9 Mar. (os) 1749, PRO. SP. 92/58; Newcastle to Pelham, 7 June 1740, NeC. 102; Weymouth to Walpole, 8 Nov. 1768, PRO. SP. 78/276.
14. Whitworth to Townshend, 29 July 1721, PRO. SP. 90/15; re Denmark, Tilson to Titley, 26 June 1736, BL. Eg. 2683.
15. Newcastle to Harrington, 29 Mar. (os) 1741, PRO. SP. 43/100.
16. Chelmsford, Essex CRO. D/D By C1.
17. R. Sedgwick (ed.), *The House of Commons 1715–1754* (2 vols, 1970) I, 140.
18. D.B. Horn, 'The Diplomatic Experience of Secretaries of State, 1660–1832', *History*, 41 (1956), pp. 88–99.
19. Bolingbroke to Strafford, 4 Mar. (os) 1713, BL. Add. 73508; Keene to Robinson, 14 Dec. 1754, Leeds Archive Office, Vyner Papers 11846.
20. Townshend to Waldegrave, 26 Oct. (os), Waldegrave to Newcastle, 4 Dec. 1727, Chewton, BL. Add. 32753.
21. Mostyn to Earl of Nottingham, 29 Dec. (os) 1723, Leicester CRO. DG/7/4952.
22. Chesterfield to Liston, 9 June, 10 July 1784, NLS. MS. 5541.
23. Aust to Liston, 22 Aug. 1786, NLS. MS. 5545.
24. Newcastle to Pelham, 7 Aug. 1748, RA. CP. 38/72.
25. Newcastle to Pelham, 23 July 1748, NeC.643.
26. Perron to Charles Emmanuel III, 9 Jan. 1755, AST. LM. Ing. 59.
27. Andrew Stone to Pelham, 26 June 1748, NeC. 596. On his political qualities, Alt to William of Hesse Cassel, 13 Feb. 1748, Marburg 249; R. Lodge, 'The Mission of Henry Legge to Berlin, 1748', *Transactions of the Royal Historical Society*, 4th ser. 14 (1932), pp. 1–38; P. Kulisheck, 'The Favourite Child of the Whigs: The Life and Career of Henry Bilson Legge, 1708–1764' (Ph.D., Minnesota, 1996), pp. 61–127; George to Pitt, 11 Dec. 1787, CUL. Add. 6958.
28. Townshend to William Finch, 21 Jan. (os), William Finch to Earl of

Nottingham, 12 Feb. 1724, Leicester CRO. DG/7/4952.

29. Fox to Hanbury Williams, 10 May (os) 1750, Farmington, Hanbury Williams 52; Newcastle to Pelham, 13 Sept. 1750, BL. Add. 35411.

30. Horatio Walpole to Trevor, 5 Dec. (os) 1740, Trevor 24.

31. Contrast Robinson to Leheup, 4 Feb. and Robinson to Horatio Walpole, 7 Feb. 1730, BL. Add. 9139 with Robinson to Stone, 14 July 1736, PRO. SP. 80/227.

32. Thomas Robinson, later 2nd Earl of Grantham, to James Grant of Grant, 24 June 1761, SRO. GD. 248/177/1/89.

33. *Craftsman*, 15 Feb. (os) 1729.

34. Cobham to Schaub, 16 Feb. 1716, New York, Public Library, Hardwicke collection vol. 42.

35. Townshend to St Saphorin, 6 Mar. (os) 1724, PRO. SP. 80/48.

36. Colman to Townshend, 24 Jan. 1723, Townshend to St Saphorin, 23 Sept. 1723, PRO. SP. 80/51, 48.

37. Woodward to Tilson, 29 July 1727, PRO. SP. 80/61.

38. Delafaye to Horatio Walpole, 1 Sept. (os) 1727, Finch to Townshend, 22 Apr., Finch to Newcastle, 10 June, Finch to Harrington, 9 Sept. 1730, PRO. SP. 78/187, 95/54–6; Diemar to General Verschuer, minister of Frederick I of Sweden, 1 Sept. 1730, Marburg, Staatsarchiv, Bestand 4, England 199.

39. Le Coq to Augustus II, 15, 19 Aug., 31 Oct. 1727, Dresden, Hauptstaats-archiv, Geheimes Kabinett, Gesandtschaften 2676 18a; Coxe, *Robert Walpole*, II, 500–1; R. Grieser (ed.), *Die Memoiren des Kammerherrn Friedrich Ernst von Fabrice* (Hildesheim, 1956).

40. Delafaye to Horatio Walpole, 1 Sept. (os) 1727, PRO. SP. 78/187.

41. Townshend to Plenipotentiaries, 12 Sept. (os) 1728, PRO. SP. 78/189.

42. Hyndford to Harrington, 4 Oct. 1741, PRO. SP. 90/52.

43. Stanhope to Sunderland, 6 July 1719, BL. Add. 61513.

44. Horatio to Robert Walpole, 10 July 1734, CUL. C(H) Mss. Corresp. 2259.

45. Wych to Tilson, 20 Aug. 1735, PRO. SP. 82/56.

46. Waldegrave to Delafaye, 31 Aug. 1732, PRO. SP. 78/201; Saladin to Hattorf, 13 July 1733, Hanover, Cal. Br. 24 Nr. 2002.

47. St Saphorin to Townshend, 9 Feb., Townshend to St Saphorin, 6 Mar. (os) 1724, PRO. SP. 80/52, 48; Titley to Tilson, 3 May 1729, PRO. SP. 75/52; Horatio to Robert Walpole, 11 Oct. 1734, CUL. C(H) corresp. 2349.

48. Horatio Walpole to Harrington, 10 Sept. 1735, PRO. SP. 84/347; Elliot to Pitt, 8 Nov. 1788, CUL. Add. 6958; G.F. Freudenreich to Burges, 4 Feb. 1792, Bod. BB. 34.

49. PRO. SP. 94/98.

50. St Saphorin to Tarouca, [Aug. 1727], PRO. SP. 80/81; Berkentin to ——, 17 Mar. 1728, PRO. SP. 80/326; Ferdinand Albrecht, Duke of Brunswick-Bevern, 3 Apr. 1728, Wolfenbüttel, Staatsarchiv, 1 Alt 22, 529.

51. St Saphorin to Townshend, 26 Aug. (os) 1727, PRO. SP. 80/61; Waldegrave to Townshend, 24 July 1728, Chewton, Robinson to Harrington, 5 Aug.

1735, PRO. SP. 80/117.

52. *Sbornik* 75, p. 126; Count Dehn, Wolfenbüttel envoy, to August Wilhelm, Duke of Wolfenbüttel, 13 July 1728, Wolfenbüttel, 2 Alt 3632; Duque de Liria, *Diario del viaje a Moscovia del Duque de Liria* (Madrid, 1889), pp. 208–9.

53. Minutes of the Lord Justices, 14 Sept. (os) 1741, PRO. SP. 43/108.

54. Newcastle to Yorke, 4 May 1753, PRO. SP. 84/463; Newcastle to Dickens, 27 Aug. (os) 1751, *Sbornik*, 148 (1916), p. 265.

55. Townshend to Waldegrave, 28 Mar. (os) 1729, PRO. SP. 80/64.

56. Draft to Grimaldi, 2 Apr. (os) 1729, PRO. SP. 100/32.

57. Draft to Elgin,—Sept. 1792, PRO. FO. 26/19.

58. R. Lodge, *Scottish Diplomatists 1689–1789* (1944); K.W. Schweizer, 'Scotsmen and the British Diplomatic Service, 1714–1789', *Scottish Tradition*, 7–8 (1977–8), pp. 115–36; Scott, *British Foreign Policy*, pp. 26–7.

59. Horatio to Robert Walpole, 19 Feb. 1724, BL. Add. 63749; Mitford to Burges, 16 Nov. 1789, Bod. BB. 18.

60. Townshend to St Saphorin, 22 Aug. (os) 1724, PRO. SP. 80/48.

61. Poyntz to Delafaye, 26 Feb. (os) 1728, Hyndford to Burrish, 27 Feb. 1752, PRO. SP. 36/5, 110/6.

62. PRO. SP. 92/58 *passim.*

63. Newport, Hanbury Williams papers, q H411 012.

64. Auckland to Malmesbury, 20 Dec. [1789], Winchester, Hampshire CRO., Malmesbury 143.

65. Horn, *British Diplomatic Service*, pp. 130–2.

66. Burnaby to Newcastle, 26 June (os) 1734, BL. Add. 32689.

67. Frankland to Robinson, 16 Jan. (os) 1741, Leeds, Archive Office, Newby Hall mss 282; Finch to Earl of Nottingham, 19 Nov. 1725, Leicester CRO. Finch mss DG/7/4952.

68. Hugh Valence Jones, Under-Secretary, to Burrish, 20 Aug. (os) 1752, Villettes to Burrish, 6 Sept. 1752, PRO. SP. 110/6.

69. Tilson to Whitworth, 6, 9 Feb. (os), Norris to Whitworth, 7 Feb. (os) 1722, BL. Add. 37388.

70. Whitworth to Tilson, 15 Mar. 1721, PRO. SP. 90/13.

71. Beauchamp to William Eden,—Apr. 1763, Trevor to Keith, 19 Nov. 1782, BL. Add. 34412, 35527.

72. Auckland to Grenville, 18 Mar. 1806, BL. Add. 58923.

73. Stepney, BL. Eg. 929 f. 63–4; Thomas Coke to his guardians, 12 Mar. 1713, C.W. James, *Chief Justice Coke. His Family and Descendants at Holkham* (1929), p. 181.

74. Hyndford to Chesterfield, 14 Feb. 1747, *Sbornik* 103 (1897), p. 210; Wych to Weston, 8 Dec. 1741, PRO. SP. 82/63; Harris to Frederick Robinson, 14 Feb. 1777, Bedford CRO. Lucas papers 30/15/26/8.

75. Fox to Hanbury Williams, 16 Nov. (os) 1750, Farmington, Hanbury Williams 52; Joseph to Philip Yorke, 22 Mar. 1754, BL. Add. 35364.

76. Holdernesse to Keith, 9 Oct. 1759, BL. Add. 35483.

77. Fitzherbert to Carmarthen, 2 Feb. 1784, BL. Eg. 3500.
78. Whitworth to Tilson, 19 Apr. 1721, PRO. SP. 90/14.
79. Whitworth to Tilson, 11 Mar. 1721, PRO. SP. 90/13.
80. Whitworth to Tilson, 25 Mar. 1721, PRO. SP. 90/13.
81. Auckland to Burges, 14 July 1792, Bod. BB. 30.
82. Haslang to Wreden, 10 Jan. 1755, Munich, London 230.
83. L'Hermitage to the Greffier, Fagel, 26 Jan. 1720, The Hague, Algemeen Rijksarchief, Archief van de Familie Fagel, nr. 3785.
84. Craggs to Stair, 23 May (os) 1720, SRO. GD. 135/141,24.
85. Waldegrave to Townshend, 21 Aug. 1728, PRO. SP. 80/61; Horatio Walpole to Newcastle, 13 Oct. 1724, BL. Add. 32741.
86. Destouches to Dubois, 3 Apr. 1719, Boutel to Rouillé, French Foreign Minister, 2 Jan. 1755, AE. CP. Ang. 323, 438; Craggs to Stanhope, 16 Sept. 1720, New York Public Library, Hardwicke papers vol. 563.
87. Mirepoix to Rouillé, 9 Jan. 1755, AE. CP. Ang. 438.
88. Perron to Charles Emmanuel III, 13 Feb. 1755, AST. LM. Ing. 59; Mirepoix to Rouillé, 6 Feb. 1755, AE. CP. Ang. 438. On Newcastle's patronage methods, R. Middleton, 'The Duke of Newcastle and the Conduct of Patronage during the Seven Years' War, 1757–1762', *British Journal for Eighteenth-Century Studies*, 12 (1989), pp. 175–86, esp. p. 179.
89. Newcastle to Sandwich, 6, 17 May (os) 1748, BL. Add. 32812.
90. Ossorio to Charles Emmanuel III, 31 May 1748, AST. LM. Ing. 54.
91. Viry to Charles Emmanuel, 6 Jan. 1758, AST. LM. Ing. 63.
92. Viry to Charles Emmanuel, 9 June, 17 Oct. 1758, AST. LM. Ing. 63.
93. Fraser to Keith, 23 May 1783, BL. Add. 35528.
94. Anon., *General Remarks on our Commerce with the Continent … to which is added, observations on British Expeditions to Germany; and on our Diplomatique Agents Abroad* [1806?], p. 49.
95. Townshend to Waldegrave, 26 Oct. (os) 1727, PRO. SP. 80/62.
96. Waldegrave Diary, Chewton. For his wine account in 1737, PRO. SP. 36/41 f. 60; Horatio Walpole to Newcastle, 3 May, 28 Oct. 1735, BL. Add. 32787, 32789.
97. Hanbury Williams to Henry Fox, 27 July 1752, 23 Jan. 1753, BL. Add. 51393.
98. Grantham to Rochford, 29 Sept. 1771, Bedford CRO. L30/15/26/1.
99. Craggs to Stair, 6 Dec. (os) 1716, SRO. GD. 135/147. For the same point, Henry Pelham to Essex, 22 Oct. (os) 1734, BL. Add. 27733.
100. Torrington to Harris, 9 Jan. 1784, Malmesbury 169.
101. Dorset to Carmarthen, 1 Apr. 1784, BL. Eg. 3499.
102. Dorset to Carmarthen, 11, 23, 24 Jan. 1784, BL. Eg. 3499.
103. Dorset to Wraxall, 24 May 1787, Beinecke, Osborn Files, Dorset.
104. Carmarthen to Hailes, 22 Oct., 6 Nov., Hailes to Carmarthen, 28 Oct. 1784, BL. Eg. 3499.
105. George Colman the Younger (ed.), *Posthumous Letters from Various Celebrated Men, Addressed to Francis Colman and George Colman the Elder* (1820), p. 16.

106. Bentinck to Newcastle, 5 Mar. 1748, C. Gerretson and P. Geyl (eds), *Briefwisseling en Aantekeningen van Willem Bentinck* (Utrecht, 1934), p. 385.
107. Newcastle to Cumberland, 11 Mar. (os) 1748, RA. CP. 32/245.
108. Harcourt to George III, 5 Mar. 1771, *Corresp. of George III*, II, 215.
109. James Stanhope to Townshend, 14 Aug. 1716, PRO. SP. 43/1.
110. Stanyan to Bolingbroke, 6 Nov. 1713, PRO. SP. 96/15.
111. Whitworth to Tilson, 30 Mar. 1724, BL. Add. 37393.
112. CUL. C(H) Mss. 10/73.
113. Newcastle to Pelham, 10 July 1748, NeC. 638.
114. Anon., *General Remarks on our Commerce*, p. 48.
115. Anon., *General Remarks on our Commerce*, p. 50.
116. Rondeau to Tilson, 30 Mar. (os) 1730, PRO. SP. 91/11.
117. Bentinck to Henry Pelham, 28 Oct. 1750, NeC. 1173.
118. Langlois to St Paul, 27 Dec. 1774, Northumberland CRO. ZBU B3/25; Wych to Harrington, 8 June 1740, PRO. SP. 82/61.
119. Harrington to Robinson, 14 Sept. (os) 1730, BL. Add. 23780; Marquis de Fleury, Saxon minister, Count Watzdorf, Saxon envoy, 30 Dec. 1730, PRO. SP. 107/2, Dresden, Hauptstaatsarchiv, Geheimes Kabinett, Gesandtschaften 2676 I.
120. Perron to Charles Emmanuel III, 13 Feb. 1755, AST. LM. Ing. 59.
121. C. Ross (ed.), *Correspondence of Charles, First Marquis Cornwallis* (3 vols, 1859), I, 196–203; The Cornwallis papers in the PRO. do not add to this account; Townshend to Du Bourgay, 15 Mar. (os) 1726, PRO. SP. 90/20.
122. Tyrawly to Newcastle, 25 Feb. 1729, PRO. SP. 88/35.
123. Tyrawly to Newcastle, 26 Aug. 1735, PRO. SP. 89/38.
124. K. Müller, *Das Kaiserliche Gesandtschaftswesen im Jahrhundert nach dem Westfalischen Frieden, 1648–1740* (Bonn, 1976), p. 249.
125. Mr Walpole's Apology, BL. Add. 9132 f. 81; R. Hatton, *Diplomatic Relations between Great Britain and the Dutch Republic, 1714–1721* (1950).
126. Destouches to Dubois, 15 Dec. 1718, AE. CP. Ang. 311.
127. B. Williams, *Stanhope: A Study in Eighteenth-Century War and Diplomacy* (Oxford, 1932).
128. Barthélemy to Montmorin, 19 Aug. 1791, AE. CP. Ang. 578.
129. *Craftsman*, 9 Sept. (os) 1727; *The British Journal*, 10 Aug. (os) 1728; *Fog's Weekly Journal*, 23 May (os) 1730; *Cirencester Flying Post and Weekly Miscellany*, 15 Mar. (os) 1742; Anon., *Political Dialogues between the Celebrated Statues of Pasquin and Marsorio at Rome* (1736), p. 5; George, 9th Earl of Dalhousie, to Francis Jackson, 10 June 1789, SRO. GD. 45/14/501.
130. Friedrich Christian von Plettenberg to his brother, Count Ferdinand, 22 Apr. 1728, Münster, Staatsarchiv, Deposit Nordkirchen NB104; Tarouca to Townshend, 14 May 1728, PRO. SP. 80/326; Eugène to Count Philip Kinsky, 20 Aug. 1728, Vienna, Palais Kinsky, papers of Count Philip 2(b); Liria to Waldegrave, 25 Apr. 1731, BL. Add. 32772; H.J. Pretsch, *Graf Manteuffels Beitrag zur Österreichischen Geheimdiplomatic* (Bonn, 1970), p. 112;

Horatio Walpole to Waldegrave, 23 Feb. 1735, Chewton.
131. *Polit. Corresp.* 5, pp. 176, 207.
132. W. Stanhope to Schaub, 29 July 1721, BL. Add. 4204.
133. Alleyne Fitzherbert to Keith, 25 Aug. 1779, BL. Add. 35517.
134. Auckland to Burges, 11 Aug. 1790, 14 July 1792, Bod. BB. 30.
135. Grenville to Gower, 15 May 1792, BL. Add. 59021.
136. Tilson to Whitworth, 9 Mar. (os) 1724, BL. Add. 37393.
137. Mitford to Burges, 16 Nov. 1789, Bod. BB. 18.
138. Whitworth to Townshend, 19 Apr. 1721, PRO. SP. 90/14.
139. Stepney to Trumbull, 17 July 1695, BL. Trumbull Papers Add. 14.

3 Effectiveness

1. John to Christian VI, 16 Oct. 1733, PRO. SP. 107/7; Frederick to Finckenstein, 12 Dec. 1781, *Polit. Corresp.* 46, p. 337. Re Hanbury Williams, Frederick to Michell, 17 Nov. 1750, 8, p. 157.
2. Wyndham, 13 Mar. (os) 1734, James Erskine, 14 Feb. (os) 1735, Cobbett, IX, 365, 822.
3. *Craftsman*, 7 July (os), 15 Sept. (os) 1739. See also *Mist's Weekly Journal*, 7 Oct. (os) 1727, [Johnson], *A Compleat Vindication of the Licensers of the Stage* (1739) in D.J. Greene (ed.), *Samuel Johnson—Political Writings* (New Haven, 1977), p. 66.
4. *Old England*, 24 Feb. (os) 1750. See also *Newcastle Courant*, 13 Oct. (os) 1750.
5. P. Thicknesse, *A Year's Journey through the Païs Bas and Austrian Netherlands* (2nd edn, 1786), pp. 244–50, quote p. 245; Sandwich to Richard Phelps, Under-Secretary, 2 Aug. 1764, BL. Stowe 259; Joseph Schornberg to Viscount Townshend, — Mar. 1769, Beinecke, Osborn Shelves, Townshend Box 11; H. Furber (ed.), *Correspondence of Edmund Burke, V* (Cambridge, 1965), p. 307.
6. Anon., *The True History of Dr. Robin Sublimate, and his Associates; or Bob turn'd Physician* (1729), p. 25; Anon., *Lord Blunder's Confession* (1733); Anon., *Political Dialogues between the Celebrated Statues of Pasquin and Marsorio* (1736), p. 5; *Champion*, 3 June (os) 1740; *Craftsman*, 6 Jan. (os), 9 Sept. (os) 1727, 20 July (os) 1734; *Westminster Journal*, 2 Jan. (os) 1742.
7. Keene to Delafaye, 16 Mar. 1731, PRO. SP. 94/107; Cobbett, XI, 287.
8. Waldegrave to Newcastle, 5 Feb. 1728, BL. Add. 32754; Robinson to Horatio Walpole (quote), 28 Sept. 1735, PRO. SP. 80/118.
9. Sir John Graham, Jacobite envoy, to John Hay, 4 May 1726, RA. SP. 93/64.
10. R.R. Sedgwick (ed.), *The House of Commons 1715–1754* (2 vols, 1970), II, 208.
11. Townshend to Du Bourgay, 19 Sept. (os) 1727, 25 Nov. (os) 1729, PRO. SP. 90/22, 25; George II to Townshend, undated, W. Coxe, *Memoirs of the Life and Administration of Sir Robert Walpole* (3 vols, 1798), II, 534.
12. Newcastle to Kinnoull, 16 May (os) 1735, PRO. SP. 97/27; Harrington to Newcastle, 27 July 1735, PRO. SP. 43/87; Fawkener to Robert Walpole, 8

May, Fawkener to Rondeau, 26 May, 1 June 1736, BL. Add. 74072.

13. Harrington to Finch, 5 June (os) 1733, PRO. SP. 84/232; Charles VI to Kinsky, 7 Jan. 1734, PRO. SP. 107/19; Newcastle to Robert Walpole, 26 July (os) 1723, BL. Add. 32686.

14. Essex to Waldegrave, 4 July 1733, 18 Apr., 4 July 1734, Chewton; Newcastle to Essex, — Oct. (os) 1734, BL. Add. 32786 ff. 61–4.

15. Molesworth to Newcastle, 21 Oct. 1724, PRO. SP. 92/31.

16. Titley to Tigh, 30 Jan., Titley to Tilson, 4, 11 Feb. 1730, PRO. SP. 75/54.

17. Burnett to Newcastle, 16 Aug., 25 Oct., Dormer to Newcastle, 17, 31 Aug., 8 Sept., 26 Oct., 3 Nov. 1726, Burnett to Newcastle, 21 Oct., Dormer to Newcastle, 28 Oct. and enclosures, Dormer to Newcastle, 13 Nov. 1727, Newcastle to Dormer, 10 Nov. (os) 1727, PRO. SP. 89/32–4.

18. Stanhope to Keene, 22 Mar. 1724, Essex to Newcastle, 12 Sept. 1733, BL. Add. 4204, 32782; Ossorio, Sardinian envoy, to Charles Emmanuel III, 12 Aug. 1733, PRO. SP. 92/87.

19. Robinson to Weston, 25 May 1741, PRO. SP. 80/145; cf. Dunant to Tilson, 23 Jan. 1737, PRO. SP. 80/125, Hanbury Williams to Robinson, re Dayrolle, 10 July 1747, BL. Add. 23825.

20. Waldegrave to ?, — July 1732, Chewton.

21. Namier and Brooke, *The House of Commons 1754–1790* II, 137–8.

22. Dorset to Hawkesbury, 19 Oct. 1787, BL. Add. 38222; Dorset to Stafford, 1, 22 Nov., 19 Dec. 1787, PRO. 30/29/1/15.

23. Puysieulx to Argenson, 7 (quote), 9 Oct. 1746, AE. CP. Hollande 462.

24. *Old England*, 14 Feb. (os) 1747; Cumberland to Newcastle, 26 Feb. (os) 1748, RA. CP. 32/120, cf. Newcastle to Cumberland, 25 Feb., 32/116.

25. Keith to Holdernesse, 28 Apr. 1756, PRO. SP. 80/197.

26. Newcastle to Horatio Walpole, 6 Nov. (os) 1723, BL. Add. 32686.

27. Keene to Newcastle, 2 Mar. 1731, Tyrawly to Newcastle, 20 Oct. 1735, Hyndford to Harrington, 9 June (os) 1740, Edward Finch to Harrington, 29 July 1741, Lambert to Newcastle, 25 July 1740, PRO. SP. 94/107, 89/38, 91/28, 36/51, 78/223; Hyndford to Chesterfield, 14 Feb. 1747, *Shornik* 103 (1897), p. 210; Gray to Bedford, 16 Jan. 1750, Bedford Estate office, papers of 4th Duke.

28. Finch to Harrington, 24 June (os) 1740 (quote), 14 Nov. (os) 1741, Paul Methuen to James Vernon, 25 Nov. 1698, Worsley to James Stanhope, 22 Dec. 1714, PRO. SP. 91/24, 29, 89/17, 23; Horatio to Robert Walpole, 19 Feb. 1724, Sandwich to Newcastle, 22 Dec. 1747, BL. Add. 63749, 32810.

29. Boyd to Bute, 13 Dec. 1762, MS 1/108; Chesterfield to Waldegrave, 24 Dec. 1728, Chewton; Cosby to Weston, 5 May 1764, BL. Add. 57927. For linguistic skills playing a role in recommendations and appointments, Molesworth to Carteret, 1 Sept. 1723, PRO. SP. 92/31; Peter, Lord King to Newcastle, 3 Apr. (os) 1724, Harrington to Robinson, 14 Sept. (os) 1730, W. Fraser to Keith, 16 Aug. 1785, BL. Add. 32687, 23780, 35535; W. Gibson, *A Social History of the Domestic Chaplain 1530–1840* (Leicester, 1997), pp. 57–9.

30. Sutton to Townshend, 5, 8 May, Woodward to Tilson, 29 May 1727, PRO. SP. 81/122, 80/61; Robinson to Tilson, 30 June 1736, Lord Mountstuart to Liston, 6 Dec. 1782, BL. Add. 23854, 36804.

31. Lady Glenorchy to Duke of Kent, 21 Dec. 1720, Bedford, CRO. L. 30/8/8/6; Poyntz to Delafaye, 25 Sept. 1723, PRO. SP. 43/5.

32. Tilson to Delafaye, 31 Aug. 1723, PRO. SP. 43/3; Aust to Liston, 15 Aug. 1786, NLS. MSS. 5545.

33. Destouches to Dubois, 9 July 1722, AE. CP. Ang. 342.

34. Harrington to Robinson, 29 Sept. 1738, PRO. SP. 80/131, cf. Townshend to St Saphorin, 26 Oct. (os) 1722, PRO. SP. 80/48.

35. Destouches to Dubois, 9 Jan. 1719, AE. CP. Ang. 322; Tilson to Delafaye, 15 Nov. 1725, PRO. SP. 43/8.

36. Fawkener to Newcastle, 30 Dec. 1735, BL. Add. 74072, cf. Stormont to Rochford, 23 Mar. 1774, PRO. SP. 78/191; Burges to Keith, 13 July 1792, Bod. BB. 48; cf. Lord Glenorchy to Duke of Kent, — 1724, Bedford CRO. L. 30/8/10/72.

37. Whitworth to Tilson, 4 Mar. 1721, PRO. SP. 90/13.

38. Manning to Sunderland, 21 Dec. (os) 1715, BL. Add. 61650.

39. Yorke to Weston, 15 Dec. 1761, BL. Add. 58213; Drake to Burges, 27 Nov. 1790, Bod. BB. 34.

40. Tilson to Chetwynd, 19 Oct. (os) 1711, Stafford CRO. D649/8/7/17; Dunant to Weston, 27 Jan. 1737, PRO. SP. 80/125; Robinson to Trevor, 5 May 1736, BL. Add. 23853.

41. Burnaby to Horatio Walpole, 1 Feb. 1735, PRO. SP. 84/341.

42. '...impressed by the general probity and efficiency of eighteenth-century administration in the naval and diplomatic fields', Richard Ollard, review of *Descriptive List of State Papers Portugal* in *Times Literary Supplement*, 13 July 1984, p. 785.

43. St Saphorin to Stanhope, 30 Oct. 1719, PRO. SP. 80/39; Count Philip Kinsky to Prince Eugène, 23 June 1733, HHStA. GK. 94b.

44. Hyndford to Harrington, 14 June 1741, PRO. SP. 90/50; cf. Polwarth to Townshend, 17 Oct. 1716, PRO. SP. 75/36.

45. Hanbury Williams to Chesterfield, 28 Oct. 1747, Sutton to Townshend, 7 Oct. 1728, PRO. SP. 88/69, 81/122.

46. Theophilus Oglethorpe to 'James III', 14 June 1720, RA. SP. 47/82.

47. Destouches to Dubois, 22 Jan. 1722, AE. CP. Ang. 340.

48. Thomas Pelham to Newcastle, 23 Apr. 1732, BL. Add. 32776; Waldegrave to —, — July, Chewton.

49. Horatio Walpole to Trevor, 28 Apr. (os) 1741, Trevor 27.

50. Newcastle to Waldegrave, 30 Mar. (os) 1734, BL. Add. 32784; Newcastle to Horatio Walpole, 22 July (os) 1737, PRO. SP. 36/41.

51. Bristol to Lord Hervey, 15 Oct. (os) 1740, *Letter Books of John Hervey, First Earl of Bristol* (3 vols, Wells, 1894), III, 255; cf. John to von Hagen, 10 July 1733, PRO. SP. 107/14.

52. Craggs to Stair, 18 Dec. (os) 1718, Graham (ed.), *Stair* II, 87; Townshend to Waldegrave, 9 July (os) 1728, PRO. SP. 80/61; Delafaye to Waldegrave, 10 Aug. (os) 1732, Chewton; Horatio Walpole to Newcastle, 3 May 1735, BL. Add. 32787. For praise of Waldegrave's 'pleghm', Henry Pelham to Essex, 2 Aug. (os) 1732, BL. Add. 27732.

53. Haslang, Bavarian envoy, to Wachtendonck, Munich, Hauptstaatsarchiv, 16 Aug. 1765, Bayr. Ges. London 342.

54. Essex to Newcastle, 13 Oct. 1733, PRO. SP. 92/35.

55. John Jeffreys MP to Philip Yorke MP, 8 Sept. 1752, BL. Add. 35630.

56. Robinson to Newcastle, 30 Sept. 1732, BL. Add. 32778; Horatio Walpole to Trevor, 9 Jan. (os) 1739, Aylesbury, Trevor 16.

57. Germain to Dorset, 6 Jan. 1784, Maidstone, CRO. U269 C192.

58. Newcastle to Robert Walpole, 7 Aug. (os), to Townshend, 11 Aug. (os) 1723, BL. Add. 32686.

59. Cadogan to Stair, 12 Jan. 1717, SRO. GD. 135/141/10.

60. Black, *A System of Ambition? British Foreign Policy 1660–1793* (2nd edn, Stroud, 2000).

4 The 'English Plan' of Diplomacy

1. Robinson to Weston, 15 Apr. 1744, Farmington, Weston 14.

2. Pollon, Sardinian envoy, to Victor Amadeus III, 7 Feb., 7 Mar. 1786, AST. LM. Ing. 88; Barthélemy to Montmorin, 14 Jan. 1791, AE. CP. Ang. 576; Auckland to Morton Eden, 1 Nov. 1791, *Journal and Correspondence of William, Lord Auckland* (4 vols, 1861–2) II, 393–5.

3. Newcastle to Horatio Walpole, 11 Apr. 1735, BL. Add. 32787.

4. Holdernesse to Mitchell, 17, 25 Feb., Joseph Yorke to Holdernesse, 11 Apr. 1758, PRO. SP. 90/71; Hardwicke to Newcastle, 23 Apr. 1758, BL. Add. 32879.

5. Townshend to Richard Sutton, 8 Nov. (os) 1728, PRO. SP. 81/122.

6. Newcastle to Dickens, 22 Oct. 1752, *Sbornik* 148, p. 366.

7. Stepney to Görtz, 25 Mar. 1698, Darmstadt, Staatsarchiv, F23 156/16; Dormer to Newcastle, 21 Apr., 4 May, 1, 15, 30 June, 2, 14 July, 31 Aug., Newcastle to Dormer, 10 May (os), 21 June (os), 19 July (os) 1726, PRO. SP. 89/33, 32.

8. Joseph to Philip Yorke, 7 Jan. 1752, BL. Add. 35362; Instructions to Yorke, 21 Nov. 1751, PRO. SP. 84/458.

9. Forbes and Rondeau to Delafaye, 23 Feb. (os) 1734, *Sbornik* 76, p. 180; Finch to Weston, 26 Jan., Finch to Harrington, 20 Feb., 3 Aug., Burnaby to Harrington, 16 Oct. 1739, PRO. SP. 95/84, 86, 87.

10. Edward Finch to Harrington, 22 Nov. (os) 1740, PRO. SP. 91/26.

11. Whitworth to Tilson, 20 Dec. 1721, PRO. SP. 90/15, cf. Tilson to Whitworth, 13, 16 Mar. (os) 1722, BL. Add. 37388; Waldegrave Journal, 17 May 1728, Chewton.

12. Earl of Ilchester and Mrs Langford-Brooke, *The Life of Sir Charles Hanbury-Williams* (1929), pp. 311–417; Mitchell to Holdernesse, 3, 7, 22 June 1756, Hanbury Williams to Holdernesse, 22 Mar. 1757 (quote), PRO. SP. 90/65, 91/65.

13. Pitt to Newcastle, 28 Jan. 1758, BL. Add. 35417.

14. Viry to Charles Emmanuel III, 14, 21 Feb., 3 Mar. 1758, AST. LM. Ing. 63.

15. Keene to Delafaye, 6 Oct. 1727, PRO. SP. 94/98.

16. Holdernesse to Keith, 13 Feb. 1759, Bute to Keith, 6 Feb. 1762, BL. Add. 3099; Andrew Stone to Pelham, 14 June (os) 1740, NeC. 103.

17. N.A.M. Rodger, 'Instigators or spectators? The British government and the restoration of the Stadholderate in 1747', *Tijdschrift voor Geschiedenis*, 106 (1993), pp. 496–514.

18. Whitworth to Tilson, 29 Apr., 24 June 1721, PRO. SP. 90/14; cf. Whitworth to Townshend, 24 Oct. 1716, BL. Add. 37363; Polwarth to Townshend, 3 Nov. 1716, PRO. SP. 75/36.

19. Malmesbury to Grenville, 27 Dec. 1793, PRO. FO. 64/31; Methuen to Trenchard, 21 Aug., 2 Oct. 1694, PRO. SP. 89/17.

20. Harrington to Hyndford, 8 Nov. (os) 1741, PRO. SP. 90/51.

21. Delafaye to Waldegrave, 7 May 1731, Chewton; Keene did not lose this caution: Horatio Walpole to Pelham, 12 Aug. (os) 1747, NeC 487.

22. Paget to Nottingham, 25 May, 8 June, 20 July, 13, 20 Aug., 28 Sept., St George Ashe, Paget's secretary, to Warre, 13 Aug., Paget to [?Warre], 20 Aug., 1690, PRO. SP. 80/17; Eden to Pitt, 20 July 1786, PRO. 30/8/110. For envoys defending the taking of the initiative, and thus responsibility, in negotiations, Whitworth to Tilson, 27 Jan. 1720, Sandwich to Newcastle, 5 May 1748, PRO. SP. 90/11, 84/434.

23. Whitworth to Halifax, 18 Oct. 1714, BL. Add. 37361.

24. Walpole to Waldegrave, 7 Mar. (os) 1737, Chewton; Burnaby to Robinson, 22 Jan. (os), Weston to Robinson, 5 Feb. (os) 1742, Fraser to Keith, 24, 28 May 1782, BL. Add. 23810, 35525; Aust to Liston, 16 Dec. 1783, NLS. Mss. 5539.

25. Joseph Yorke to Philip Yorke, 9 Dec. 1755, BL. Add. 35364.

26. Dorset to Carmarthen, 22 Feb. 1784, BL. Eg. 3499; Essex to Newcastle, 1 Aug. 1735, PRO. SP. 92/35.

27. Whitworth to Tilson, 4 Mar. 1721, PRO. SP. 90/13.

28. Lumley to Carteret, 19 Dec. 1722, Newcastle to Dormer, 17, 31 Jan. (os), 14 Mar. (os), Dormer to Delafaye, 10 Apr. 1727, PRO. SP. 89/30, 32.

29. Hastings to Henry Crabb Botton, 29 Jan. 1770, BL. Add. 29126.

30. *Ipswich Journal*, 11, 25 May 1765; *Bristol Gazette and Public Advertiser*, 4 July 1771.

31. Trevor to Keith, 5 Apr. 1782, BL. Add. 35525.

32. Yorke to Keith, 19 May 1782, BL. Add. 35525.

33. Carmarthen to Fitzherbert, 22 Feb. 1783, Matlock, Derbyshire CRO. 239 M/O 521.

34. Mountstuart to Liston, 26 Dec. 1783, NLS Mss. 5539; Duchess to Duke of Manchester, 7 May 1783, Huntington CRO. dd M21 B.
35. Malmesbury to Ewart, 29 Aug. 1789, Williamwood 147.
36. Fox to Portland, [20 Jan.], Dorset to Hawkesbury, 8 Jan. 1789, BL. Add. 47561, 38471, Hawkesbury to Dorset, 13 Jan., 3, 6, 20 Feb. 1789, Maidstone KAO C182; Dorset to Wraxall, 27 Nov., 11 Dec. 1788, 29 Jan., 5 Feb. 1789, Beinecke, Osborn Files, Dorset; Dorset to Stafford, 11 Dec. 1788, 22 Jan. 1789, PRO. 30/29/1/15.
37. Philip, 2nd Earl of Hardwicke, 'A Memorial of Family Occurences', Cambridge CRO. 408/F 6(I), p. 10; Keith to Harris, 22 June 1784, Winchester, Malmesbury 158.
38. Holdernesse to Keith, 23 Mar. 1756, BL. Add. 35480.
39. Dickens to Newcastle, 25 Oct. 1753, PRO. SP. 91/66. For concern about the unauthorized disclosure of material by Dickens earlier in the year, Newcastle to Yorke, 12 Jan. 1753, PRO. SP. 84/462.
40. M.M. Escott, 'Britain's Relations with France and Spain 1763–1771' (Ph.D., Wales, 1988), p. 516.
41. Viry to Charles Emmanuel, 4 July 1758, AST. LM. Ing. 63, reporting Pitt's comments on Bristol.
42. Townshend to Du Bourgay, 27 Dec. (os) 1728, PRO. SP. 90/24.
43. Villettes to Robinson, 21 Jan. 1742, BL. Add. 23810.
44. Harrington to Robinson, 20 July (os) 1733, PRO. SP. 80/97.
45. Harrington to Hyndford, 16 Sept. (os) 1746, *Sbornik* 103 (1897), p. 105. For criticism of Thomas Coke, Chancellor at Constantinople, Harbord to Nottingham, 17 Apr. 1692, PRO. SP. 80/17.
46. Townshend to St Saphorin, 30 June (os) 1724, PRO. SP. 80/48.
47. Hanbury Williams to Henry Fox, 17 June 1751, BL. Add. 51393; Robinson to Delafaye, 18 Nov. 1733, PRO. SP. 80/101.
48. Harrington to Hyndford, 8 Nov. (os) 1741, PRO. SP. 90/51.
49. Paget to Nottingham, 21 Dec. 1690, Townshend to Du Bourgay, 25 Nov. (os) 1728, Robinson to Carteret, 13 July, Carteret to Robinson, 24, 27 July 1743, PRO. SP. 80/17, 90/25, 80/160.
50. Newcastle to Villettes, 5 Aug. (os) 1742, PRO. SP. 92/44; Ossorio to Charles Emmanuel, 21 Mar. 1742, AST. LM. Ing. 48.
51. Wentworth to Newcastle, 9 July 1747, BL. Add. 32808.
52. Trevor to Harrington, 21 Jan. 1746, PRO. SP. 84/416.
53. Mitchell to Weston, 2 Feb. 1762, Farmington, Weston 5.
54. Horatio Walpole to Newcastle, 26 June 1726, BL. Add. 32746.
55. Keith to Harris, 7 Feb. 1784, Winchester, Hampshire CRO. Malmesbury 158.
56. A. Boyer, *Political State of Great Britain*, XV (1718), p. 237.
57. Robinson to Weston, 1 Apr. 1739, Farmington, Weston 12; Viry to Charles Emmanuel, 17 Feb. 1757, AST. LM. Ing. 61.
58. Mitchell to Weston, 14 Nov. 1761, Farmington, Weston 21.

59. Yorke to Newcastle, 21 May 1762, BL. Add. 32938.
60. Delafaye to Tilson, 12 Aug. (os) 1729, PRO. SP. 43/80.
61. Horatio Walpole to Waldegrave, 26 Mar. 1735, Chewton.

5 Means of Control

1. Trevor to Pelham, 12 May 1744, Beinecke, Osborn Shelves, Pelham box, cf. 15 May.
2. Burges to Liston, 6 Nov. 1789, Bod. BB. 45.
3. Harris to Ewart, 15 Mar. 1785, Winchester, Malmesbury 204, pp. 30, 35–40; 3rd Earl of Malmesbury (ed.), *Diaries and Correspondence of James Harris, First Earl of Malmesbury* (4 vols, 1844), II, 112–13. He offered a different view to Elliot, 17 Jan. 1786, NLS. Mss. 12999 f. 116.
4. Tyrawly to Robert Walpole, 29 Sept. 1734, CUL. C(H) corresp. 2342; Villettes to Mann, 10 Dec. 1738, PRO. SP. 105/281.
5. Essex to Earl of Scarborough, 24 Mar. 1734, BL. Add. 27733; Dunant to Tilson, 23 Jan. 1737, PRO. SP. 80/125. cf. Tyrawly to Delafaye, 15 Jan. 1734, PRO. SP. 89/37; Hanbury Williams to Henry Fox, 23 Jan. 1753, BL. Add. 51393.
6. Robert Murray Keith to Carmarthen, 30 Jan., 12 Feb., Carmarthen to Keith, 12 Feb., 16 May, 11 July 1788, PRO. FO. 7/15–16, BL. Add. 35540; Straton to Keith, 15 Aug., Keith to Ewart, 28 Sept. 1788, BL. Add. 35541; Keith to Carmarthen, 20, 22 Mar., Keith to Pitt, 20, 21, 22 Mar., Keith to Trevor, 25 Apr. 1789, NLS. Acc. 9769 72/2/71–2, 74–6, 78.
7. Eden to Pitt, 6 June 1786, PRO. 30/8/110.
8. C. Middleton, *British Foreign Policy*, p. 10, and 'The Foundation of the Foreign Office', in R. Bullen (ed.), *The Foreign Office 1782–1982* (Frederick, Maryland, 1984), which, though very useful on the Foreign Office up to 1830, contributes little to an account of its foundation.
9. M.A. Thomson, *The Secretaries of State 1681–1782* (Oxford, 1932), pp. 90–1.
10. Horatio Walpole to Trevor, 26 Aug. 1736, Aylesbury, Trevor 4.
11. Joseph Yorke to Philip Yorke, 5 May 1752, BL. Add. 35363.
12. Stanyan to Bolingbroke, 6 Nov. 1713, PRO. SP. 96/15.
13. Carmarthen to Keith, 7 Mar. 1788, PRO. FO 7/15.
14. Thomas Jackson to Harris, 28 Sept. 1787, 7 Mar. 1788, Malmesbury 158.
15. Carmarthen to Eden, 28 July 1786, PRO. FO. 27/19.
16. Destouches to Dubois, 15 Dec. 1718, AE. CP. Ang. 311; Craggs to Stair, 25 Jan. (os) 1720, SRO. GD. 135/141/24, 16; Gibson, *Domestic Chaplain*, pp. 142–3; Destouches to Dubois, 15 Jan. 1722, AE. CP. Ang. 340; Davenant to Philip Kinsky, 29 July 1733, Eugène to Kinsky, 2 Jan. 1734, Vienna, Palais Kinsky, papers of Count Philip, boxes 2 (c) and (d); Robert Daniel to Waldegrave, 10 Feb. 1734, Chewton.
17. Tilson to Robinson, 7 July 1730, BL. Add. 23780.
18. Fawkener to Porter, 20 Nov. 1748, BL. Add. 74074; Langlois to St Paul, 8

Nov. 1774, Northumberland CRO. ZBU B 3/25.

19. Holdernesse to Mitchell, 1, 8, 22 Nov., Mitchell to Holdernesse, 25 Dec. 1757, PRO. SP. 90/70.

20. Mitchell to Holdernesse, 17 Sept. 1757, PRO. SP. 90/70; Delafaye to Waldegrave, 18, 22, 8, 26 Mar. (os) 1731, Chewton. For delays in the post from England to Portugal e.g. Paul Methuen to Vernon, 8 Dec. 1696, PRO. SP. 89/17, and with Paris, Couraud to Waldegrave, 9, 26 Sept. (os), 31 Oct. (os), 16 Dec. (os) 1734, Chewton.

21. Harbord to Nottingham, 14 Dec. 1691, Chesterfield to Harrington, 20 Jan. (os) 1745, PRO. SP. 80/17, 84/408.

22. Dorset to Carmarthen, 17 June 1784, BL. Eg. 3499; William to his brother, the Marquess of Buckingham, 30 July 1787, HL. STG. Box 39(3).

23. Malmesbury to Grenville, 29 Nov. 1793, PRO. FO. 64/31; Malmesbury to Burges, 3, 14 Dec. 1793, 28 May 1794, Bod. BB. 37; Poyntz to Thomas Townshend, 24 Sept. 1724, Beinecke, Osborn Shelves C 201; Morton Eden to Grenville, 18 Dec. 1794, PRO. FO. 245/4.

24. Methuen to Nottingham, 8 Aug., 5 Sept. 1693, Methuen to Trenchard, 12 June 1694, Dormer to Newcastle, 19 Aug., Dormer to Townshend, 13 Sept. 1725, Dormer to Newcastle, 19 Dec. (os) 1727, Tyrawly to Newcastle, 23 Mar. (os) 1728, Parker to Newcastle, 28 Apr. 1735, PRO. SP. 89/17, 31, 34, 35, 94/217.

25. Holdernesse to Mitchell, 6 Aug. 1756, PRO. SP. 90/65.

26. Hyndford to Carteret, 21 Nov. (os) 1744, *Sbornik*, 102 (1898), p. 156.

27. Doctor Lidderdale to Horatio Walpole, 26 Sept., Stanhope to Horatio Walpole and Poyntz, 30 Sept., Stanhope to Keene, 12 Oct., Stanhope to Newcastle, 5, 14 Oct., Stanhope and Keene to Newcastle, 27 Oct. 1729, BL. Add. 32763; Finch to Harrington, 9 May 1740, PRO. SP. 41/24.

28. Woodward to ——, 30 Dec. 1726, PRO. SP. 80/60; Burges to Elgin, 5 Nov. 1792, Bod. BB. 48.

29. Harbord to Nottingham, 3, 17 Jan., 18 Feb., 1692, PRO. SP. 80/17; Fawkener to Newcastle, 8 Oct., 10 Nov., 30 Dec. 1735, BL. Add. 74072.

30. Barker, Paget's secretary, to Warre, 18, 22, 28, 31 Dec., Paget to Earl of Nottingham, Secretary of State, 26 Dec. 1689, cf. Lexington to Vernon, 23 Feb., 12 Mar. 1695, Wych to Harrington, 21 Mar. 1742, PRO. SP. 80/17, 91/31.

31. Horatio to Robert Walpole, 20 Jan. 1715, BL. Add. 74063; Auckland to Burges, 7 Jan. 1791, Wickham to Burges, Bod. BB. 30, 46 f. 111.

32. Robinson to Carteret, 11 June 1743, PRO. SP. 80/159.

33. Glenorchy to Duke of Kent, 25 Nov. 1724, Bedford, CRO. L30/8/8/37.

34. Ward journal, BL. Add. 6235 f. 49.

35. Stepney to [Sir John Trenchard], [between 29 Apr. and 6 May 1693], Burnett to Newcastle, 23 June, Cayley to Townshend, 25 June, 7 July 1725, PRO. SP. 80/17, 89/31; Hedges to Robinson, 9 July 1727, Leeds, District Archive, Vyner papers 6018; Newcastle to Essex, 6 June (os) 1735, PRO. SP. 92/39.

36. Vice-Consul Irvine (Ostend) to James Wallace, 17 July 1757, PRO. SP. 110/6.

37. Trevor to Carteret, 25 Sept. 1744, PRO. SP. 84/406; Harrington to Newcastle, 24 July 1735, PRO. SP. 43/87; Tilson to Waldegrave, 15 July 1735, Chewton.

38. Carmarthen to Robert Murray Keith, 18 July, Carmarthen to Ainslie, 19 Dec. 1786, PRO. FO. 7/12, 78/7. For consideration of a shorter postal route, Harbord to Nottingham, 29 June 1692, PRO. SP. 80/17, and a cut in transmission times for despatches from the Balkans, C.J. Heywood, 'English Diplomatic Relations with Turkey, 1689–1698', in W. Hale and A.I. Bagis (eds), *Four Centuries of Turco-British Relations. Studies in Diplomatic, Economic and Cultural Affairs* (Walkington, 1984), pp. 35–7.

39. Auckland to Eden, 1 Mar. 1792, BL. Add. 34441.

40. Horace Mann to Humphry Morice, 4 May 1784, Northumberland CRO. ZSW. 554/45.

41. Pulteney to Pitt, 6 Apr. 1787, CUL. Add. 6958.

42. Hardwicke to Newcastle, 31 July 1762, BL. Add. 32941.

43. Bedford to Bute, 20 Sept., 5 Nov. 1762, 10 Jan. 1763, MS. 5/160, 162, BL. Add. 38200.

44. Choiseul to Solar, 26 Aug., Choiseul to Nivernais, 14 Sept. 1762, AE. CP. Ang. 446–7.

45. Grafton to Lord Chancellor Northington, 23 Sept. 1765, Bury St Edmunds, Grafton papers 423/213.

46. St Helens to Burges, 17 June, reply 24 June 1794, Bod. BB. 38 f. 161, 164.

47. Udney to Burges, 14 Feb. 1794, Bod. BB. 44.

48. Thomas Brand to Robert Wharton, 20 Aug. 1793, Durham University Library, Wharton papers.

49. Weston to Burrish, 11 Dec. (os) 1750, PRO. SP. 110/6.

50. Sutton to Townshend, 7 Oct. 1728, PRO. SP. 81/122, cf. Hedges (Turin) to Robinson, 12 July, Leeds District Archive, Vyner papers 6018.

51. Kinnoull to Robinson, 5 June (os) 1733, BL. Add. 23788.

52. Keene to Robert Walpole, 24 Apr. 1739, CUL. C(H) corresp. 2860.

53. Keene to Robinson, 12 Jan. 1755, Leeds, Archive Office, Vyner papers no. 11864.

54. Whitworth to Stanhope, 20 May 1717, BL. Add. 37363.

55. Auckland to Burges, 25 Sept. 1790, Bod. BB. 30.

56. Hanbury Williams to Keith, 4 Nov. 1753, BL. Add. 35480; Titley to Harrington, 12 Oct. 1734, PRO. SP. 75/65. For other complaints, e.g. Essex to Newcastle, 7 Feb. 1733; Robinson to Weston re Villiers, 25 May 1741, PRO. SP. 92/35, 80/145; Thomas Kennedy to Robert Murray Keith, 22 July 1777, BL. Add. 35512 re Yorke's complaints.

57. Robinson to Delafaye, 7 Feb. 1733, PRO. SP. 80/93.

58. Townshend to William Finch, 17 July (os) 1724, Leicester CRO. DG/7/4/4752; Newcastle to Sandwich, 12 Jan. (os) 1748, BL. Add. 32811.

59. Hanbury Williams to Fox, 17 June 1751, BL. Add. 51393; Eliot to Burges, 31 Aug. 1793, Bod. BB. 34.
60. Tilson to Delafaye, 17 May (os) 1734, PRO. SP. 36/31.
61. Robinson to Hanbury Williams, 15 July 1747, Farmington, Hanbury Williams, 25; Mitchell to Keith, 15 Mar. 1762, BL. Add. 35484.
62. Eden to Pitt, 8 June 1786, PRO. 30/8/110.
63. Holdernesse to Keith, 11 June 1756, PRO. SP. 80/197.
64. Steinberg to Hyndford, 19 July 1746, Hanover, Cal. Br. 24 Nr. 6618.
65. Carteret to Schaub, 8 Jan. (os) 1722, New York, Public Library, Hardwicke papers vol. 67; Tilson to Titley, 26 June 1736, BL. Eg. 2683.
66. Horatio Walpole to Weston, 8 Sept. 1739, Farmington, Weston vol. 12; Grenville to Morton Eden, 9 Sept. 1798, BL. Add. 73765.
67. Trevor to Harrington, 1 Aug. 1740, PRO. SP. 84/386.
68. Holdernesse to Keith, 11 June 1756, BL. Add. 35480.
69. Coxe, *Robert Walpole* III, 201.
70. 'Notes relating to my coming here' [Paris, 1725], Chewton.
71. Keith to Sandwich, 12 Aug. 1748, Stafford CRO. D615/P (S)/1/10/25.
72. Sandwich to Newcastle, 14 July 1748, PRO. SP. 84/434.
73. Newcastle to Sandwich, 20 Oct. (os) 1747, BL. Add. 32810.
74. Canning to J.H. Frere, 17 Jan. 1801, BL. Add. 38833.
75. Mitchell to Keith, 9 June 1762, BL. Add. 35485.
76. Nivernais to Praslin, 16 Dec. 1762, AE. CP. Ang. 448.
77. Newcastle to Mitchell, 9 July 1756, BL. Add. 6832. cf. Horatio Walpole to Robinson, 19 Nov. 1735, BL. Add. 23796; Horatio Walpole to Waldegrave, 26 Mar. (os) 1736, Chewton; Horatio Walpole to Trevor, 30 Jan. (os), 17 Mar. (os) 1741, Aylesbury, Trevor, 25–6.
78. Peterborough to Dubois, 20 Nov., Peterborough to Orléans, 20 Nov. 1717, SRO. GD. 135/141/23; Peterborough to Stanhope, 20 Nov. 1719, Philip, Viscount Mahon (later 5th Earl Stanhope), *History of England from the Peace of Utrecht to the Peace of Versailles* (3rd edn, 7 vols, 1853–4) II, lxxxix.
79. Stanhope to Townshend, 29 Aug. 1716, PRO. SP. 43/1.
80. Addison to Peterborough, 6 May (os) 1717, HHStA. England Varia 7; Dubois to Schaub, 27 Jan. 1721, AE. CP. Ang. 339.
81. Chammorel to Dubois, 4 May 1722, AE. CP. Ang. 341.
82. Horatio to Robert Walpole, 28 Aug. 1724, BL. Add. 63749; Peterborough to Townshend, 9 Sept. 1724, PRO. SP. 35/52. See also A. Bakshian, '"A Hangdog Whom I Dearly Love": The Third Earl of Peterborough', *History Today*, 31 (1981), pp. 14–19.
83. Newcastle to Waldegrave, 2 Mar. (os) 1733, BL. Add. 32780.

6 The Diplomatic Life

1. Etherege to Charles, 2nd Earl of Middleton, Secretary of State for the Northern Department, 19 Jan. 1686, Bod. BB. 44.

2. Elliot to Pitt, 2 Dec. 1788, PRO. 30/8/132/2; Finch to Weston, 15 Nov. 1740, PRO. SP. 91/26.

3. Paget to Nottingham, 15 Dec. 1689, 5 Jan., 30 Mar., 5, 27 Apr., [no date, received 10 July], 8, 12, 19, 26 Oct., 2 Nov., 10 Dec. 1690, Instructions for Robert, Lord Sutton as envoy to Leopold, — Apr. (os) 1694, PRO. SP. 80/17. For issue of protocol at royal audiences in Lisbon, Henry Worsley to Bolingbroke, 2 June, Worsley to James Stanhope, 7 Dec. 1714, and of protocol problems over wording of letters, Worsley to Robert Pringle, 21 Jan. 1715, PRO. SP. 89/23.

4. 'Observations on the methods used at the Congress of Cambray for preserving the equality between the two crowns of England and France, then mediators' [c. 1724], BL. Stowe 186 f. 73.

5. Etherege to Middleton, 20 Mar. 1687, BL. Add. 11513; Waldegrave to Townshend, 24 July 1728, Chewton.

6. Eden to Lord Sheffield, 10 June 1788, BL. Add. 61980.

7. Malmesbury to Burges, 6 Jan. 1793, Bod. BB. 37.

8. Robinson to Harrington, 10 Mar. 1734, PRO. SP. 80/104; Smyth (ed.), *Memoirs and Correspondence of Sir Robert Murray Keith*, I, 466.

9. Thomas Burnett to Newcastle, 21 Nov. 1724, 15 June 1726, Scott to Tilson, 7 Nov. 1721, PRO. SP. 89/31, 33, 88/28. For competition in entertaining, Lady Miller, *Letters from Italy* (3 vols, 1776), I, 194–5; Smyth (ed.), *Keith*, I, 477–8.

10. Titley to Weston, 19 Feb. 1763, Weston-Underwood.

11. Macartney to Lord Holland, 19 Aug. 1765, BL. Add. 51388.

12. Newcastle to Sandwich, 11 Mar. (os) 1748, Legge to Fox, 10 Sept. 1748, BL. Add. 32811, 51388; Chavigny to Chauvelin, 9 Oct. 1731, AE. CP. Allemagne 379.

13. Hanbury Williams to Robinson, 3 Sept. 1747, BL. Add. 23826.

14. Horatio Walpole to Weston, 25 Aug. 1739, Farmington, Weston papers, vol. 12.

15. Titley to Weston, 27 Sept. 1746, Farmington, Weston papers, vol. 18.

16. Tyrawly to Sir, 6 June (os) 1739, PRONI. T. 28/2/8/47; Stanyan to Townshend, 12 July 1725, PRO. SP. 97/25; Essex to Newcastle, 12 Sept. 1733, BL. Add. 32782.

17. For example, *Centinel* 23–4 Nov. 1757.

18. Titley to Robinson, 18 Nov. (os) 1725, Leeds, Vyner 6018; Hume to James Oswald, 29 Jan. (os) 1748, volume of autograph letters from Oswald's correspondence no. 39. I consulted this at Hockworthy House in 1999, but the collection has since been moved.

19. Hanbury Williams to Fox, 22 Mar. 1748, BL. Add. 32811.

20. Richard Grenville to Keith, 23 Dec. 1783, BL. Add. 35530.

21. Finch to Harrington, 17 Oct. 1733, PRO. SP. 95/64.

22. Elliot to Pitt, — Aug. 1788, CUL. Add. 6958.

23. Vernon to Stair, 20 Dec. 1715, SRO. GD. 135/141/2.

24. Dalrymple to Liston, 21 Jan. 1784, NLS. Mss. 5540.
25. Gardiner to Burges, 3 Aug. 1793, Bod. BB. 35.
26. Robinson to Weston, 20 May 1741, PRO. SP. 80/145.
27. Hyndford to Baron Grote, 10 Apr., 11 May 1749, Hanover, Cal. Br. 24 Nr. 6618; Whitworth to Tilson, 23 Aug. 1724, BL. Add. 37395.
28. Eden to Pitt, 23 Aug. 1787, BL. Add. 34426; Methuen to Stair, 10 June 1715, SRO. GD. 135/141/3A.
29. Macartney to Lord Holland, 30 June 1766, BL. Add. 51388.
30. Bubb to Stair, 5 Aug., 14 Oct., 30 Mar., 2 Nov. 1716, SRO. GD. 135/141/2,3A,6.
31. Dormer to Newcastle, 6 Nov. 1725, Tyrawly to Newcastle, 16 Jan. 1733, PRO. SP. 89/31, 37; Tyrawly to Sir Robert Walpole, 29 Sept. 1734, CUL. C(H) corresp. 2342.
32. Albemarle to Newcastle, 14 July 1732, BL. Add. 32687.
33. Mann to Newcastle, 18 Jan. 1746, PRO. SP. 98/51.
34. Carteret to Schaub, 21 Feb. 1722, Delafaye to Schaub, 27 Feb. 1723, New York, Public Library, Hardwicke papers vol. 67; Chesterfield to Waldegrave, 1 Feb. 1729, Delafaye to Waldegrave, 25 July (os) 1733, Chewton; Sandwich to Duke of Bedford, 17 Mar. 1748, *Correspondence of John, Fourth Duke of Bedford* I (1842), pp. 331–2.
35. BL. Add. 32693 ff. 401–2; Colchester to Burges, 22 July 1793, Bod. BB. 19, cf. Vernon to Sutton, 15 Aug. (os) 1699, PRO. SP. 80/17.
36. P. Thicknesse, *Useful Hints to those who make the Tour of France* (1768), pp. 158–60.
37. *Fog's Weekly Journal*, 31 Jan. (os) 1730.
38. Thomas Pelham to Waldegrave, 24 Jan. 1732 and file at Chewton; Methuen to Vernon, 29 May 1694, PRO. SP. 89/17.
39. Burnett to Temple Stanyan, 27 Feb. 1724, 15 Feb., 19, 21 Apr., 5, 26 May 1725, Stert to Delafaye, 24 May, 18 Sept., 8 Dec. 1727, Stanyan to Temple Stanyan, 14 May 1725, PRO. SP. 89/31, 34, 97/25; Lady Suffolk to Essex, 6 Aug. (os) 1733, BL. Add. 27732; Holdernesse to Hanbury Williams, 28 Mar., reply 17 June 1755, Newport, Public Library, M411 0.12.
40. Hanbury Williams to Fox, 17 Dec. 1752, BL. Add. 51393; Fox to Hanbury Williams, 28 Aug. (os) 1752, Farmington, Hanbury Williams 67; Rondeau to Tilson, 27 Apr. (os) 1730, Holzendorf to Tilson, 1 May 1731, Methuen to Trenchard, 13 Mar. 1694, Methuen to Vernon, 25 Jan., 20 Aug. 1696, Paul Methuen to Vernon, 4 Feb. 1698, Worsley to James Stanhope, 22 Dec. 1714, 28 Mar. 1716, PRO. SP. 91/11, 84/581, 89/17, 23–4; Dorset to Carmarthen, 19 Feb., 8 July 1784, BL. Eg. 3499; Fawkener to Newcastle, 18 May, Fawkener to Harrington, 11 June, Fawkener to Robinson, 6 Aug. 1736, BL. Add. 74072; Robert to George Ainslie, 22 Apr. 1789, Bod. BB. 18; Lexington to Vernon, 14 Jan. 1696, PRO. SP. 80/17.
41. J.M. Graham (ed.), *Annals and Correspondence of the Viscount and First and Second Earls of Stair* (2 vols, 1875) I, 290–3; Davenant to Townshend, 25 Mar. 1721,

Poyntz to Delafaye, 15 Jan. 1729, PRO. SP. 79/14, 78/190; Walpole to Waldegrave, 21 Mar. (os), 14, 21 Apr. (os), 1735, Stone to Waldegrave, 18 Sept. (os) 1735, 23 Dec. (os) 1736, Delafaye to Waldegrave, 15 Apr. (os) 1731, 10, 22 Jan. (os) 1733, Couraud to Waldegrave, 28 Nov. (os) 1734, Henry Pelham to Waldegrave, 3 Feb. (os) 1732, Chewton; Waldegrave to Couraud, 6 Dec., Pelham to Stone, 30 Dec. (os) 1735, Burnett to Newcastle, 5 Aug. 1724, 26 May, 14 Nov. 1725, Dormer to Newcastle, 14 Oct., 6 Nov. 1725, Trevor to Stone, 23 Dec. 1735, PRO. SP. 78/210, 203, 89/31, 84/581.

42. Tyrawly to Delafaye, 15 June 1733, PRO. SP. 89/37.

43. Bubb to Stair, 2 Nov., Craggs to Stair, 6 Dec. (os) 1716, SRO. GD. 135/141/6, 135/147.

44. Kinnoull to Delafaye, 19 Aug. 1730, PRO. SP. 97/26.

45. Newcastle to Kinnoull, 31 Mar. (os) 1730, PRO. SP. 97/26.

46. Horace Walpole to Mann, 15 Nov. (os) 1742, W.S. Lewis et al. (eds), *The Yale Edition of Horace Walpole's correspondence … with Horace Mann II* (1955), p. 104.

47. Sutton to Tilson, 17 May 1729, PRO. SP. 81/123.

48. Essex to Waldegrave, 18 Apr., 4 July 1734, Chewton.

49. Robinson to Waldegrave, 26 Jan. 1732, Chewton.

50. Waldegrave to ——, [1725], Chewton.

51. Chesterfield to Waldegrave, 12 Oct., 10 Dec. 1728, Chewton.

52. Chesterfield to Waldegrave, 27 Nov. 1731, Chewton. For the successes of foreign envoys in London, Lynch, *The Independent Patriot* (1737), pp. 27–8.

53. Davenant to Stair, 8 Dec. 1716, SRO. GD. 135/141/6.

54. Memoir by Lady Louisa Stuart as introduction to *Letters and Journals of Lady Mary Coke* (4 vols, 1889–96), I, lii-liv.

55. Woodward to Robinson, 25 July 1730, BL. Add. 23780.

56. Perron to Charles Emmanuel III, 23 Jan. 1755, AST. LM. Ing. 59.

57. Blacow to Thomas Bray, 28 Dec. 1754, Exeter College, Oxford, Bray papers.

58. Black, 'Fit for a king', *History Today*, 37 (Apr. 1987), p. 3.

59. Yorke to Hardwicke, 12 Nov. 1749, BL. Add. 35355.

60. Lady Mary Wortley Montagu to Countess of Bute, 30 May 1757, *Letters and Works* edited by Lord Wharncliffe (2 vols, 1898) II, 316.

61. I. Grundy, *Lady Mary Wortley Montagu* (Oxford, 1999), pp. 568–9.

62. Namier and Brooke, *House of Commons*, III, 486–7.

63. Lord Cobham to Townshend, 20 Feb. 1715, BL. Blakeney Mss. 18.

64. Waldegrave Journal, Chewton.

65. Harrington to Burrish, 30 Sept. (os) 1746, PRO. SP. 81/95; Hyndford to Steinberg, 11 Oct., 8 Nov. 1746, Hanover, Han. 92 LXXV 13.

66. Keene to Delafaye, 13 Apr., 23 Aug. 1731, PRO. SP. 94/107, 108.

67. Tyrawly to Carteret, 27 Sept. 1744, Keene to Newcastle, 2 Sept. 1752, BL. Add. 23361, 32840; Rochford to Bute, 9 Sept. 1767, MS. 7/186; Burges to Grenville, 12 July 1792, Bod. BB. 48.

68. Molesworth to Stanyan, 7 Oct. 1722, PRO. SP. 92/31.

69. Whitworth to Tilson, 31 Aug. 1721, PRO. SP. 90/15.
70. Glenorchy to Duke of Kent, 8 Sept., 3, 7 Nov., 12 Dec. 1722, Bedford CRO. L30/8/10/46–51; St Saphorin to Townshend, 18 Mar. 1722, Townshend to St Saphorin, 21 Dec. (os) 1724, St Saphorin to Tilson, 22 June 1724, PRO. SP. 80/46, 48, 52. For Stair's losses, Graham, *Stair* II, 2; *Weekly Miscellany* (Dublin), 9 May (os) 1734; for Robinson, Robinson to Delafaye, 11 July 1732, PRO. SP. 80/89; cf. Cunningham (Venice) to Stanhope, 7 Aug. 1716, PRO. SP. 99/61; Lord Glenorchy to Duke of Kent, 22 Nov. 1720, Bedford CRO. L 30/8/10/15; Molesworth (Turin) to Carteret, 10 Oct. 1722, PRO. SP. 92/31; Keith to Andrew Drummond, 28 Sept. 1785, G. Smyth (ed.), *Memoirs and Correspondence of Sir Robert Murray Keith* (2 vols, 1849), II, 180.
71. Horatio Walpole to Trevor, 7 Mar. (os) 1738, Aylesbury, Trevor 11.
72. Thomas Jeans to Keith, 22 June 1775, BL. Add. 35509.
73. Namier and Brooke, *House of Commons*, III, 477.
74. Malmesbury to Burges, 16 Apr. 1794, Bod. BB. 37.
75. Delafaye to Stanhope, 2 June 1719, PRO. SP. 43/61; *Calendar of Treasury Books and Calendars I, 1729–30*, p. 134.
76. Robinson to Harrington, 2 May, Harrington to Robinson, 30 Mar. (os) 1731, PRO. SP. 80/73.
77. Burges to Hammond, 5 Sept. 1793, Bod. BB. 48.
78. Titley to Weston, 20, 27 Sept. 1746, Farmington, Hanbury Williams 18.
79. Thompson to Newcastle, 14 Sept. 1743, PRO. SP. 78/228; Keith to Sandwich, 12 Aug. 1748, Stafford CRO. D 615/P (S)/1/10/25.
80. Hyndford to Chesterfield, 14 Feb. 1747, *Sbornik*, 103 (1897), p. 211.
81. Hanbury Williams to Fox, 2, 28 Jan. 1751, BL. Add. 32724.
82. Elliot to Keith, 27 Mar., 20 July 1775, BL. Add. 35509.
83. Hampden to [Earl of Sunderland], [1722], Norris to Newcastle, 27 June (os) 1751, BL. Add. 61650 f. 117–19, 32724.
84. Tilson to Lord Polwarth, 11 Dec. 1723, Henry Pelham to Essex, 22 Oct. (os) 1734, BL. Add. 32792, 27733.
85. Macartney to Holland, 30 June 1766, BL. Add. 51388.
86. Whitworth to Tilson, 12 Nov. 1714, BL. Add. 37361; Whitworth to Delafaye, 23 Apr. 1720, PRO. SP. 90/12. cf. Molesworth (Turin) to Robert Walpole, 1 Dec. 1723, PRO. SP. 92/31.
87. Tyrawly to Newcastle, 26 Aug. 1735, PRO. SP. 89/38.
88. Stanyan to Sunderland, 2 Oct., 29 May, 12 June 1717, Woodward to Robinson, 25 July 1730, Hanbury Williams to Henry Fox, 9 Apr. 1752, BL. Add. 61537, 23780, 51393; C(H) Mss. 91/121; Waldegrave Diary, 12 Aug. 1730, Chewton; Lexington to Vernon, 11 Dec. 1694, Whitworth to Tilson, 5 Apr. 1721, PRO. SP. 80/17, 91/13; Langlois to St Paul, Northumberland CRO. ZBU B3/25. For Paget's expenses, Paget to Nottingham, 5 Apr. 1690, for Stepney's, Stepney to Vernon, 24 June 1693, for Lexington's, Lexington to Vernon, 8 Jan. 1695, all PRO. SP. 80/17, Stair's expenses, undated memo SRO, GD. 135/147 no. 25, and for Cadogan's expenses on trip to Vienna

in 1720, BL. Add. 61494 f. 17. For expense claims see, for example, Raby's for 1703, BL. Add. 63471 ff. 22–43, Henry Newton's for Genoa and Florence in 1707, Whitworth's 'Journies to Muscovy and back', Thomas Ward's extraordinaries, PRO. SP. 98/83, 91/107, 84/579 f. 478; Whitworth's bills for 1715–16, Edward Finch's extraordinaries (Dresden, 1727), Everard Fawkener's expenses (Constantinople 1735–42), BL. Add. 37362 f. 436–7, Blakeney Mss, vol. 32, Add. 74073; extraordinaries of Edmund Allen, Consul at Naples, CUL. C(H) Mss. papers 63/62. For problems, Worsley to James Stanhope, 8 Mar. 1715, Fitzherbert to Carmarthen, 2 Feb. 1784, PRO. SP. 89/23, BL. Eg. 3500. For postal costs, Bod. Ms. Rawl. D 870 f. 312. For concern to get satisfactory pay, Harris to Carmarthen, 24 Aug. 1784, PRO. 30/8/155. For the situation earlier—both good and bad—G.M. Bell, 'Elizabethan Diplomatic Compensation: Its Nature and Variety', *Journal of British Studies* (Spring 1981), pp. 1–25, and *Handlist of British Diplomatic Representatives*, pp. 13–14.

89. Burges to Fawkener, 28 June 1791, BL. Add. 74077.
90. Whitworth to Tilson, 19 Apr. 1721, PRO. SP. 90/14.
91. Jackson to Burges, 8 June 1791, Bod. BB. 36.
92. Thomas Walpole to Burges, 24 Oct. 1792, Bod. BB. 44.
93. Mountstuart to Keith, 11 Sept. 1782, BL. Add. 35526; Arbuthnot to Burges, 3 Aug. 1795, Bod. BB. 46.
94. Hamilton to Burges, 24 Mar. 1795, Bod. BB. 20.
95. Newcastle to Essex, — Oct. (os) 1734, BL. Add. 32786; Bury St Edmunds, West Suffolk CRO. 941/47/25, 484.
96. Gray to Robinson, 11 Nov. 1747, BL. Add. 23826.
97. Gray to Robinson, 6 Jan. 1748, BL. Add. 23827.
98. Poyntz to Tilson, 19 May 1728, Norwich, Norfolk CRO. Bradfer Lawrence papers.
99. St Saphorin to Schaub, 4 Mar. 1720, PRO. SP. 80/40.
100. Chesterfield to Liston, 9 June, 10 July (quote) 1784, NLS. MS. 5541.
101. Malmesbury to Burges, 18 Jan. 1794, Bod. BB. 37.
102. Jackson to Burges, 8 June 1791, Bod. BB. 36.
103. Robinson to Delafaye, 4 July 1733, PRO. SP. 80/97.
104. Keene to Newcastle, 2 Sept. 1752, BL. Add. 32840.
105. Robinson to Delafaye, 12 Mar. 1732, PRO. SP. 80/226, to Newcastle, 30 Sept. 1732, BL. Add. 32778.
106. Hedges to Robinson, 9 July 1727, Leeds, District Archive, Vyner papers 6018.
107. Thomas Jeans to Keith, 22 June 1775, BL. Add. 35509.
108. Robinson to Horatio Walpole, 25 Aug. 1731, Trevor to Horatio Walpole, 8 Feb. 1737, BL. Add. 63750, 73891.

7 Diplomats and the Information Society

1. Instructions for Sutton, 25 Mar. (os) 1727, PRO. SP. 81/122.
2. Porter to Weston, 10 Dec. 1764, BL. Add. 57927.
3. M.S. Anderson, 'Eighteenth-century Theories of the Balance of Power', in R.M. Hatton and Anderson (eds), *Studies in Diplomatic History* (1970), pp. 183–98; Black, 'The Theory of the Balance of Power in the First Half of the Eighteenth Century', *Review of International Studies* (1983), pp. 55–61.
4. Huntingdon CRO. DD. M36/8, p. 48; PRO. SP. 80/136; HL. Lo. 7669.
5. A 398-page memorandum by St Saphorin about Austria was sent in June 1721, New York, Public Library, Hardwicke papers vol. 41 and BL. Add. 61707. For his 1727 memorandum on the Mecklenburg dispute, PRO. SP. 80/61. Tilson to Trevor, 26 July (os) 1737, Aylesbury, Trevor 9; Waldegrave to Newcastle, 22 May 1735, Chewton; Earl of Halifax, Secretary of State, to Hay, 26 Mar., Hay to Halifax, 18 May 1765, PRO. SP. 89/60.
6. Auckland to Burges, 24 Aug. 1791, Bod. BB. 30.
7. Heslop's bill, BL. Add. 73524 HH; 3rd Earl of Malmesbury (ed.), *Diaries and Correspondence of James Harris, First Earl of Malmesbury* (4 vols, 1844), II, 304–6; Grenville, Foreign Secretary, to George III, 25 Sept., George III to Grenville, 26 Sept. 1792, BL. Add. 58857; Canning to John Hookham Frere, 20 June 1800, BL. Add. 38833.
8. Stone to Waldegrave, 10, 25 Apr. (os) 1735, Chewton; Fawkener to Rondeau, 21 Nov. 1736, BL. Add. 74072; Cressener to Burrish, 9 Apr. 1757, PRO. SP. 110/6.
9. Titley to Weston, 3, 9, 27 Mar. 1762, Farmington, Weston, vol. 5.
10. Keith to Grenville, 5 Aug. 1791, PRO. FO. 7/27.
11. P. Fraser, *The Intelligence of the Secretaries of State and Their Monopoly of Licensed News 1660–1688* (Cambridge, 1956); P.M. Handover, *A History of the London Gazette, 1665–1965* (1965).
12. R.M. Hatton, 'The "London Gazette" in 1718: Supply of News from Abroad', *Bulletin of the Institute of Historical Research*, p. 108; Circular letter from Carteret, 11 Feb. (os) 1723, draft PRO. SP. 92/31; Francis Colman, Secretary in Vienna, to Tilson, 4 Mar. 1724, PRO. SP. 80/51; Weston to Robinson, 28 July (os) 1728, Weston to Tyrawly, 16 Mar. (os) 1744, BL. Add. 23802, 23630; Holdernesse to Hanbury Williams, 19 Aug. 1755, Newport.
13. For example, Stepney to Vernon, 20 June 1693, John Molesworth to Carteret, 30 Mar. 1723, Colman to Townshend, 17 Feb., 10 Mar., 7 Apr. 1723, 5 Apr., 31 May, 28 June 1724, Colman to Tilson, 5 Sept. 1723, Charles Holzendorf, secretary at The Hague, to Tilson, 28 July 1728, Waldegrave to Townshend, 3 July 1728, Keene to Delafaye, 23 Aug. 1731, Colman to Delafaye, 26 Apr. 1732, Burrish to William Chetwynd, Under-Secretary, 23 May, 10 July 1747, PRO. SP. 80/17, 92/31, 80/51, 84/301, 80/61, 94/108, 98/84, 81/96; Waldegrave to Tilson, 22 Oct. 1729, Chewton; Horatio

Walpole to ——, 1, 19, 26 Mar., 9 Apr. 1715, Tilson to Robinson, 14 July (os) 1730, Robinson to Weston, 28 Apr. 1736, George Aust, Senior Clerk in Northern Department, and Deputy Writer of the *Gazette*, to Keith, 27 Oct. 1789, BL. Add. 74063, 23780, 23853, 35541.

14. Handover, *Gazette*, p. 57.
15. For example, Destouches, French envoy in London, to Dubois, French foreign minister, 9, 19 Nov. 1722, AE. CP. Ang. 343; Prince Eugène to Count Philip Kinsky, Austrian envoy in London, 3 Mar., 20 June 1731, HHStA. Grosse Korrespondenz 94(b); Baron Wachtendonck, Palatine foreign minister, to Baron Haslang, Palatine envoy in London, 27 Aug. 1759, Munich, Bayerisches Haupstaatsarchiv, Bayr. Ges. London 235.
16. Henry Worsley to James Stanhope, 16, 30 Aug., 12 Oct. 1715, Finch to Newcastle, 31 Aug. 1725, PRO. SP. 89/23, 84/579.
17. Finch to Tilson, 24 Oct., 18 Nov., Tilson to Finch, 20 Oct. (os) 1727, PRO. SP. 84/294.
18. Townshend to Hermann, 7 May, Glenorchy to Townshend, 7, 24 Aug., 5 Oct., Wych to Townshend, 4 June 1728, PRO. SP. 75/51, 84/45.
19. Horatio Walpole to Newcastle, and to John Couraud, 8 July 1735, PRO. SP. 84/344.
20. Horatio Walpole to Harrington, 12 Aug. 1735, PRO. SP. 84/346.
21. Couraud to Waldegrave, 4 Sept. (os) 1738, Chewton.
22. Stone to Trevor, 16 Dec. (os) 1737, Aylesbury, Trevor 9; Trevor to Horatio Walpole, 3 Jan. 1738, BL. Add. 73891.
23. Hatton, *George I* (1978), pp. 54–68.
24. There are two copies in the British Library, 10805 aa 42 and 900 C23 (1).
25. In the List and Index Society report *State Papers France 1732–1738* (1984), pp. 2, 208, Renard is inaccurately given as the book's printer, one of several errors in the volume.
26. Renard to Dayrolle, 13 Aug. 1732. Two copies survive, one forwarded to Hanover, the other sent to Waldegrave, PRO. SP. 84/319 f. 119, Chewton.
27. Dayrolle to Waldegrave, 15 Aug. 1732, Chewton.
28. Dayrolle to Tilson, 16 Aug. 1732, PRO. SP. 84/319. For action in the United Provinces, Dayrolle to Tilson, 19, 23 Aug., Dayrolle to Harrington, 23 Aug. 1732, PRO. SP. 84/319.
29. Delafaye to Waldegrave, 14 Aug. (os) 1732, Chewton.
30. Waldegrave to Delafaye, 31 Aug. 1732, PRO. SP. 78/201.
31. Missing.
32. Waldegrave to Delafaye, 3 Sept. 1732, PRO. SP. 78/201.
33. Walpole to Trevor, 14 Mar. (os) 1741, Aylesbury, Trevor 26. There is no additional material in State Papers Holland.
34. Trevor to Walpole, 21, 24, 31 Mar. 1741, Aylesbury, Trevor 26.
35. Horatio Walpole to Newcastle, 3, 14 Aug., Horatio Walpole and William Stanhope to Newcastle, 25 Sept. 1728, BL. Add. 32757–8.
36. Worsley to Tilson, 2 Apr. 1717, Hanbury Williams to Newcastle, 1 Aug.

1750, PRO. SP. 89/25, 88/71; Torrington's journal, 22 May 1788, Stafford CRO., Bradford Mss. 18/9; Carteret to Lumley, 5 Feb. (os) 1723, William White to Temple Stanyan, 21 Apr. 1727, PRO. SP. 89/30, 34; Du Bourgay to Tilson, 9 Dec. 1724, PRO. SP. 90/18.

37. Woodward to Tilson, 28 May 1729, PRO. SP. 88/35.

38. Hyndford to Harrington, 5 May 1741, PRO. SP. 90/52.

39. Hop to Fagel, 11 Aug. 1739, PRO. SP. 107/31.

40. Reverend Patrick St Clair to Ashe Windham, 9 Oct. (os) 1730, Norwich, Norfolk RO. Ketton-Cremer Mss, WKC 6/24 401 X; Horatio Walpole to Titley, 23 Oct. 1736, BL. Eg. 2683.

41. Samson to Trevor, 19 Aug. 1736, Aylesbury, Trevor 4.

42. Trevor to Weston, 29 Apr. 1740, PRO. SP. 84/385.

43. Waldegrave to Stone, 8 July 1740, PRO. SP. 43/91.

44. Couraud to Waldegrave, 1, 5 Dec. (os) 1735, Chewton.

45. Essex to Newcastle, 13 July 1732, PRO. 92/34.

46. Wolters to Weston, 28 July 1761, Farmington, Weston 21, cf. 28 Aug.

47. Burges to Whitworth, 26 Mar. 1793, Bod. BB. 48, p. 191.

48. Robethon to Stair, 24 Aug. 1716, SRO. GD. 135/141/7.

49. Scott, *British Foreign Policy*, p. 18.

50. Whitworth to Tilson, 24 June 1721, PRO. SP. 90/14.

51. Robinson to Tilson, 14 Sept. 1735, PRO. SP. 80/118.

52. Newcastle to Dickens, 12 Oct. 1753, *Sbornik* 148 (1916), pp. 505–6, cf. 26 Oct., 6 Nov.

53. K. Ellis, *The Post Office in the Eighteenth Century: A Study in Administrative History* (1958) and 'The Administrative Connections between Britain and Hanover', *Journal of the Society of Archivists*, 3 (1969), pp. 556–66); P. Fritz, 'The Anti-Jacobite Intelligence System of the English Ministers, 1715–1745', *Historical Journal*, 16 (1973), pp. 265–89, and *The English Ministers and Jacobitism between the Rebellions of 1715 and 1745* (Toronto, 1975). Fritz has little to say about the situation after 1727.

54. Ellis, *Post Office*, p. 70.

55. Mr Thomas to C. Lechmere, 1 May 1838, PRO. SP. 107/1A.

56. SP. 92/85–7 contains the intercepted correspondence of the Sardinian envoy for 1733, 94/246 Spanish intercepts for 1737–8, 89/92 Portuguese material for 1762–80, and 78/325 French intercepts for 1777–80.

57. Townshend to Stephen Poyntz, William Stanhope and Horatio Walpole, 15 July 1729, PRO. SP. 78/193. See also, for example, Stepney to Vernon, 19 Sept. 1693, Worsley to James Stanhope, 8 Feb., 22 Mar., 5 Apr., 16 Aug. 1715, anonymous undated note, PRO. SP. 80/17, 89/23, 30 f. 219.

58. Hull, University Library, Hotham papers 3/3.

59. BL. Add. 61567–76. For intercepts of Portuguese diplomatic material in the papers of Horatio Walpole, BL. Add. 73981–3.

60. Hedges to Robinson, 9 July 1727, Leeds, District Archive Office, Vyner Mss. 6018; Chesterfield to Waldegrave, 30 Jan. 1731, Chewton.

61. Ellis, *Post Office*, pp. 66–8, 127–42; J.C. Sainty, *Officials of the Secretaries of State 1660–1782* (1973), pp. 51–2; W. Gibson, 'An Eighteenth-Century Paradox: The Career of the Decipherer-Bishop, Edward Willes', *British Journal for Eighteenth-Century Studies*, 12 (1989), pp. 69–76.

62. Corbiere to Newcastle, 27 Jan. (os) 1731, PRO. SP. 36/22; Burges to Auckland, 20 July 1790, Bod. BB. 47.

63. Ellis, *Post Office*, p. 74, 'Administrative Connections', pp. 560–1, and 'British Communications and Diplomacy in the Eighteenth Century', *Bulletin of the Institute of Historical Research*, 31 (1958), p. 163; B. Peterson, '"The Correspondent in Paris": en engelsk informationaskalle udner 1700–talet', *Scandia*, 27 (1961), pp. 387–99; S.P. Oakley, 'The Interception of Posts in Celle, 1694–1700', in Hatton and Bromley (eds), *William III and Louis XIV* (Liverpool, 1968), pp. 95–116.

64. *Polit. Corresp.* 7, pp. 281–2, 290; Willes to Burges, 18 Oct. 1790, Bod. BB. 45.

65. Chesterfield to Tilson, 10 Oct. 1730, PRO. SP. 84/308.

66. Robert Wolters, Consul in Rotterdam, to Sir Everard Fawkener, Cumberland's secretary, 15 Dec. 1747, RA. CP. 30/121.

67. Newcastle to Henry Pelham, 26 July 1752, BL. Add. 35412.

68. B. Williams, *The Life of William Pitt, Earl of Chatham* (2 vols, 1913) I, 399; Oakley, 'Interception', p. 95; BL. Add. 32309; Sir John Fortescue (ed.), *The Correspondence of King George the Third from 1760 to December 1783* (6 vols, 1928), III, 39–40.

69. Charles Arbuthnot to Burges, 3 Aug. 1795, Bod. BB. 46.

70. Thomas Walpole to Keith, 4 Nov., Morton Eden to Keith, 5 Nov. 1784, BL. Add. 35532.

71. P. Cunningham (ed.), *The Letters of Horace Walpole* I (Edinburgh, 1906), p. cxxxviii; W. Coxe, *Sir Robert Walpole* II, 300–6; Newcastle to Harrington and Poyntz, 7 May (os), 1730, Newcastle to Waldegrave, 1 Apr. (os) 1731, Broglie to Chauvelin, 9 Apr. 1731, BL. Add. 32767, 32772.

72. Newcastle to Townshend, 30 June (os) 1725, BL. Add. 32687; Sinzendorf to Palm, 23 Mar. 1727, CUL. C(H) Mss. corresp. 1290; Frederick William I to Borck, envoy in London, 19 Jan. 1736, BL. Add. 33064.

73. Richard Neville Aldworth to Duke of Bedford, 26 Apr. (os) 1750, Bedford papers; Newcastle to George II, 4 Apr. (os) 1730, PRO. SP. 36/18; undated correspondence between George II and Townshend, Coxe, *Walpole*, II, 536–7.

74. Reichenbach to Grumbkow, 14, 18 Apr. 1730, Hull, DD HO 3/3.

75. Cobbett, IX, 222, 229; *London Journal*, 2 Mar. (os), *Daily Courant*, 13 July (os) 1734.

76. Robert Walpole to Waldegrave, 7 Mar. (os) 1737, Chewton.

77. 'Interrogation du ... Thomas Limpous', 27 July 1738, AE. CP. Ang; Eden to Pitt, 27 July 1786, PRO. 30/8/110.

78. Wager to Admiral Norris, 7 Oct. 1734, BL. Add. 28156.

79. Newcastle to Waldegrave, 24 Apr. (os), Waldegrave to Newcastle, 16

May, 16, 25 June BL. Add. 32772; Black and A. Reese, 'Die Panik von 1731', in J. Kunisch (ed.), *Expansion und Gleichgewicht. Studien zur europäischen Mächtepolitik des ancien régime* (Berlin, 1986), pp. 69–95; Waldegrave to Delafaye, 18 Oct. 1733, PRO. SP. 78/204.

80. Albemarle to Bedford, 29 Nov. 1749, Bedford papers; cf. Rochford to Robert Walpole, 22 Sept. 1770, PRO. SP. 78/280.

81. Holloway, Consul in Malaga, to Newcastle, 23 Sept., 11, 18 Nov. 1727, Cayley to Keene, 15 May, Cayley to Newcastle, 19 Apr., 17 May, 21 June, 9 Aug. 1729, PRO. SP. 94/215, 219.

82. Parker to William Poyntz, 19 Aug. 1716, Newcastle to Thompson, 19 Feb. (os), Thompson to John Couraud, 22, 30 Mar., 26 Apr., 6, 20 May, Thompson to Weston, 18 July, 22 Aug., Thompson to Harrington, 29 Aug., Sorell, Thompson's secretary, to Couraud, 16 Sept., Thompson to Couraud, 8, 15 Nov. 1741, 19 Dec. 1742, Thompson to Newcastle, 11 June 1743, PRO. SP. 89/24, 78/225, 227, 228.

83. Memoranda on Spanish preparations, — Apr., 29 July 1790, BL. Add. 59279; Merry to Leeds, 15, 19, 29 Apr., Fitzherbert to Leeds, 16 June, 'State of the Intelligence', 13, 26 June, Walpole to Leeds, 28 Apr., 26 May 1790, PRO. FO. 63/13; Worsley to Thomas Tickell, 5 Aug. 1720, PRO. SP. 89/28. Cf. Thomas Lumley, envoy in Lisbon, to Carteret, 22 June 1722, Newcastle to Dormer, 21 June (os) 1726, PRO. SP. 89/30, 32.

84. Jackson to William Poyntz, 9, 17 Mar., 23 Apr., 26 June, Jackson to Craggs, 29 July, 28 Aug., 18 Dec. 1719, PRO. SP. 89/27; Reports from Goldsworthy and Renard, 13, 24 Jan. 1744, PRO. ADM 1 3828, pp. 867, 875, 879.

85. Castres to Thomas Corbett, 18 Jan. 1744, PRO. ADM. 1 3828, p. 859.

86. N. Tracy, *Navies, Deterrence, and American Independence* (Vancouver, 1988), pp. 13–22. See also F.P. Renaut, *Le Secret Service de l'Amirauté britannique au temps de la guerre d'Amérique 1776–1783* (Paris, 1936); E. Sparrow, *Secret Service. British Agents in France 1792–1815* (Woodbridge, 1999); M. Duffy, 'British Naval Intelligence and Bonaparte's Egyptian Expedition of 1798', *Mariner's Mirror*, 84 (1998), pp. 278–90; S.E. Maffeo, *Most Secret and Confidential: Intelligence in the Age of Nelson* (Annapolis, 2000) is weak.

87. Worsley to Craggs, 8 Jan. 1720, Thompson to Couraud, 11 Feb. 1741, PRO. SP. 89/28, 78/225; Tracy, *Navies*, p. 13.

88. Thompson to Newcastle, 14 Oct. 1742, PRO. SP. 78/227.

89. Pelham to Delafaye, 21 July 1731, PRO. SP. 78/198 and enclosures; Poyntz to Waldegrave, 19 July (os) 1731, Chewton.

90. Duncan to Aust, 17, 21, 22 Nov., Duncan to Elgin, 8 Dec. 1792, BL. Add. 34445, PRO. FO. 26/19.

91. E.g. John Methuen (Lisbon) to Sir John Trenchard, 19 Sept., 3, 21, 31 Oct., 14 Nov. 1693, PRO. SP. 89/17. On the value of neutral listening posts, Puysieulx, French Foreign Minister, to Montaigu, envoy in Venice, 13 Feb. 1748, Paris, Bibliothèque Nationale, nouvelles acquisitions françaises 14911.

92. Weston to Burrish, 26 Feb. (os) 1742, PRO. SP. 110/6.

93. Cressener to Fawkener, 5, 8, 15 Dec. 1747, RA. CP. 30/72, 85, 152; Albemarle to Bedford, 29 Nov. 1749, Bedford papers; Paris intelligence in Cressener report of 2 May 1758, BL. Add. 32879. The only available study deals largely with his career after the Seven Years' War, A. Schulte, *Ein englischer Gesandter am Rhein: George Cressener* (Bonn, 1971). The French supported Cressener's expulsion from Liège, Rouillé to Mirepoix, 19 Feb., 15 June 1755, AE. CP. Ang. 438–9.

94. Holdernesse to Yorke, — Feb. 1756, BL. Add. 3447.

95. M. Antoine and D. Ozanam (eds), *Correspondance Secrète du Comte de Broglie avec Louis XV* (2 vols, Paris, 1956–61); M. Braubach, *Die Geheimdiplomatie des Prinzen Eugen von Savoyen* (Cologne, 1962).

96. I. de Madariaga, *Britain, Russia and the Armed Neutrality of 1780* (1962); Hatton, 'Gratifications and Foreign Policy: Anglo-French Rivalry in Sweden during the Nine Years War', in Hatton and J.S. Bromley (eds), *William III and Louis XIV. Essays 1680–1720 by and for Mark A. Thomson* (Liverpool, 1968), pp. 68–94; D.A. Miller, *Sir Joseph Yorke and Anglo-Dutch Relations 1774–1780* (The Hague, 1970); M.F. Metcalf, *Russia, England and Swedish Party Politics 1762–1766: The Interplay between Great Power Diplomacy and Domestic Politics during Sweden's Age of Liberty* (Stockholm, 1977); M. Roberts, *British Diplomacy and Swedish Politics 1758–1773* (1980).

97. L. Wiesener, *Le Régent, l'Abbé Dubois et les Anglais* (3 vols, Paris, 1891–9); E. Bourgeois, *Le Secret du Régent et la politique de l'Abbé Dubois* (Paris, 1907).

98. Horn, *British Diplomatic Service*, pp. 282–3.

99. E.g. Newcastle to Colman, 27 Aug. 1725, PRO. SP. 98/83.

100. Horatio to Robert Walpole, — Mar., 24 Mar. 1725, BL. Add. 63749. For Horatio as spymaster, see also BL. Add. 73858, 73994–74002.

101. Essex to Newcastle, 4 Nov. 1733, PRO. SP. 92/35 re. Stosch.

102. *Polit. Corresp.* XI, 294, cf. p. 193.

103. Black, 'Sir Robert Ainslie: His Majesty's Agent-Provocateur? British Foreign Policy and the International Crisis of 1787', *European History Quarterly*, 14 (1984), pp. 253–83.

104. Townshend to Robert Walpole, 25 Oct. 1723, BL. Add. 32686. Townshend was their brother-in-law. The three kept a close eye on Schaub, Townshend to Robert Walpole, 20 July 1723, PRO. SP. 43/4.

8 Diplomacy and British Foreign Policy

1. Northampton to ——, 23 Oct. 1762, BL. Stowe 257.

2. *Owen's Weekly Chronicle*, 17, 31 Mar. 1764.

3. Black, 'The Crown, Hanover and the Shift in British Foreign Policy in the 1760s', in Black (ed.), *Knights Errant and True Englishmen. British Foreign Policy, 1660–1800* (Edinburgh, 1988), pp. 113–34.

4. U. Dann, *Hannover und England 1740–1760. Diplomatie und Selbsterhaltung* (Hildesheim, 1986).

5. This is not intended to deny the continued role of Hanoverian concerns, S. Conrady, 'Die Wirksamkeit König Georg III für die hannoverschen Kurlande', *Niedersächsisches Jahrbuch für Landesgeschichte*, 39 (1969), pp. 150–91; T.C.W. Blanning, '"That horrid Electorate" or "Ma patrie germanique"? George III, Hanover and the *Fürstenbund* of 1785', *Historical Journal*, 20 (1977), pp. 321–6.

6. E.D. Adams, *The Influence of Grenville on Pitt's Foreign Policy, 1787–1798* (Washington, 1904) should be read alongside M. Duffy, 'Pitt, Grenville and the Control of British Foreign Policy in the 1790s', in Black (ed.), *Knights Errant*, pp. 151–77.

7. M. Morris, *The British Monarchy and the French Revolution* (New Haven, 1998).

8. R. Pares, *King George III and the Politicians* (Oxford, 1953), pp. 143–81; C. Middleton, 'The Impact of the American and French Revolutions on the British Constitution: A Case Study of the British Cabinet', *Consortium on Revolutionary Europe. Proceedings 1986*, pp. 317–26.

9. Black, *Foreign Policy in an Age of Revolutions*, pp. 474–6.

10. E.A. Smith, *George IV* (New Haven, 1999).

11. Sheffield Public Library, Wentworth Woodhouse papers RI-2124.

12. For a similar conclusion from the nineteenth-century perspective, R.A. Jones, *The British Diplomatic Service 1815–1914* (Waterloo, Ontario, 1983), pp. 30–1.

13. Jackson to Burges, 6 May 1791, Bod. BB. 36 f. 68.

14. Mann to Newcastle, 29 Oct. 1748, BL. Add. 32815. Consuls were particularly responsible for preserving commercial rights and privileges, Bedford to Goldsworthy, 28 Nov. (os) 1748, PRO. SP. 98/55. For the situation elsewhere, A. Mézin, *Les Consuls de France au Siècle des Lumières, 1715–1792* (Paris, 1997).

15. Entry book, BL. Add. 72558; P.S. Lachs, *The Diplomatic Corps under Charles II and James II* (New Brunswick, 1965), pp. 36, 62; Etherege to Trumbull, 10 Sept. 1686, BL. Add. 11513.

16. Wych to Harrington, 17 Aug. 1734, PRO. SP. 82/54.

17. Paget to Nottingham, 23 Mar. 1690, PRO. SP. 80/17; John Balaquier to Shaub, 5 July 1722, New York, Public Library, Hardwicke collection vol. 67.

18. Tyrawly to Newcastle, 25 Sept. 1728, Tyrawly to Delafaye, 25 Feb. 1729, PRO. SP. 89/35, cf. Tyrawly to Robert Walpole, 29 Sept. 1734, CUL. C(H) corresp. 2342; Keene to Newcastle, 4 Dec. 1736, Chewton; Cayley to Keene, 22 June 1728, PRO. SP. 94/218.

19. Sandwich to Alexander Burnet, in charge, in Mitchell's absence, of affairs in Berlin, 15 Jan. 1765, PRO. SP. 90/84.

20. Essex to Newcastle, 13 Sept. 1734, PRO. SP. 92/35.

21. Burrish to Holdernesse, 12 Aug. 1755, PRO. SP. 81/105.

22. Ryder diary, 5 Jan. 1754, Sandon Park, Harrowby mss; Sedgwick, *History of Parliament* I, 596–7.

23. J.O. McLachlan, *Trade and Peace with Old Spain, 1667–1750: A Study of the Influence of Commerce on Anglo-Spanish Diplomacy in the First Half of the Eighteenth Century* (Cambridge, 1940).

24. Bladen, '… the Matters which gave rise to the Conferences at Antwerp', PRO. SP. 80/136, ff. 138–47; P.G.M. Dickson, 'English Commercial Negotiations with Austria, 1737–1752', in A. Whiteman, J.S. Bromley and Dickson (eds), *Statesman, Scholars and Merchants* (Oxford, 1970), pp. 81–112; Instructions for Craufurd, 2 Sept. 1784, and for Eden, 10 Mar. 1786, PRO. FO. 27/13, 19.

25. J. Ehrman, *The British Government and Commercial Negotiations with Europe 1783–1793* (Cambridge, 1962).

26. Newcastle to Burges, — Apr. (os) 1731, 29 Sept. (os) 1734, Burges to Newcastle, 4, 25 June 1734, PRO. SP. 99/63.

27. K. Wilson, *The Sense of the People. Politics, Culture and Imperialism in England, 1715–1785* (Cambridge, 1995).

28. For the themes of flexibility and inclusiveness, P. Langford, *Public Life and the Propertied Englishman, 1689–1789* (Oxford, 1991).

29. Rochford to Shelburne, 5 Nov. 1766, PRO. SP. 78/271.

30. Barrillon to Louis XIV, 10, 13 Sept. 1685, AE. CP. Ang. 156.

31. BL. Add. 72546.

32. George Hamilton to Waldegrave, June and Nov. 1738, Chewton; (quote) Thomas Jeans to Keith, 22 June 1775, BL. Add. 35509; Vernon to Sutton, 30 June (os) 1699, PRO. SP. 80/17.

33. Scott to Tilson, 10 June 1721, Whitworth to Townshend, 11 Nov. 1721, Harrington to Woodward, 9, 30 Mar. (os), Woodward to Harrington, 12 May 1733, PRO. SP. 88/28, 90/15, 88/41.

34. Stepney to Vernon, 5 Aug. 1693, Townshend to Chesterfield, 14 May (os) 1728, PRO. SP. 80/17, 84/300.

35. Paget to Nottingham, 2 Mar. 1690, Molesworth to Newcastle, 21 June, 1, 25 July, 21 Oct. 1724, Newcastle to Hedges, 6 July (os) 1727, PRO. SP. 80/17, 92/31–2.

36. Lord Finch to the Earl of Nottingham, 4 Feb. (os) 1724, Leicester CRO. DG/7/4952.

37. Elliot to Keith, 20 July 1775, BL. Add. 35509.

38. Auckland to Pitt, 30 Jan. 1792, CUL. Add. 6958.

39. Auckland to Burges, 11 Sept. 1790, Bod. BB. 30.

40. Black, 'The Development of Anglo-Sardinian Relations in the First Half of the Eighteenth Century', *Studi Piemontesi*, 12 (1983), pp. 48–60.

41. Viry, report, 27 May 1768, AST. LM. Ing. 74; Châtelet to Choiseul, 27 May 1768, AE. CP. Ang. 483.

42. Scarnafis, report, 16 Apr. 1771, AST. LM. Ing. 77.

43. Brand to Robert Wharton, 16 May 1787, Durham, University Library, Brand papers; Leeds to Eden, 24 July 1789, PRO. FO. 72/15.

44. Elliot to William Eden, 11 July 1776, BL. Add. 34413.

45. Cobbett, XX, 667.
46. Hammond to Drake, 7 Dec. 1790, Exeter, Devon CRO. 1700 M/CP 122; memorandum recommending creation of Secretaries of Legation [1786–7], PRO. FO. 366/525.
47. Mrs E. Stuart Wortley, *A Prime Minister and his Son* (1925), pp. 198–203.
48. Mason to Burges, 16 Aug. 1789, Bod. BB. 18.
49. Craufurd to Burges, 25 Apr., 30 June, Burges to Craufurd, 11 Aug. 1795, Bod. BB. 32; H. Mitchell, *The Underground War Against Revolutionary France: The Missions of William Wickham 1794–1800* (Oxford, 1965); M. Hutt, *Chouannerie and Counter-Revolution. Puisaye, the Princes and the British Government* (Cambridge, 1983).
50. Black, *The Collapse of the Anglo-French Alliance 1727–31* (Gloucester, 1987), pp. 63–5; HHStA. Grosse Korrespondenz 85a.
51. Leeds to Burges, 29 Aug. 1790, Bod. BB. 37; Gower to Pitt, 22 Oct. 1790, CUL. Add. 69583 no. 858; Pitt to Elliot, — Oct., Elliot to Pitt, 26 Oct. 1790, PRO. 30/8/102, 139; C.P. Miles (ed.), *The Correspondence of William Augustus Miles on the French Revolution, 1789–1817* (2 vols, 1890), I, 150–71; H.V. Evans, 'William Pitt, William Miles and the French Revolution', *Bulletin of the Institute of Historical Research*, 43 (1970), pp. 196–8.
52. Yorke to Hanbury Williams, 10 Sept. 1751, Farmington, Hanbury Williams 12; Frederick II to Mitchell, 28 Sept. 1751, *Polit. Corresp.* 8 (1882), p. 464. Important series held outside Windsor include the papers of Owen O'Rourke, long-serving Jacobite agent in Vienna, HHStA. England Varia 8. For the extensive literature on Jacobite diplomacy, a good starting point is G.H. Jones, *The Main Stream of Jacobitism* (Cambridge, Mass., 1954). On Jacobite diplomats, E. Gregg, 'Monarchs without a Crown', in R. Oresko, G.C. Gibbs and H.M. Scott (eds), *Royal and Republican Sovereignty in Early Modern Europe: Essays in Memory of Ragnhild Hatton* (Cambridge, 1997), pp. 391–2.
53. E. Cruickshanks, *Political Untouchables. The Tories and the '45* (1979), p. 23. For an example that could be readily repeated, Newcastle to Dormer, 10 May (os) 1726, PRO. SP. 89/32.
54. Burges to Fawkener, 28 June, Fawkener to Grenville, 1, 12, 28 July 1791, BL. Add. 74077, 59023; A. Cunningham, 'Robert Adair's Mission to St. Petersburg', in Cunningham, *Anglo-Ottoman Encounters in the Age of Revolution* (1993), pp. 32–50.
55. Earl of Carlisle, 'Anecdotes about numerous people', Castle Howard, J14/65/2.
56. Historical Manuscripts Commission, *Carlisle Manuscripts*.
57. Grenville to Marquess of Buckingham, 30 July 1787, HL. STG. Box 39 (3); Gardiner to Burges, 1 Sept. 1792, Bod. BB. 35.
58. Thurlow to Burges, 5 Dec. 1789, Cabinet minute, 30 Nov. 1789, Bod. BB. 18, 52.
59. L. and M. Frey, '"The Reign of the Charlatans is Over". The French

Revolutionary Attack on Diplomatic Practice', *Journal of Modern History*, 65 (1993), pp. 706–44.

60. Dorset to Leeds, 17 July 1789, PRO. FO. 27/32; Charles Sackville to Hotham, 31 July 1789, Hull UL. DDHo./4/23.

61. Dorset to Leeds, 28 July 1789, PRO. FO. 27/32.

62. Dorset to Leeds, 27, 28, 30 July, Dorset to Montmorin, 26 July 1789, PRO. FO. 27/32.

63. Eden to Pitt, 3 Oct. 1789, PRO. 30/8/111; Richmond to Pitt, 29 Aug., 1 Sept. 1788, CUL. Add. 6958; Richmond to Grenville, 4 Feb. 1792, BL. Add. 58937; Leeds to Fitzgerald, 5 Mar. 1790, PRO. FO. 27/134.

64. O. Browning (ed.), *The Despatches of Earl Gower 1790–92* (Cambridge, 1885).

65. Burges to Grenville, 15, 17 Aug., 3 Sept., Dundas to George III, 17 Aug., Dundas to Gower, 17 Aug., Burges to Auckland, 17 Aug. 1792, Broomhall 60/2/22; Auckland to Burges, 21 Aug. 1792, Bod. BB. 30.

66. To visit George III.

67. Burges to his wife, 1 Sept. 1792, Bod. BB. 48.

68. Aust to Grenville, [27 Aug.?], [28 Aug.?], 8 Sept., Burges to Grenville, 1, 8 Sept. 1792, BL. Add. 58968; Pitt to Edward Eliot, 31 Aug. 1792, Ipswich, Suffolk CRO. HA 119 T108/39; Auckland to Burges, 21 Aug., Lindsay to Burges, 3, 5 Sept. 1792, Bod. BB. 30, 45.

69. Burges to William Eliot, 30 July 1793, Bod. BB. 48.

70. PRO. FO. 29/4–5.

71. Heathcote to Grenville, 9 Aug. 1796, PRO. FO. 154/1.

72. Grenville to Whitworth, 6 Aug. 1799, PRO. FO. 65/27.

73. Miles to Pitt, — Oct. 1785, Beinecke, Miles file.

74. G.S. Rowe and A.W. Knott, 'The Longchamps Affair (1784–1786), The Law of Nations, and the Shaping of Early American Foreign Policy', *Diplomatic History*, 10 (1986), pp. 199–220.

75. Thornton to Burges, 25 Apr. 1796, Bod. BB. 21.

76. Thornton to Burges, 26 May 1796, Bod. BB. 21.

77. Hammond to Grenville, 1 Nov. 1791, BL. Add. 58939; G.S. Graham, *Sea Power and British North America 1783–1820. A Study in British Colonial Policy* (Cambridge, Mass., 1941), pp. 79–83; C.R. Ritcheson, *Aftermath of Revolution: British Policy towards the United States 1782–1795* (Dallas, 1969); J.L. Wright, *Britain and the American Frontier, 1783–1815* (Athens, Georgia, 1975), pp. 1–85; R.C. Stuart, *United States Expansionism and British North America, 1775–1871* (Chapel Hill, 1988), pp. 28–41.

78. C. Williamson, *Vermont in Quandry: 1763–1825* (Montpelier, Vermont, 1949), pp. 151–64.

79. H.C. Syrett (ed.), *The Papers of Alexander Hamilton* 7 (New York, 1963), pp. 70–4; J.P. Boyd, *Number 7, Alexander Hamilton's Secret Attempts to Control American Foreign Policy* (Princeton, 1964), pp. 4–13; Ritcheson, *Aftermath of Revolution*, pp. 103–4, 112–15.

80. A.H. DeGroot, 'Ottoman North Africa and the Dutch Republic in the

Seventeenth and Eighteenth Centuries', *Revue de l'Occident Musulman et de la Méditerranée*, 39 (1985), pp. 131–47.

81. E. Ingram, *Commitment to Empire: Prophecies of the Great Game in Asia, 1797–1800* (Oxford, 1981); S. Förster, *Die Mächtigen Diener der East India Company. Ursachen und Hintergründe der britischen Expansionspolitik in Südasien, 1793–1819* (Stuttgart, 1992).

82. Staunton to Burges, 12 Nov. 1793, Bod. BB. 46 f. 31.

83. Fawkener to Newcastle, 10 June 1736, BL. Add. 74072; D.K. Richter, 'Native Peoples of North America and the Eighteenth-Century British Empire', in P.J. Marshall (ed.), *The Oxford History of the British Empire, II. The Eighteenth Century* (Oxford, 1998), p. 350.

84. J. Merrell, *The Indians' New World: Catawbas and Their Neighbors from European Contact Through the Era of Removal* (Chapel Hill, 1989), pp. 134–66; E. Hinderaker, *Elusive Empires. Constructing Colonialism in the Ohio Valley, 1673–1800* (Cambridge, 1997), pp. 72–5, 121–2.

85. E. Cashin, *The King's Ranger: Thomas Brown and the American Revolution on the Southern Frontier* (Athens, Georgia, 1989).

86. E. Cashin, *Lachlan McGillivray, Indian Trader, The Shaping of the Southern Colonial Frontier* (Athens, Georgia, 1992); D. Usner, *Indians, Settlers and Slaves in a Frontier Exchange Economy: The Lower Mississippi Valley Before 1783* (Chapel Hill, North Carolina, 1990).

87. H.H. Peckham, *Pontiac and the Indian Uprising* (Princeton, New Jersey, 1947).

88. R. White, *Middle Ground: Indians, Empires, and Republics in the Great Lakes Region, 1650–1815* (Cambridge, 1991). Other important recent works include, C. Calloway, *The Western Abenakis of Vermont, 1600–1800* (Norman, Oklahoma, 1990); N.M. McConnell, *A Country Between: The Upper Ohio Valley and its Peoples, 1724–1774* (Lincoln, Nebraska, 1992).

89. J.R. Alden, *John Stuart and the Southern Colonial Frontier* (Ann Arbor, Michigan, 1944); W.R. Jacobs, *Diplomacy and Indian Gifts: The Northern Colonial Frontier, 1748–1763* (1950).

90. C. Calloway, *Crown and the Calumet: British-Indian Relations, 1783–1815* (Norman, Oklahoma, 1987); I.K. Steele, *Warpaths. Invasions of North America* (Oxford, 1994); R.D. Hurt, *The Ohio Frontier, Crucible of the Old Northwest, 1720–1830* (Bloomington, Indiana, 1996).

91. P.E. Hair and R. Law, 'The English in Western Africa to 1700', in N. Canny (ed.), *The Oxford History of the British Empire. I. The Origins of Empire* (Oxford, 1998), p. 261. See also Law, 'King Agaja of Dahomey, the Slave Trade, and the Question of West African Plantations: The Mission of Bulfinch Lambe and Adomo Tomo to England, 1726–32', *Journal of Imperial and Commonwealth History*, 19 (1991), pp. 138–63.

92. C.H. Alexandrowicz, *The Law of Nations in the East Indies*; M. Fisher, *Indirect Rule in India: Residents and the Residency System, 1764–1858* (1991).

93. Diary of George Paterson, — July 1770, BL. IO. MSS. Eur. E379/1, p. 272.

94. W.A.C. Halliwell, 'Peace negotiations with Sindhia and the Raja of Berar',

Wellington Studies, II (1999), pp. 48–68.

95. R.D. Choksey, *A History of British Diplomacy at the Court of the Peshwas 1786–1818* (Poona, 1951); S.N. Sen, *Anglo-Maratha Relations 1785–96* (Bombay, 1974).

96. Cornwallis to Campbell, 12 Apr., Cornwallis to Nizam, 30 Apr., Nizam to Cornwallis, 2 Nov., Cornwallis to Pitt, 1 June 1788, PRO. 30/11/159, 106, 175; Cornwallis to Kennaway, 16 June, and to Directors of East India Company, 3 Nov. 1788, Charles Ross (ed.), *Correspondence of Charles, 1st Marquis Cornwallis* (3 vols, 1859), I, 537–42; Cornwallis to Lansdowne, 10 Nov. 1788, Bowood, papers of the 1st Marquess of Lansdowne, vol. 40. I would like to thank Brendan Carnduff for letting me read his draft *New DNB* entries for Collins, Kennaway and Kirkpatrick.

97. Thomas Trigge to Henry Addington, 1 Feb. 1804, Exeter, Devon RO. 152M OC 10.

98. Samuel Manesty to Addington, 18 Apr. 1804, Exeter, Devon RO. 152M/CI 804/OF2; E. Ingram, 'An Aspiring Buffer-State: Anglo-Persian Relations in the Third Coalition, 1804–1807', *Historical Journal*, 16 (1973), pp. 509–33; M.E. Yapp, *Strategies of British India: Britain, Iran and Afghanistan, 1798–1850* (Oxford, 1980).

99. Black, *From Louis XIV to Napoleon. The Fate of a Great Power* (1999).

100. Jones, *British Diplomatic Service*, pp. 215–16; Cunningham, *Anglo-Ottoman Encounters in the Age of Revolution*, pp. 54–7. For a similar, although slightly more positive recent account for another state, C. Storrs, *War, Diplomacy and the Rise of Savoy, 1690–1720* (Cambridge, 1999), pp. 142–4.

101. See also, Bell, *British Diplomatic Representatives*, pp. 11–15.

Appendix: Sources

1. Grenville to Elgin, 5 Sept. 1792, PRO. FO. 26/19.
2. Stanhope to Stair, 14 Jan. (os) 1715, SRO. GD. 135/141/2.
3. Burges to John Ewart, 28 Jan. 1792, Williamwood 147; John Ewart to Burges, 29 Jan. 1792, Bod. BB. 34; Morton Eden to Auckland, 14 Aug., Auckland to Grenville, 21 Aug. 1792, BL. Add. 3444, 58920.
4. *Private Papers of British Diplomats 1782–1900* (Royal Commission on Historical Manuscripts, Guides to Sources for British History no. 4, 1985) is invaluable.
5. Chesterfield to Harrington, 11 Jan. 1732, PRO. SP. 84/316.
6. Robinson to Harrington, 5 Jan. 1732, PRO. SP. 80/84.
7. Wych to Tilson, 23 Mar., Wych to Townshend 1725, Harrington to Wych, 19 Dec. (os) 1735, PRO. SP. 82/42, 56.
8. Wych to Tilson, 23 Mar. 1725, PRO. SP. 82/42.
9. Townshend to Edward Finch, 14 Sept. 1725, PRO. SP. 88/30. More generally, see Black, 'Anglo-Russian Relations 1714–1750: A Note on Sources', in J.M. Hartley, *The Study of Russian History from British Archival Sources*

(1986), pp. 67–87.

10. Black, 'British Intelligence and the Mid-Eighteenth-Century Crisis', *Intelligence and National Security*, 2 (1987), pp. 209–29, and 'Eighteenth-Century Intercepted Dispatches', *Journal of the Society of Archivists*, 11 (1990), pp. 138–43.

11. *Report on the Manuscripts of J.B. Fortescue, Esq., preserved at Dropmore* (10 vols, 1892–1927). For another example of the limited extent of published material, G. Hogge (ed.), *The Journals and Correspondence of William Lord Auckland* (4 vols, 1860–2). Editions of the Malmesbury and the Trevor correspondence provide more evidence of this.

12. Leeds to Alleyne Fitzherbert, 20 Nov. 1789, BL. Eg. 3500.

13. Stanyan to Sunderland, 31 July 1717, BL. Add. 61537.

14. BL. Add. 73508.

15. BL. Add. 73765.

16. Whitworth to George Tilson, 12 Nov. 1714, BL. Add. 37361.

17. Elliot to William Eden, 19 Mar. 1776, BL. Add. 34413.

18. D/EP. F318.

19. Much of this correspondence was printed in *Colonel St. Paul of Ewart*, edited by George Butler (2 vols, 1911).

20. Some of his papers were cited and published by his grandson, the 3rd Earl of Malmesbury: *Diaries and Collection of James Harris, 1st Earl of Malmsbury* (4 vols, 1844) and *A Series of Letters of the 1st Earl of Malmesbury, his Family and Friends* (2 vols, 1870).

21. Mss. Rawl. A. 326.

22. Mss. Eng. Hist. D. 164.

23. Mss. Eng. Hist. D. 117–18.

24. Mss. Eng. Hist. D. 147.

25. Mss. Rawl. A. 285.

26. Mss. Rawl. A. 286, c. 391–2.

27. Mss. Eng. Lett c. 18.

28. Mss. Eng. Lett. c. 336–40. See G. Rice, 'British Consuls and Diplomats in the Mid-eighteenth Century: An Italian Example', *English Historical Review*, 92 (1977), pp. 834–46.

29. Mss. Lyell empt. 37.

30. Mss. Eng. Hist. C. 62.

31. Mss. Eng. Lett. D. 109; Black, 'Anglo-Russian relations after the Seven Years' War', *Scottish Slavonic Review*, 9 (1987), pp. 27–37.

32. Some material was published in J. Hutton (ed.), *Selections from the Letters and Correspondence of Sir James Bland Burges* (1885).

33. For one series, Black, 'Anglo-Dutch Relations 1728–1732. The Chesterfield-Waldegrave Correspondence', *Nederlandse Historische Bronnen*, 10 (1992), pp. 132–62.

34. H.M. Scott, *British Foreign Policy in the Age of the American Revolution* (Oxford, 1990).

35. Letters from Elliot and his secretary J. Johnstone to Ewart, Williamwood vol. 131; Ewart to Elliot, 11 Sept., 31 Oct. 1788, NLS. 13022.

36. S. Checkland, *The Elgins 1766–1917. A Tale of Aristocrats, Proconsuls and their Wives* (Aberdeen, 1988), pp. 21–2.

37. Auckland to Elgin, 18 Aug. 1792, Broomhall, 60/1/106.

38. On the dispersal, A.H. Smith, G.M. Baker and R.W. Kenny, *The Papers of Nathaniel Bacon of Stiffkey*, 1 (1979), xx–xxxvii. The records still there have been listed by the Norfolk RO, HMC. no. 86/14.

39. See K.W. Schweizer (ed.), *Lord Bute: Essays in Re-interpretation* (Leicester, 1988); J.D. Nicholas, 'The Ministry of Lord Bute, 1762–3' (Ph.D. Aberystwyth, 1988); Schweizer and J.L. Bullion, 'The Use of the Private Papers of Politicians in the Study of Policy Formulation during the Eighteenth Century: The Bute Papers as a Case Study', *Archives*, 22 (1995), pp. 39–43.

40. National Registry of Archives report 22339; K.W. Schweizer, 'A Handlist to the Additional Weston Papers', *Bulletin of the Institute of Historical Research*, 51 (1978), pp. 99–102.

41. T.C.W. Blanning, "That Horrid Electorate" or "Ma Patrie Germanique"? George III, Hanover and the *Fürstenbund* of 1785', *Historical Journal*, 20 (1977), pp. 342–4.

42. There are all too few works comparable to Brian Hutton's 'The Creation, Dispersal and Re-Discovery of the papers of George, First Earl Macartney', *Familia*, 2, no. 5 (1989), pp. 81–6.

43. Huntington Library, HM. 18940, pp. 270, 353.

44. L. Scott, 'Under Secretaries of State, 1755–1775' (M.A. Manchester, 1950).

45. For the earlier history of the papers, Earl of Ilchester and Mrs Langford-Brooke, *The Life of Sir Charles Hanbury-Williams* (1929), pp. 12–15.

46. Black, 'Non-Walpolean Manuscripts in the Lewis Walpole Library', *Yale University Library Gazette*, 67 (1992), pp. 58–67.

47. R. Massini, *Sir Luke Schaub, Ein Basler im diplomatischen Dienst Englands* (Basle, 1953).

48. G. Rice, 'Archival Sources for the Life and Career of the Fourth Earl of Rochford …', *Archives*, 20 (1992), p. 261.

49. Holdernesse to Yorke, 26 Mar. 1754, BL. Eg. 3445.

Selected Further Reading

For Diplomacy
M.S. Anderson, *The Rise of Modern Diplomacy 1450–1919* (Harlow, 1993).

For British Diplomatic Service
P.S. Lachs, *The Diplomatic Corps under Charles II and James II* (New Brunswick, New Jersey, 1965).
D.B. Horn, *The British Diplomatic Service, 1689–1789* (Oxford, 1961).
M.A. Thomson, *The Secretaries of State, 1681–1782* (Oxford, 1932).
C.R. Middleton, *The Administration of British Foreign Policy, 1782–1846* (Durham, North Carolina, 1977).

For British Foreign Policy
D.B. Horn, *Great Britain and Europe in the Eighteenth Century* (Oxford, 1967).
J.M. Black, *A System of Ambition? British Foreign Policy 1660–1793* (2nd edn, Stroud, 2000).
R.M. Hatton, *George I* (2nd edn, New Haven, 2001).
J.M. Black, *British Foreign Policy in the Age of Walpole* (Edinburgh, 1985).
J.M. Black, *America or Europe? British Foreign Policy, 1739–63* (London, 1998).
H.M. Scott, *British Foreign Policy in the Age of the American Revolution* (Oxford, 1990).
J.M. Black, *British Foreign Policy in an Age of Revolutions 1783–1793* (Cambridge, 1994).

Index